TELEVISION

TELEVISION

MICHAEL WINSHIP

RANDOM HOUSE NEW YORK

Library of Congress Cataloging-in-Publication Data
Winship, Michael.
Television.
1. Television—History. I. Title.
PN1992.2.W56   1988   791.45'09   87-42662
ISBN 0-394-56401-4

Photo credits are on pages 357–58.

Manufactured in the United States of America
Typography and binding design by J. K. Lambert
First American Edition

FOR KATHLEEN AND AMANDA

PREFACE

I was standing next to Jim Lehrer, the co-anchor of *The MacNeil/Lehrer Newshour*, in a darkened TV studio. We were waiting, which is something you do a lot of in television, waiting for a light to be repositioned or a camera to be fixed or a tape to be rewound and reset—"reracked."

"The thing you've got to understand," Lehrer said, in frustration, "is that television is not a feasible medium."

For a long time, those of us involved with a project called *Television* thought it might not be feasible either. We struggled with the contents of the eight programs that make up the series. What should we include, what can we leave out, how do we make this a comprehensive series about our industry?

We're talking about a truly remarkable invention. In just half a century, television has covered the planet, becoming a global power with a profound impact on everything from buying habits and fashion styles to politics and language. There are now more than 750 million TV sets in almost 160 countries, watched by more than 2.5 billion people. For every child born in the world, a television set is manufactured—a quarter of a million every day. More people have access to television than to telephones. There are more than sixty thousand transmitters on the earth's surface or orbiting over our heads. In fact, because of all that activity, in some low frequencies, the earth gives off more energy than the sun.

Think about how TV affects your daily life. Even if you're not the type who clicks on *Good Morning America* first thing in the morning and signs off at night with David Letterman, *Mary Tyler Moore Show* reruns, and "The Star-Spangled Banner," television is all around you. People talk about last night's *Dynasty* in the corridors of office buildings, get up in the wee hours of the morning to watch the latest royal wedding, and set the timer on their VCR to tape *Out of Africa* on Home Box Office. When I walk down the hall of my apartment building on Thursday nights, I can hear *The Cosby Show* blasting away behind almost every door.

There's no escape.

For news and sports, there's nothing like it. With the three networks, local coverage, and the twenty-four-hour service of Cable News Network, we can be whisked away, live, to virtually anyplace in the world—or out of it. We can watch a hijacked airliner sitting on the tarmac at Beirut Airport, or we can dive to the depths of the Atlantic to see for the first time the ghostly remains of the *Titanic*. Men walk on the moon, space probes transmit close-up pictures of Halley's Comet, and seven astronauts vanish in a violent explosion, smoke curling in the sky like the head of a scorpion.

Television scholar Joshua Meyrowitz writes that because of TV "children are taken across the globe before we give them permission to cross the street."

One of my sisters-in-law tells me that my niece has learned to tell time—with a slight hitch. "Mom," she asks, "is it almost nine o'clock, eight o'clock Central?"

Another sister-in-law remembers living in El Paso, Texas, during the mid-sixties when my brother-in-law was drafted into the army. The high point of their day, she says, was the *CBS Evening News*. When Walter Cronkite signed off with "And that's the way it is," the whole family would cry out, "Walter, don't go! Don't leave us!" They felt he was their only contact with the real world.

Television, using Cronkite and Barbara Walters as de facto intermediaries, helped set in motion peace talks between Menachem Begin and Anwar Sadat. Television has helped win elections—and not just in this country. Corazon Aquino, denied almost any access to the Marcos-controlled television system, got her message out to the Filipino people with an elaborate network of home videocassettes. In exchange for two blank cassettes, voters got a cassette of Aquino on the campaign trail.

There has been an explosion of access. When I was growing up, in western New York, we could receive four stations—NBC and CBS affiliates in Rochester and Syracuse. When I was a teenager, the inauguration of ABC stations in both those cities was a cause for major celebration. Now, my mother, with her cable hookup, can receive almost thirty channels. And with the VCR she got for Christmas, she can watch movies or Jane Fonda herself into a frenzy. In the United States, we rent more videocassettes than we take books out of public libraries.

And then there's the money involved in commercial television. The amounts are staggering. Consider:

- Advertisers spend about $21 billion a year on television.
- A thirty-second commercial on the 1987 Super Bowl cost around $600,000. A similar thirty-second spot on the phenomenally successful *Cosby Show* costs $440,000. *Fortune* magazine reported that the series generates around $75 million in revenue for NBC per year.
- WOR-TV, a New York–area independent station, was sold by RKO to MCA for $387 million.
- Capital Cities bought ABC for $3.52 billion.
- General Electric bought RCA, NBC's parent company, for $6.3 billion.

So the television business appears to be an automatic moneymaking machine. Television is an extremely lucrative game.

Well, yes and no.

With the growth of independent stations, the availability of so much inexpensive advertising space on cable stations, and the boom in home video, network advertising revenues were down in 1986, the first time since 1971, when cigarette ads were banned from the air.

Another factor is the skyrocketing cost of programming: about seventy percent of a network's money is spent on programming. American television spends about $4 billion on shows every year. The cost is increasing as much as twenty-five to thirty percent a year.

The upcoming massive miniseries *War and Remembrance* reportedly cost more than $100 million to produce. Episodes of *Miami Vice* often run around $1.5 million an episode; *Moonlighting,* around $900,000 per episode. *The Washington Post* said that *Moonlighting*'s elaborate "Taming of the Shrew" parody, called "Atomic Shakespeare"—not, incidentally, a ratings success—cost $3 million.

The studios are losing money on these shows. Some are beginning to refuse to produce certain series for the networks unless there's a guarantee of income. Most half-hour shows lose about $100,000 per episode. The hope is that the money will be retrieved—and then some—in syndication.

For some, that dream comes true. WOR-TV in New York has paid $30 million for a three-and-a-half-year package of *Cosby* shows. KPIX in San Francisco, a smaller market, is paying $20 million for that same package. In fact, Viacom, the syndication company handling *Cosby,* will make as much as $500 million in *Cosby* sales—just in the first go-around.

Two of the three major networks are losing money, the studios say they're taking a beating, and some of the independents are filing for bankruptcy. But some of the players are making a mint.

And what is the future of *public* television, where

a PBS producer once had to cancel a guest for a news special because they could not afford enough chairs? In the current atmosphere of cutthroat competition and deregulation, can it, with its smaller audiences and sometimes rarified programming, survive?

There are other problems and issues as well, issues of a more social nature: Does television breed violence? Is it a dumbing and addictive drug? Is it educating the world or driving us crazy? Is it destroying society or bringing us closer together? What about censorship: Are the nude talk shows and soft porn of the Playboy Channel and some of the public access cable stations eating away at the core of American morality? What about the lyrics and sexual innuendos of MTV rock videos? For that matter, what about the fundamentalist evangelists, filling the air with consternation, outrage, and pleas for more tithing?

"Television is busily destroying the world," producer Herbert Brodkin claimed.

"Television is not a luxury, it's a necessity," visionary and author Arthur C. Clarke said. "People demand information and entertainment."

And Reuven Frank, former NBC News head said, "Mankind might be better off if television had never been invented."

Bernard Greenhead, an Englishman who worked as an engineer with EMI in Britain in the early days of television experiments, remembered a demonstration at which Russian émigré inventor Issac Schoenburg was present. "After the visitors had gone, Schoenberg came back into the control room and said, 'Well, gentlemen, you seem to have perfected the greatest time waster of all mankind. I hope you use it well.'"

We wail and moan about television, but the bottom line is, of course, we all watch it. "How can you attack it?" Federico Fellini asked an interviewer.

"To attack television would be as absurd as launching a campaign against the force of gravity."

Television is certainly as pervasive as gravity, but immune from neither criticism nor scrutiny. As Edward R. Murrow said, in words that are inscribed on the Alfred I. duPont Award for broadcast journalism:

This instrument can teach, it can illuminate; yes, it can even inspire. But it can do so only to the extent that humans are determined to use it to those ends. Otherwise, it is merely lights and wires in a box.

With so much attention being paid to television, so much to discuss, and so much to remember, it seemed like the perfect time to produce a series like *Television.* Certain colleagues accused us of "navel gazing," of being too wrapped up in our business and thinking other people would be just as fascinated as we are. Frankly, I think people *are* as fascinated with television as we are. It's an essential part of all of our lives.

The *Television* project began in February 1985.

I was just wrapping up my final script for the *Smithsonian World* series when Jack Sameth, who would become *Television*'s American executive producer, told me about an exciting new series being shown on British television, produced by Granada TV, one of Britain's leading broadcasting companies. It was a series that undertook nothing less than a full-scale examination of the television industry.

WNET, the public station in New York City, and KCET, the public station in Los Angeles, were in the process of acquiring the United States rights to the series, Jack said. He had been put in charge of creating a new American version of the series, using Granada's as the bedrock and building on it with updates, new interviews, and more material about

American television. Would I be interested in working on it with him?

Absolutely, I said. I'm a self-confessed TV junkie. Coproducer Susan Kim and I are of the first generation who can't remember a time when there wasn't television. I was brought up on the Nelson family, *Leave It to Beaver*, and *Captain Kangaroo* (until the day he died, my father kept on his desk a pencil box I fashioned from a milk carton—made under the careful tutelage of the Captain). I was a contestant in the Howdy Doody Lookalike Contest, a five-year-old whose birthday party was produced with a *Mickey Mouse Club* motif, and at six, I did passable Perry Como and Edward R. Murrow imitations.

I love television, and I love working in it. I feel about TV the way Orson Welles felt about movies: "the greatest set of electric trains a boy ever had." When I hear that a friend has left the business to pursue another profession, I can never understand why.

Most of my work has been in public television, although I've also worked on cable projects for Ted Turner, Showtime, and The Entertainment Channel (a pay-cable effort that took a $34 million bath in pre-tax losses and drowned).

You're also reading the words of a man who scripted a videocassette called *Haircuts at Home.*

Maybe not the broadest experience, but certainly varied.

As a viewer, television has widened my horizons, while at the same time exposing me to some of the most incredible tripe and nonsense ever. As a participant, it has brought me into contact with extraordinary people and extraordinary events. Because of television, I stood in the hearing room of the House Judiciary Committee as they debated the articles of impeachment against Richard Nixon. I got to hang out with players from the Steelers and the Cowboys at Super Bowl X in 1976. I traveled to the bottom of a salt mine underneath Lake Erie to view a massive experiment to detect proton decay, a key to understanding the forces that created the universe. I have spent time in Georgia with Charlayne Hunter-Gault of *The MacNeil/Lehrer Newshour* working on a show that reexamined the time in early 1961 when she integrated the University of Georgia, written about everything from Abscam to reindeer racing, and collaborated with a wild variety of talent—from Bill Moyers and Robert Mac-Neil to Dinah Shore and Julie Andrews.

It's a wonderful life—mostly. There have been moments when I felt like running away to Djakarta and becoming a bicycle messenger. Sometimes the pressure can be close to overwhelming. Deadlines, last-minute script revisions, surly stars—they all happen. But ultimately, this is a great business.

Our eight programs, we hope, will entertain and enlighten and make us all think about the effect that television has had upon ourselves and our society. It's an opportunity for us to examine the television revolution—its ability to inform, entrance, and seduce.

The groundwork laid for us by the original Granada series was invaluable. Their production team spent three years filming all over the world, combing historical archives, and interviewing the most interesting and distinguished people in the industry. Many of the voices speaking from these pages are those of men and women who were interviewed by Granada, others have been interviewed for the American series, and still others have been tracked down exclusively for this book. Our thanks to all of them.

What follows is a look at the television industry—its history, success stories, comic disasters, current problems and trends, and a glimpse at its possible future—a story told by the men and women who make it happen.

ACKNOWLEDGMENTS

This book is a companion volume to the eight-part, public television series, *Television*, coproduced by WNET/New York and KCET/Los Angeles and based on a series of the same name produced by Granada Television of Great Britain. It could not have been completed without the loving support and friendship of the series' production team, especially that of old friends and colleagues Jack Sameth, the series executive producer; and coproducer Susan Kim. Their hard work, good humor, and understanding—in the face of long hours, impossible deadlines, a too-small staff, and a too-tight budget—made it possible. Someday I may be able to repay them.

Associate producer Ann Leifeste and project assistant Susan McLaughlin worked stalwartly against the endless flow of paperwork and technical details that go into putting together a series of this scale. May visions of sandy beaches, free weekends, and long naps soon dance in their heads. Videotape editor David Pentecost, consultant Andrea Sheen, production manager Beth Harrison, tape operator Phil Fortunato, production aide Chelle Tutt and interns Christine Caruso, Elisabeth Wassmann, and Jonathan Tobias made invaluable contributions to the *Television* series and hence to this book. The executives in charge of the series were Robert Kotlowitz of WNET and Phylis Geller of KCET. Their enthusiasm and cooperation were essential.

Thanks also must go to the people responsible for the original Granada series in Great Britain: executive producer Norman Swallow and his team of producers, especially Leslie Woodhead, who offered counsel and support at several critical moments. Film librarian Monica Ford at Granada's headquarters in Manchester and Susan Temple at Granada International in London were always available for information and advice.

What's more, as Susan Kim wrote for the closing credits of each episode of the *Television* series, "Special thanks to the hundreds of producers, directors, writers, performers, musicians, and craftspeople who provided their cooperation and gracious permission" to use examples of their work. Add to that our very special and appreciative thanks to ABC, CBS, NBC, PBS, and the many studios, production companies, and program distributors who gave their utmost support to what otherwise would have been an impossible task.

Neither series nor book ever would have happened if not for the diligent work of Irene Smookler, WNET's director of program marketing; and the gracious financial backing of *Television*'s corporate underwriter, the MCI Communications Corporation; the Corporation for Public Broadcasting, the member stations of the Public Broadcasting Service, and the Marilyn M. Simpson Charitable Trust.

As for the book specifically, there are many without whom it never would have been completed. At Random House, editor Carolyn Reidy, copy editor Mitchell Ivers, and editorial associate Irena Vukov-Kendes kept the process rolling and offered steadfast opinions and cogent criticism every step of the way. At WNET, photo editor Hazel Hammond, assisted by intern David Cheifetz, took on the awesome assignment of tracking down the hundreds of pictures in this book. David Kessler became the unofficial manuscript production manager, smoothing potential bumps, expediting payments and attending to the logistical details that would drive less tolerant people mad. Vicki Herman helped arrange many of the interviews in Los Angeles and conducted the four interviews in Chapter Ten. Patricia Hayes and Alan Ellington were the faithful programmers who packed all of this manuscript into a word processor.

Through it all was a person whose love and forbearance as late night after late night and weekend after weekend slipped away were equaled only by her relentless ability as a fact checker: my wife, Kathleen Campion. Thank you.

Finally, I must point to the person who first hired me away from Washington to come to work at WNET in 1974, and whose faith and support even managed to survive this whole mad pursuit, Leonard Mayhew. I hope that the end result proves that his confidence and trust were well founded. I thank him.

Michael Winship

CONTENTS

INTRODUCTION
BY EDWIN NEWMAN

Television speaks for itself. It may be argued that it is better watched than written about and read about. I am not so sure. We ought to try to pull together a coherent and systematic view of what television has accomplished; also, of course, what it has failed to accomplish, what its effects have been, and what they might have been. Television, from its network beginnings, has been with us for about forty years. Full blast, so to speak, it has been with us for about thirty-five. It is time to take stock. This book, and the series on which it is based, do that.

Here I must correct myself. I spoke of "us." Television, as it exists and has existed, especially in the United States, Britain, and other countries called "advanced," has not existed in the same way and to the same extent in countries called "developing" or "underdeveloped." Nor has it been the same in countries where governments use it as an instrument of policy or, in their own interest, suppress it. The consequences of these differences can be tremendous. So can the consequences of an end to those differences or of a narrowing of them. Television has been, for example, a key part of Mikhail Gorbachev's *glasnost* in the Soviet Union, not only because of what it has told the Soviet people about their country but also because of the impression it has created abroad.

In somewhat the same way, footage of South Korean student riots, seen abroad, has surely been a factor in the calculations of the government in Seoul, while South Africa's ban on television coverage of disturbances there has been damaging to the government in Pretoria, though probably less damaging than permitting the disturbances to be seen. Perhaps those in authority in South Africa had in mind the effect on public opinion of television's coverage of the turmoil in the United States brought on by the civil rights movement of the 1960s and '70s, coverage that greatly speeded up the reforms that black Americans had waited for for so long.

Inevitably, much of what television has done was not planned. Turn an invention of such potential loose, and there is no telling what may come out of it. My own case may be instructive. I began in the news business—there was, happily, no talk of "media" in those days—in a wire service. The next step was newspaper work, then writing radio news, then on the air in radio, and as television moved in, staring into cameras and saying who I was, and where. None of this was planned: I had no visions of speaking to larger audiences or getting across this or that vital message. True, there was more money in radio and television than in working for a paper, but in those early days, most of us were happy just to have a job. There was no grand design. Television had come along; it offered employment and, incidentally, the work was easier. Why not get aboard?

Permit me, if you will, another reminiscence. The first television work I did was for the BBC, on a 1950 series called *An American Looks at Britain.* I was not, however, the American originally hired to do the looking. Howard K. Smith, then of CBS in London, was. He was called away and had to miss the second of the three programs. He recommended me as a substitute. In short, accident took over.

Are you nervous, the first time you do television? Indeed you are. It was even more nerve-racking in those beginning days when there were no Tele-PrompTers, or even cue cards (less respectfully called idiot cards) held above or below the camera lens with the script hand-printed on them in large letters. With no prompter and no cue cards, you memorized the script, because it was thought undesirable for you to be looking down and losing "eye contact." No wonder some of those who were prominent in radio resented and resisted television. It seemed to them merely a more troublesome way of doing what they had been doing all along.

Going back to that first day at the BBC, nobody on the production team had ever heard of me, so it was lonely at the desk, under the lights, heavily made up, sounding outlandishly American in that nest of English accents, waiting for the signal to speak, and hoping that my memory would not fail. Few things in television are more embarrassing than having the "takes" mount up during a taping, having the floor manager shout, "Scene one, take ten!"—or fifteen or twenty or whatever it may be. One thing that is more embarrassing, however, is flubbing live, on the air. Evidently, I did not flub, because the producer of *An American Looks at Britain,* Norman Swallow, became a friend. These many years later, he was executive producer, for Granada Television, of the original series from which the eight-part *Television* series was adapted by WNET in New York and KCET in Los Angeles for showing on PBS. Accident again. It should be added that Swallow himself is part of television's history.

In any case, because of having taken part in his program, I found myself making occasional appearances on other BBC and Independent Television shows. One result was that I was sometimes recognized as I went about. You get used to being recognized. You come to enjoy it; what is distressing is not being recognized, being ignored. There is also a larger significance: The wire service or newspaper journalist is unknown to the general public (unless, that is, he or she turns up from time to time on television). Television newspeople are, to a greater or lesser degree, celebrities. That may affect their outlook. It may affect the public's view of their reporting. Newspaper people are judged by what they write; we are judged also by how we sound,

how we look, and whether we seem to be "sincere." We are much more readily accused of being biased. Some television anchors cannot cover stories; they would attract too much attention and distract attention from the story itself.

Because we are recognizable, and because we are present with cameras, we have a special place. Go to scenes of devastation, particularly devastation spawned by political oppression, and people cry out, "Tell the world! Tell the world!" It might at times be said of television newspeople, "Thine is the burden of a whole world's weeping."

The chapters of this book tell where television has made its mark. For television can, and does, do extraordinary things, things that would once have been thought miraculous. Put this in terms of news: As this is written, the Persian Gulf, with the Iran-Iraq war and the escorted convoys passing through the Strait of Hormuz, is a big story. It is very nearly taken for granted that if something happens there during the day, we will know about it—and see it—that night. Imagine the technological progress that has made that possible; imagine also the expense involved in getting the reporting and camera crews there, keeping them there, and getting their reports out.

Knowing this, it is hard for some of us not to think back to the early days of television news. I remember being told to go to what was then French Morocco, to do what would now seem thoroughly rudimentary stories about life on the American air bases there. And to Kenya at the time of the Mau Mau uprising, and the Suez Canal Zone to see whether the British would pull out, and if they did, how soon. We did our best to appear nonchalant, but we were tremendously excited. We were pioneers.

Take Kenya: American print journalists had

been there, but so far as we knew, television had not. NBC had a trailblazing program at that time, *Background,* which offered a half-hour documentary each week. The Mau Mau rebellion was being presented in the press as primarily a black uprising against whites. In fact, the number of whites killed was tiny. It was blacks who were being slaughtered, in some cases for tribal reasons, in others because they were thought to be subservient to the British. We went to the "white highlands," where the only settlers were white, and there found a couple who ran a large ranch. The wife was an American, small and blond. She wore a revolver in a holster on her hip—good pictures. We interviewed a white who said that British rule could not possibly last and put on blacks to speak for themselves. We got a stirring recording of singing by blacks being trained as soldiers against the Mau Mau. We shipped the recording to New York by commercial air and—this was not uncommon in those days—it was lost.

The film it was to accompany was, luckily, not lost. It took a few days to reach New York, and there the developing and printing and editing process took a few days more. Program schedules then took account of such things. The delays were annoying to some accustomed to radio or to wire service or newspaper work, but they were worth it. How many Americans had ever seen Kenya? We were able to give some idea of what was happening there and some idea of the country's physical magnificence.

We had a lot to learn. In the Suez Canal Zone, we wanted an interview with the British commanding general, and we wanted the interview to take place in the desert. This involved going to the trouble of pretending that the general and I had met in the desert by accident, that he just happened to be riding around out there and so did we, and that we

had with us all our bulky equipment and film, just in case our paths crossed. We wouldn't bother to do that now. We would simply say that this is what almost all the Canal Zone looks like, and "General, I can't help wondering why it is thought to be worth holding on to?" As for the equipment, it might be one tenth the size.

In those days—a phrase I keep using—the mere fact that we went somewhere gave a place a degree of importance. There was a thrill in seeing a Kenyan game reserve for the first time, or the pyramids and the Sphinx. The audience must have felt it, too. Still, our achievements did not stand. Television was moving far too quickly for that.

How quickly? This book, and the PBS series to which it is a companion, is appearing in 1988, an American election year, ten presidential elections since the first election in which television played even a modest part. Some political experts thought that the stiffness and, as it seemed, arrogance of the 1948 Republican candidate, Thomas E. Dewey, helped elect President Truman. The number of people who actually saw Dewey on television must have been tiny by today's standards, but in a very close election, so the theory went, it might have been enough to make the difference.

Now, of course, television substantially shapes our politics. Take, as a case in point, the first debate between President Ford and Jimmy Carter in 1976: They had come together, under the auspices of the League of Women Voters, in the Walnut Street Theater in Philadelphia. ABC was the pool producer for television—that is, it provided the cameras and the sound and lighting equipment, and the technicians to run them, with picture available to all. In addition, the networks were there, like other news organizations, covering the event. That, at any rate, was the pretense employed to comply with the requirements of the Federal Communications Act: It was not a television debate but a debate television happened to be covering.

When a piece of equipment failed and the sound was lost, the debate was suspended and the networks filled the time with their own correspondents; Mr. Ford and Mr. Carter fell silent. The audience in the theater sat and waited. Twenty-seven minutes went by before Jack Sameth, ABC's director (and in 1987 executive producer of the *Television* series), passed along word that the sound had been restored and I, as moderator, called for the debate to be resumed. Go on with this non-television event without television? Ridiculous. Moreover, for news value, the technical snafu overshadowed anything else that emerged from the debate.

From the 1950s and '60s and even '70s, when network television gobbled up the conventions and elections, there has been a great change. For example, unless there is a genuine contest for the nomination, which the primary system makes unlikely, conventions are no longer covered "gavel to gavel." The novelty has worn off; the thrill is gone. The attitude was summed up during last year's British general election—the story achieved wide circulation—by a British mother. She was able to get the children away from the television set and into bed early. "Darlings," she told them, "it's only men talking."

Debates, it is true, because of their gladiatorial aspects and the possibility that those participating will be caught off guard, may still be eagerly watched. Yet even they may be less important than a characteristic product of television—the political commercial. We have reached the point where it is difficult for a candidate to get himself or herself taken seriously without the slick appeals produced by "media consultants." This is because political commercials are expensive. If a candidate does not have them, that means the candidate has not been able to raise the necessary money. A candidate in those circumstances tends to be shrugged off.

It is not only politics that yields to television's pressures. Changes in diplomatic positions may be signaled on television rather than in more formal ways. Israel's Menachem Begin and Egypt's Anwar Sadat did exactly that, on programs with Barbara Walters and Walter Cronkite, before they reached their peace agreement with the help of President Carter at Camp David in 1978. Equally, grilling by reporters may force those in authority to define their attitudes more precisely than they would have preferred. Moreover, when something happens that appears to call for a response from Washington, American administrations may feel compelled to have their positions set out in time for the evening news shows. Lloyd Cutler, counselor to President Carter, has written of decisions made too hastily, so that Washington would not be open to the charge that it was taken by surprise.

If administrations do make such mistakes, television should not be blamed. After all, the words *no comment* have not disappeared from the English language.

On a similar point, the argument that television coverage plays into the hands of airplane hijackers is wide of the mark. No doubt the hijackers relish the publicity, and no doubt the coverage is frequently excessive, sometimes grotesquely so. Yet perhaps the attention given the hijackers by television keeps the hostages alive. That is possible, too.

Another criticism of television coverage seems to me highly doubtful: that if, for example, television had been present at Gettysburg, the North might not have gone on, or that cameras at Iwo Jima might have weakened American resolve. The fact is, they might just as easily have done the opposite. The Vietnam experience is not relevant here. Vietnam was a war millions of Americans thought we should not be fighting. Television provided a daily reminder of that.

Television was once expected to cement the family as an institution. After all, the family would be together, gathered around the set, seeing the same programs and comparing individual reactions. Yet the mighty success of television coincided with a weakening of the family as an institution and increased rates of illegitimacy, teenage pregnancy, and drug use. Was there a connection? NBC devoted an entire night of prime-time viewing period to a documentary we called *The American Family: An Endangered Species.* Might it have been less endangered without television? or more? I wish I knew.

A family scene I will never forget was built around television. It was in the 1960s, and we were making a documentary called *Poverty Is People,* the Johnson administration's "War on Poverty" having brought on a spate of such programs. We were filming in New York, in Harlem, and we went into the grim apartment of a family on welfare. The mother and children were sitting around a television set—the only thing they had, so far as we could tell, that was not an absolute necessity—almost inanimate, but watching, getting glimpses of lives they could not hope to duplicate or even approach, seeing products they could not hope to own. Did television dull their understanding and simply hold them captive? That seemed to be the case. Would those same programs arouse resentment and envy in others? That was probably the case, as well. And what impressions of the United States do those programs create abroad? I remember being told that one effect of showings of *Dallas* overseas was an influx of foreign nurses wanting to work in so rich and glamorous a city.

Let's take up, finally, the matter of television as an educational tool. In the early days, hopes were high that television would be a great instructor, that it would banish ignorance and illiteracy. It does educate, of course, whether it intends to or not, in the sense that it implants ideas, impressions, attitudes. Some of what it does—in the conscious and deliberate production of tripe—is deplorable.

Because my career has been overwhelmingly in news, that has tended to determine my judgment and measurement of television. Still, I have been the host of some musical programs—concerts by the Boston Symphony Orchestra from Tanglewood among them—and I have done some work for NBC Sports and on religious programs. I have taken part in comedy shows, including *Saturday Night Live,* and in situation comedies, usually carrying out the daunting task of playing myself, and in game shows and quiz shows. I have also been the host of dramatic series on cable. All this has given me some sense of television's variety. Thanks to that variety, television's impact varies. It varies also from country to country. We Americans should understand that our television is not typical, despite the popularity of some American programs overseas, not typical by a long shot.

It would be foolish to try to assess the relative importance of television and of other twentieth-century inventions. There would be no point in an argument between supporters of television and supporters of the airplane, or of nuclear energy, or of—let this stand for a host of medical advances—the Salk vaccine. We can let it go at this: Television has been monumentally important, incalculably influential, even for people who do not watch it.

For those who make their livings in it, there are questions that come up endlessly. One is this: Which programs do you enjoy doing most?

The answer is that enjoyment matters less than the conviction that you have, at times, done a necessary job well. Usually, this involves some melancholy event that you wish had not happened at all. I had a large hand in NBC's coverage of the shootings of President Kennedy, Robert Kennedy, Martin Luther King, Jr., George Wallace, and President Reagan. In the course of those assignments, I did not feel that I had any obligation to "hold the country together" or anything of that sort. That would have been highly presumptuous.

The obligation is the age-old obligation of the reporter: to establish the facts so far as they can be established, to make plain where the facts are missing, to try to put what is known into perspective, and to offer some enlightenment about what the consequences may be. If the country in some way benefits from that, so much the better.

I remember one such program. It dealt with drugs and alcohol use among teenagers, and I suggested an opening to NBC's producer, Patrica Mauger. Each teenager appeared before the camera and told what substances he or she had used; how the addiction began; whether his or her parents knew; and where the money for the addiction had come. The opening could not have been more direct, or more frightening.

I tell this story to suggest not that I am a directorial genius but rather that this is often the nature of effective television: getting to the point, whether through the tiny blonde in Kenya decades before with the gun on her hip or the succession of teenagers personifying the grim problem of drug use in the United States.

There were also regrets. One of the earliest documentaries I worked on was *The Orient Express*, in the early 1960s, when an NBC camera crew and I rode the famous train from Paris to Istanbul. It was a lighthearted show, and I was given free rein. Although Istanbul is in European Turkey and not Asian Turkey, I still wish I had sung that old Al Jolson favorite, with a few words changed, "Nothing could be finer than to be in Asia Minor in the morning." Who knows what it might have done for my career?

So, again: Enjoyment? Sometimes. Gratification? Sometimes. And over the years, along with the letdowns and disappointments, a sense that I should count myself fortunate to have worked in television, and for all its faults, more fortunate still to have seen it.

TELEVISION

1. THE BEGINNING

Even in the thirties, the movies were wary of this newfangled menace called television. Posed behind a nightmarish device that Hollywood thought resembled a TV camera of the future, Mary Astor starred in a 1936 feature called Trapped by Television.

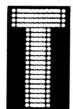here was no sudden flash of inspiration that came to a single lone inventor. Television was an idea that existed long before its realization, a natural progression in a world that had seen the birth of telephones, radio, and motion pictures. At the turn of the century, for example, it was the subject of a *Tom Swift* novel. Even before that, cartoonists such as Albert Robida in France and George Du Maurier in Britain had fun imagining the potential uses—and abuses—of "living pictures" in the sanctity of the home.

Nor can television be claimed as the sole prize of a single nation. Parallel research and development were going on in many countries, including the United States, Britain, Germany, France, Japan, and the Soviet Union.

Serious work began toward the end of the last century, with such inventions as the Nipkow Disc, created by Paul Nipkow in Germany. The disc was a fundamental component of "mechanical" television systems in which discs rotated in both the camera and the receiver. Light passing through the discs created crude television images.

The advocates of the mechanical system—such as John Logie Baird in Great Britain and Charles Francis Jenkins and Ernst Alexanderson in the United States—were challenged by other inventors who favored an electronic system. Vladimir Zworykin, a Russian émigré who came to the United States, was one of the men who believed in the notion of electronic TV. He worked first at Westinghouse, where his experiments were tolerated but not taken seriously, and then at RCA.

RCA was at the forefront of the development of television in America, largely because of the entrepreneurial spirit and enthusiasm of one man—David Sarnoff. His story has become a legend of

AT&T was one of the leading experimenters in early television. In 1927, they scored a political coup when they successfully transmitted pictures between New York and Washington. AT&T President Walter Sherman Gifford, Research Director H. R. Arnold, and Vice President General J. J. Carty in New York (left) exchanged greetings with then–Secretary of Commerce Herbert Hoover and two unidentified men (right) in Washington.

sorts. He too was a Russian émigré, a poor kid who worked as an office boy, earning less than a dollar a day. He learned telegraphy and later created a largely apocryphal story that he picked up the first radio signals reporting the news of the *Titanic* disaster. President William Howard Taft, the story went, ordered all radio stations on the East Coast shut down so that Sarnoff could pick up the faint signals relaying the news of the tragedy's survivors. Sarnoff *did* actually assist in the monitoring of transmissions, but he was neither the first nor the only. In any case, the story did much to enhance his reputation.

He became an up-and-coming executive, first with American Marconi and then with RCA. One of the first to see the vast entertainment potential of radio, he created the first network—NBC—and in 1923 wrote a memo stating, "I believe that television, which is the technical name for seeing as well as hearing by radio, will come to pass in the future." Sarnoff underwrote Zworykin's research.

While work on both mechanical and electronic television proceeded at a steady pace in Britain, in America it was slowed by patent wrangles involving, among others, Sarnoff, Zworykin, and a young Mormon named Philo T. Farnsworth. Farnsworth was a leader in the development of electronic television. His wife, Elma, worked closely with him.

"It was in 1919 that Phil first heard about mechanical television. He had been raised on a farm and there hadn't been money for books and he was just information starved," she said. But Farnsworth discovered that the previous occupant of the Idaho farm on which he was living had left behind a stack of *Popular Science* magazines and scientific journals. In them, he read articles about the potential for mechanical TV. According to Mrs. Farnsworth, this seemed "very crude to him. . . . He didn't see

how you could get the speed of the discs high enough, and he thought it might be potentially dangerous."

But an interest in electricity—he was already in charge of the farm's power system—sent his thinking in other directions. "He was fascinated by electrons," Mrs. Farnsworth said. "He read that you could manipulate electrons in a vacuum by a magnetic force," a basic principle of electronic television.

Farnsworth had his "Eureka!" moment when he was fourteen, plowing the fields. "He turned at this little high spot to see if his rows were straight, and it just hit him like a thunderbolt—'I can scan a picture that way, by taking the dots, the electrons, back and forth as you would read a page.'" Within a year, he had diagramed what he believed to be a feasible electronic TV system.

He worked his way through Brigham Young University, graduating in 1925, his obsession with television intact. His zeal caught the imagination of a financial backer, George Everson, a California fundraiser who persuaded Farnsworth to move west, while he set about finding additional backers.

Television also drew Farnsworth's new wife under its spell, although it first did so with a bit of a shock.

"We married quite quickly because Phil had to leave for California. On our wedding night he had to see George Everson. It turned into hours, and I was getting very upset, and then I began to worry for his safety. When he did come back, he apologized for having been gone so long, and he said, 'You know, there is another woman in my life.'

"I didn't say anything, I was so dumbstruck. Then he said, 'Her name is television. And in order to have enough time together, I want you to work with me. We are going to be working right on the edge of discovery. It is going to be very exciting, and I want you to be part of it.' That's how we started and we were that way all our married life."

Work progressed in California, interrupted by occasional frustration and unintentional hilarity. "During Prohibition, it was quite frowned upon to make your own liquor," Mrs Farnsworth said.

I guess we looked a little suspicious to the neighbors. Because of the things we were doing with light, we had to set the blinds when we were demonstrating.

These policemen came to the door—two of the biggest policemen I ever saw. They said, "We have a report that you are operating a still here."

I said, "Well, come on in." Phil took over, and he said to them, "This is what we're doing," and he showed them all that we were trying to do. It was all set up on the dining room table.

George Everson was caught by two policemen at the back door. The two from the front said, "Joe, it's all right.

They're doing some kooky things called visions, but they're not doing any stilling." George had come in with his hands full of shellac. He was winding coils in the back yard and he had wanted to ask Phil a question. He had his hands up because he didn't want to get shellac on anything, and it looked very suspicious.

The big day came on September 7, 1927.

In the previous year, Phil had gotten more backing, and the agreement was that he promised to get a transmission in a year. He came in two weeks early.

It was a beautiful morning. I went into the office to do some sketches in his notebooks.

He called me in. My brother Cliff, who had made the tubes, was in the transmitting room, which was behind a partition. Phil said, "Put in a slide, Cliff," and we saw a line. It was a curvy, thick line. He adjusted it, and it became sharper. He asked Cliff to turn the slide on its side, and the line turned. Phil looked at us and he said, "Well, there you have television."

For the Television *series, television engineer Bill Elliott built a replica of Scottish inventor John Logie Baird's mechanical television system to demonstrate the kind of image Baird was able to create in the mid-twenties. As his subject, Elliott had the same ventriloquist dummy's head used by Baird, a puppet named Stukey Bill.*

I could tell he was very excited. He was beaming all over. I was jumping about in my nineteen-year-old excitement.

One of the first things he said was, "Remember, there is a lot to do yet."

First and foremost was the need to make television a moneymaking proposition. This desire was not only Farnsworth's, but his backers, of course. "There was one colorful person, he was a sort of product of the Gold Rush days," Mrs. Farnsworth said. "They called him Daddy Fagan, the executive vice president of the Crocker Bank. . . . All of the backers came to the lab, and we were all sitting around waiting while Phil went in to make sure everything was all right at the transmitter. Mr. Fagan called out, 'When are we going to see some dollars in this thing, Farnsworth?' And immediately, a dollar sign appeared on the screen."

Farnsworth had close encounters with many of the other key players in the race for television,

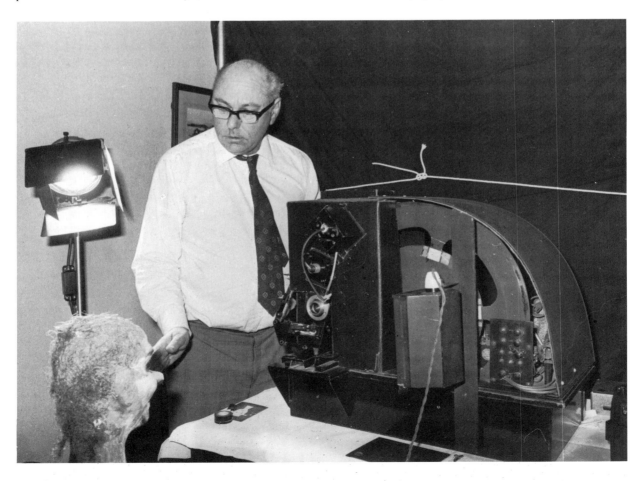

including Vladimir Zworykin. "Dr. Zworykin was a very charming person. We entertained him in our home. When he saw the first television picture in Phil's lab—this was in 1930, and we had a good picture, a clear picture—he said, 'Beautiful. I wish I had invented it myself.'"

In 1930, much to David Sarnoff's chagrin, Farnsworth was awarded a patent for electronic television. RCA wanted to buy this and other television-related patents from Farnsworth. He refused, insisting on royalty payments instead. Eventually, a licensing agreement was reached. According to broadcast historian Erik Barnouw, "The RCA attorney is said to have had tears in his eyes as he signed the contract." As a result, it can be said that American television as we know it today is largely an invention that combined the genius of RCA's Zworykin and Philo Farnsworth.

Farnsworth wound up holding more than 165 patents. He worked for Philco briefly and eventually formed his own company, the Farnsworth Radio and Television Corporation, which would become part of ITT. He was also involved in radar and atomic energy research, but he never lost interest in television.

"He was disappointed in the programming to begin with," Mrs. Farnsworth said, "but he realized it was in its infancy and had to go through growing pains. When he saw the first man walk on the moon, he said, 'It's been all worthwhile.'" Farnsworth died in 1971.

Simultaneously with RCA and Farnsworth's electronic efforts, American inventor Charles Francis Jenkins was continuing his work with mechanical television. He had conducted many experimental broadcasts from Washington, D.C., and created the Jenkins Television Corporation in New Jersey, which manufactured receivers and had its own broadcast service. Its program manager was Irma Kroman, to whom early TV was an adventure.

"I was working in New York City as a desk clerk when a friend of mine, who was an engineer, came to me and asked if I would like to be program manager of the Jenkins Television Corporation," she said.

This was in 1930. I said, "What's a program manager?" He said he didn't know, so I went out to Jenkins Television, which was in Jersey City, and was interviewed by a Mr. Replogle. He listened to my so-called qualifications—I had a bachelor's in literary interpretation, and I had done a lot of stage work—and he said, "Well, I think you are the person we're looking for," and I got the job.

He didn't know what a program manager for television was, and I certainly didn't, so I had a job I could manufacture, all by myself. There was nobody in the whole country, maybe in the whole world, who knew how to be the program manager of a television corporation!

I had no idea about the future of television at that time. Television was extremely primitive, and as far as making a program schedule, I was a novice. I would take a piece of paper and I would list the things that we were going to broadcast. We would show a Charlie Chaplin film or another movie, but in between there were blank spaces, and we had nothing to put on. *Amos 'n' Andy* was very popular on radio, so I created a female character similar to theirs. I put her on the air once a day doing all kinds of nonsense. I'd make up programs as I went along. I'd drag in one of the engineers—you know, engineers are not noted for being verbose, so I had to dig words out of them in front of the camera—but it really didn't matter because there were not many people outside watching what we were doing.

The picture was about six by six inches. We were using a neon tube with a 365-degree scanning wheel in front of it. This resulted in a red background. The figure appeared as a black silhouette. The picture looked very much like a shadow play. I was never stopped on the street. No one said, "I recognized you." They couldn't have recognized me. They could not have known my features, because they could not have seen any. I was just an outline in black.

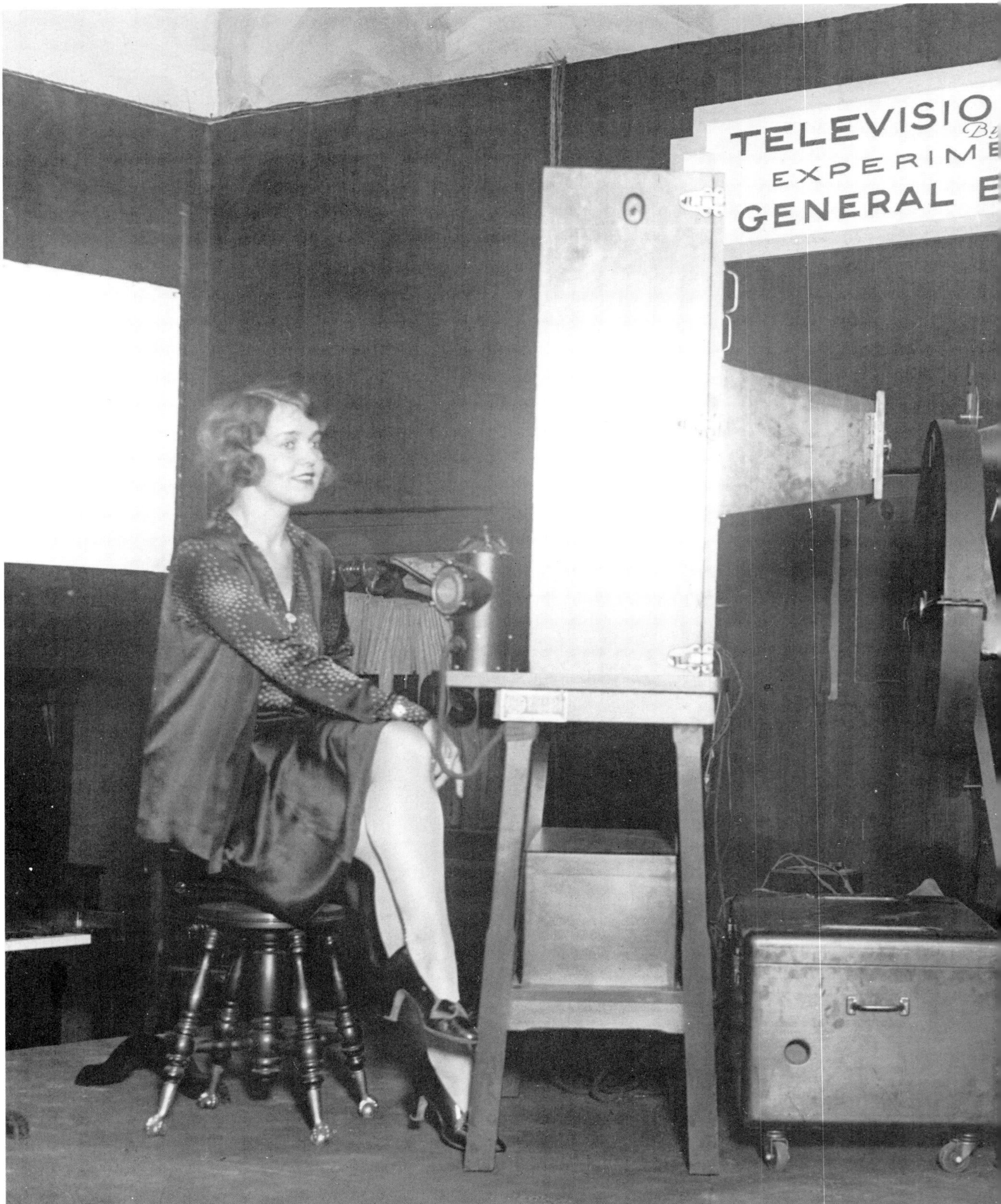
TELEVISIO
EXPERIME
GENERAL E

Miss Marie Delroy was the camera's focus of attention when General Electric demonstrated its experimental mechanical television system at a radio trade show in New York City in the late twenties.

I do know that there *were* people out there seeing our shows. People were buying Jenkins television sets. They got them for—I think—$57.50 or $58.50. . . .

Working conditions were chaotic. You never knew what was going to happen next. We were on the eighth floor of a loft building in Jersey City. On the roof was our sending apparatus. Whenever we had a thunderstorm and the lightning would come cracking, someone was designated to go up on the roof, crawl into this broadcasting shack—and because there were wires all along the top of it you had to crawl along the floor to get to the switches—and turn it off so none of us would get electrocuted downstairs.

The studio walls were concrete, and the floor was concrete, and the studio itself was a room maybe twelve by eight feet, filled with banks of light on each side. When you were broadcasting, the glare was such that you squinted your eyes when you tried to look in the camera. That didn't make any difference because nobody could see your eyes anyway.

It was so hot in the studio that even on a freezing winter day you were perspiring heavily. The engineers would stay all night and experiment with the equipment because they were so fascinated with this new development in broadcasting. I would come in in the morning to start our daily broadcasting, and they'd say, "Now watch out for this wire. See, it's red at this end, that's live. Don't step on it, you might get electrocuted." So you had to go hip-hopping around the studio to get to the place where the camera could reach you. . . .

We brought some very famous people into the studio. Ruth Etting was one; Ethel Barrymore was another. They came because they wanted to know about this new broadcasting medium. They knew nothing about it. . . . They were scared to death of the cameras.

One performer who expressed no fear whatsoever before the cameras was a twenty-one-year-old who would would go on to become "Mr. Television," Milton Berle. He appeared on an early experimental TV broadcast in Chicago in 1929. "I was at the Coliseum as master of ceremonies, and somebody contacted my mother and said, 'I have a television station over here.'

Percy Kilbride (left), who gained fame as the movies'
Pa Kettle, played the owner of a country drugstore in
The Fortune Hunter, *one of the first dramas to be*
transmitted by NBC's regular television service in
October 1939.

12

"My mother said, 'A *what* station?' What the hell
did we know? We thought TV meant tired vaudeville. . . . So we went over there. It was called the
United States Television Company, and the studio
was like a closet with lights. They put makeup on
me—black lipstick. I looked like Pola Negri, or
Garbo, years ago in silent pictures—whiteface and
all that. Was it hot!

"People ask me when I started in television. I say
1929. They never believe me."

By the end of the twenties, when Berle made his
first TV appearance, there were twenty-eight licensed "visual broadcasting" stations in the United
States. Research would make it clear that the mechanical television systems were a failure. The picture transmitted by electronic systems was far
superior. Depression economics and the wrangling
by different companies over different television designs soon drove individuals like Irma Kroman's
boss, Charles Francis Jenkins, out of business.

Only companies like RCA, with the huge profits
generated by radio sales and its NBC radio network,
could afford to continue research. Vladimir Zworykin had told David Sarnoff that perfecting his electronic television system would cost $100,000.
Sarnoff wound up spending $50 million.

Sarnoff and others, including Philo T. Farnsworth, urged the speedy introduction of television
on a commercial basis. Competitors balked. Why
hurry, they asked, when the picture still needed to
be perfected and radio was so profitable?

Sarnoff persevered. The CBS network, founded
in 1928 by William S. Paley, had begun experimental broadcasts, but NBC was poised for a major
launch. Arthur Hungerford was an eyewitness to
the first NBC broadcasts.

"I came from a small town with a graduating
class of twenty," Hungerford recalled.

In my very early teens, I made radios. I read some place
that you go to MIT if you want to make radios, so I was the
first student to ever go from my little town to the Massachu-
setts Institute of Technology.

I hadn't been there very long when I heard about television. It turned out there was an experimenter there named
Hollis Baird, who was putting on some experimental programs. In the fraternity house we had a television set that
we put together so we could watch. We sent some of our
brothers over, they would appear, and we would try to recognize them. We were bit by the television bug very early—
this would be about 1931.

I graduated from MIT with useful connections, and I was
able to get a job with the National Broadcasting Company.
After being there about a year and a half, a friend and I
tried to get into television.

It was very secret—Studio 3-H. No one could go in; it was
under lock and key. Of course, the real reason for this was
that we were trying to beat the British, who were ready to
start a program service.

The British succeeded in November 1936.

"My friend and I watched all the newspapers and
magazines from England," Hungerford continued.

One of NBC's first remote broadcast trucks. Cameramen transmit man-on-the-street interviews from New York's Times Square.

We put out a little television newspaper, which we then sent to many of the big shots in New York—all the heads of the advertising agencies and so on.

All of a sudden, we were called into the offices of our big bosses. They said, "Do you really want to be in television?"

"We certainly do."

"Well, if you stop your magazine, we will give you a job."

That's all we wanted from our reports anyway! That's how I got into television and went through that magic door for the first time, into that studio where there was just one camera, just beginning to get ready for the opening show in July of 1936.

We were given very menial jobs. My buddy was given the job of pushing the dolly on which the camera was to be mounted, and I was given the job of running a microphone boom.

The first program—July 7, 1936—began with James Harbord, who was the chairman of the board of RCA, David Sarnoff, who was the president of RCA, and Lenox Lohr, who was the president of NBC. They all wanted to be in on this act, the big beginning of television in America. They ap-

peared in an office scene, and they told how television was just around the corner.

Then we aired a variety show. The first thing that I remember is a fashion show with three lovely models and a narrator. Then there was a bit of a comedy scene with Ed Wynn, followed by Graham McNamee, who was one of the best sports announcers. To show drama, we brought over Henry Hull, the star of a long-running show called *Tobacco Road*. Then, as a sort of climax, we had the Pickens Sisters, and some dancing. Russell Market came over from the Radio City Music Hall, which was just across the street, to see what place we had for dancers. It turned out that instead of the one hundred and twenty dancers that they used on the Music Hall stage, we had room for three! So he worked out a routine for our program, we showed a film to prove that we could transmit motion pictures, and that was about it.

This show, incidentally, was for the RCA licensees and people who were close RCA family. Two or three hundred were brought upstairs to the top of the Empire State Building, where sets were placed so that they could look at the program.

A woman crew member (below left) trains light on the singer Yvette as she performs before television cameras in the mid-forties. Entertainers were eager for a chance to appear on early TV, even though radio and the movies were still the most popular entertainment mediums.

From the very beginning, broadcasters realized the need to make the most prosaic information visual and interesting. A weatherman (below right) at WNBT-TV in New York (now WNBC) buttons up tight to deliver the forecast against the backdrop of an appropriate winter scene.

Hungerford, too, remembers the problems of those early broadcasts. "One of the limitations in the television studios in those days was the light level," he said. "We had to have one thousand footcandles of light in order to get a decent picture. This caused a lot of problems for us. I remember one young singer. She was standing in front of a piano and singing. I was the floor manager on the show, and it became apparent that she was having great difficulty. I thought she was going to faint, but in the way you learn to signal back and forth, she indicated that she would be able to finish the song.

"So we went to the end of it and turned the lights off and got her out of there, and it turned out that the mascara on her eyes had melted on her eyelashes and had been seeping into her eyes all the time she was singing that song. It impressed us, the stamina of this young artist, who later became one of the best known American stars in television—Dinah Shore."

Burke Crotty was one of NBC's first producers. "The truth of the matter is that everything was experimental, everything was a challenge," he said. "It was invigorating. It was a thrilling thing to do,

With a camera close-up, viewers of this early TV drama could see the consternation of a naval officer as he pitched to and fro, but would never notice the wooden rocker device built by clever stage carpenters to achieve the special effect of a ship rolling at sea.

and as I look back at it today, I think I've never been so frightened in my life, and I am not prone to frighten very easily. . . . I will never forget the gang that we worked with, including the studio people. I never knew anyone to put in such long hours of their own. There was no overtime; there was no money for that, but they all worked overtime on their own."

NBC's experimental broadcasts continued for almost three years. Then it began a regular program service. As its curtain raiser, the network telecast to approximately a thousand viewers a major event—

Family Battle aired every Thursday over WENR-TV, ABC's Chicago affiliate, from 8 to 8:30 P.M., 1952–1953. Pictured here are the show's stars, six of the eight Kloses (Deborah and Victoria were too young to appear), and Daniel McMaster, curator of the Museum of Science and Industry, who was the show's host. All questions were viewer supplied.

President Roosevelt at the opening ceremonies of the 1939 New York World's Fair. Later that same day, Sarnoff dedicated RCA's pavilion at the fair with a telecast that announced the new era of commercial television. RCA TV sets were waiting for consumers to rush in and buy, Sarnoff said; initial sales were less than brisk.

"There may have been many for sale," Crotty said. "But there weren't too many of them bought. In the early days of television, in New York, there weren't more than 120 of them in all the city, and the majority of those were in one of two places— RCA executives' homes or bars.

"The first set was called the TRK 660. It was a huge thing, stood possibly four or four and half feet high. It had a hinged lid with a mirror inside, and you lifted the lid and looked at the picture reflected in the mirror, because the picture tube—which was then known as a kinescope—was so huge that there was no way of putting it in a cabinet horizontally. It would stick out into the room.

"I bought a brand new car in 1940 for a thousand dollars, and they wanted $660 for this TV set when there was virtually nothing on the air. At that price and at that size, no one wanted them."

Progress ground to a halt with America's entry

In 1954, all four television networks—ABC, CBS, NBC, and Du Mont—simultaneously carried a two-hour special marking the seventy-fifth anniversary of the invention of the light bulb. Light's Diamond Jubilee *featured such stars as Kim Novak, Walter Brennan, Helen Hayes, Lauren Bacall, and here, Judith Anderson, who appeared as the woman who posed for Bartholdi's Statue of Liberty.*

into World War II. The production of television equipment for commercial use was banned a few months after Pearl Harbor. TV engineers were put to work on radar development. "We did not stop broadcasting immediately," Crotty said. "What happened was that we were almost forced to stop, because we had very brilliant engineers, and the armed services needed their research talents far more than we did. So they reached in and took them."

When the war ended, the race to mass-produce televisions and make commercial television a reality went into full gear. At the time of Pearl Harbor there had only been a few hundred sets in the country. By 1947, there were 170,000, and by the end of 1948, a quarter of a million. Shows like Milton Berle's *Texaco Star Theater* were emptying city streets on Tuesday nights. A movie house manager in Ohio placed a sign on his theater door: CLOSED TUESDAY—I WANT TO SEE BERLE, TOO!

Before the war, CBS had lagged behind NBC in television experimentation. But William Paley proved to be a worthy rival for David Sarnoff. If Sarnoff was the visionary of television broadcasting, Paley was the visionary of television programming. In 1948, he scored a number of coups, stealing from NBC some of the network's biggest radio stars, including Jack Benny, Red Skelton, and Edgar Bergen. Paley would put them to work on television.

That same year, CBS named Worthington Miner manager of TV program development. He had come to work at CBS Television before the war began. "We had the same studios the whole time I was with television," he said, "above the main waiting room at Grand Central Station. At the west end were my office and Gilbert Seldes's office—he was in charge of programming at the time—and at the east end were the control room and the power supply."

The frustrations were enormous. Miner remembers conditions similar to those described by Hungerford. "I went home to my wife one night and said, 'The equipment we are being given is so inept, it is never going to sell television to the public.' There were complaints all around." One of the major problems remained the fiery intensity of the lights necessary to get a decent picture. The prodigious Vladimir Zworykin came up with the answer: a tube called the image-orthicon that was extremely sensitive to light. "One of the great romantic and dramatic moments of the early years of television," Miner said, was being invited by RCA to Madison Square Garden to see the new Zworykin tube.

We went with considerable apprehension. We had been gypped by Philco and RCA so many times. They boasted beyond their capacity to produce. . . .

The demonstration was very simple. We were all on the north side of the Garden, and on the south side were the engineers and their equipment—cameras and a man on a horse. The man on the horse was brightly lit for the cameras, but there was still a dull image on the screen. . . .

All of a sudden, every light in Madison Square Garden went black. There we were, in total and utter blackness. At that point, the rider struck a match and lit a candle—one candle. On the screen, the horse appeared and the rider appeared.

The story to all of us was complete. Where before we had needed this abnormal and harmful amount of light, all of a sudden, with one footcandle, we could light a scene, we could get a mood, we could create a character.

At that moment, Miner said, he realized that "television couldn't miss. It was going to be able to take dramatic shows into the home. . . . All of a sudden, we had an instrument that reproduced a quality picture with the atmosphere and mood that Hitchcock or Bergman might require."

CBS Chairman Paley determined that a quality picture was useless without quality programming. Placed in charge of new programs in 1948, Miner's mandate was to create "one grade A television show of an hour's duration, one variety show of an hour's duration, one half-hour situation comedy, and one children's show." The grade A show was one of the classics of the Golden Age of live television—*Studio One,* for which he also worked as a producer and writer. The comedy was *The Goldbergs,* another classic, successfully transplanted from radio. The kid's show was *Mr. I. Magination,* starring Paul

Before sports dominated the Sunday afternoon schedules, many public affairs series were offered by the networks. CBS's The Search *traveled to college campuses around the country to examine various research programs. One show, featuring Yale University's Child Study Center, even included a childbirth on camera, an unusual TV event in 1954.*

Tripp. The variety show was the killer—what could be created to compete with NBC's redoubtable Milton Berle? "If we were going to get a show to compete," Miner decided, "we had to have two things: One was a nonperforming emcee; the other was an emcee who had the most superb taste in discovering, choosing, and balancing talent to make a show that was exciting." Miner knew that his choice for the emcee, Broadway newspaper columnist Ed Sullivan, "physically, was not the most attractive of men," but he presented his idea at a meeting of CBS executives.

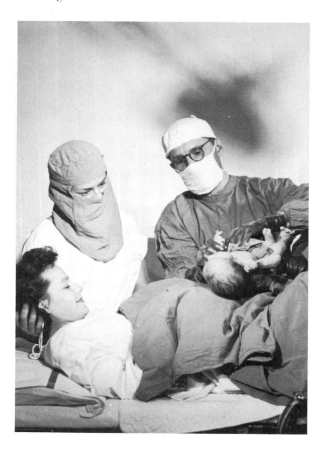

They were bored stiff. Everyone thought I had gone off my rocker. Frank Stanton, who was then executive vice president, said, "Well, let's move on to some of the other matters we have to cover."

At that moment, Bill Paley walked in and said, "Well, how do we stand on Berle?" In a rather embarrassed voice, Mr. Stanton said, "Tony Miner has given us his idea. We don't feel that it's adequate to compete with Berle, but I've asked him if he has an alternative suggestion to make. He said, 'No, none as good as that,' so there we sit."

Paley said, "I want to hear it." I relayed the concept and the reasoning. . . . There was a long pause as I finished, and unexpectedly, Paley said, "I like it."

Ed Sullivan's show went on the air on June 20, 1948. The critics' reaction was devastating. They had committed themselves to Berle. Berle's great public was kids and barflies, and that was not what Ed Sullivan was about.

I made a bet, a very small bet of five dollars, that *The Ed Sullivan Show*, which was then called *Toast of the Town*, would outlast Milton Berle. Milton Berle lasted seven years, if I'm not mistaken. NBC signed a contract whereby Berle was on salary for life, a mistake. Ed Sullivan produced a show for twenty-three years.

The year 1948 is often cited as a benchmark year for television, the year when commercial television finally took off, when it was taken seriously as a real force in the worlds of entertainment and communications. Four television networks were on the air—NBC, CBS, ABC (which had been formed in 1943, when NBC sold one of its two radio networks), and the Du Mont Television Network. The Du Mont network was created by television inventor Allen B. Du Mont, who had been a colleague of Charles Francis Jenkins. The network owned three stations in New York, Washington, and Pittsburgh, and it provided the first TV exposure for such stars as Jackie Gleason and Bishop Fulton J. Sheen before it ceased operation in 1955.

There were many more exciting developments to come in television technology. By the late 1940s,

20

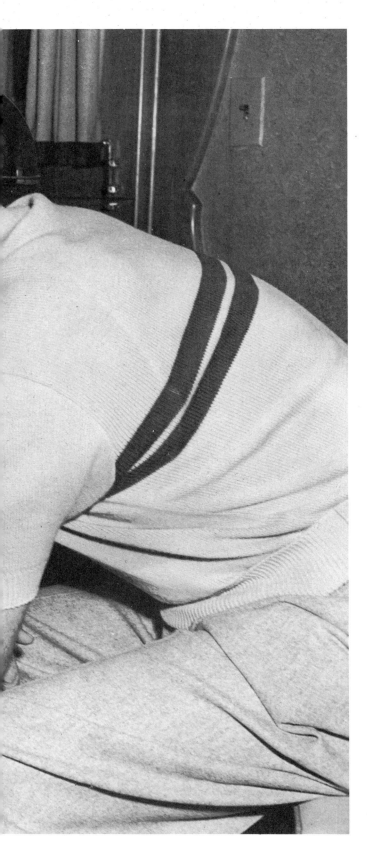

Bob Hope explains the intricacies of a 1948 television set to his son, Kelly. When Paramount Pictures, Hope's home studio, opened TV station KTLA, the first commercial station west of the Rockies, in 1947, Hope appeared on its first telecast. Since then he has become TV's hardiest perennial.

scientists and engineers were getting closer and closer to the invention of color television, but once again progress was slowed by a wrangle between advocates of mechanical and electronic systems. CBS's resident genius, Peter Goldmark, had devised a "color wheel" apparatus, but it would have required new kinds of cameras and home receivers. Sarnoff held out for a "compatible" electronic system, that is, one in which shows transmitted in color could still be seen on a black-and-white set. He won.

Videotape, home video systems, and satellites that allow us to beam pictures from all over the world are all extraordinary inventions, tools that have helped make television the astonishing revolution that it is. But the first days of network television were probably the most remarkable. An exceptional group of people came together to create those first shows and what has become known as the Golden Age.

Television was still a miracle then.

2. THE GOLDEN AGE

Ed Wynn (center) was another vaudeville and radio veteran who made the jump to television. His variety series, The Ed Wynn Show, *was one of the first national series to be produced from Los Angeles. Here, Wynn appears in a sketch with British character actors Elsa Lanchester and Reginald Gardiner.*

Everyone was learning, almost everything was live, and anything could happen. Stage fright, flubbed lines, accidents on the set—all manner of catastrophe could befall those early days of network television—and did.

But that seemed simply to add to the spirit of adventure and discovery. The improvisational nature of those first steps could also result in moments of magic. People were allowed to do just about anything they wanted precisely because nobody really knew what they were supposed to be doing in the first place. The Golden Age was a serendipitous time, especially for television drama.

Many of television's first viewers were affluent city dwellers, familiar with the theater, so live drama was an important part of the broadcast schedule in those days. The networks hired people with experience in the logistics and economics of stage production. Appropriately, many of the early television dramas were re-creations of Broadway plays.

But at the same time, original dramas, created expressly for television were being produced—TV plays that were character studies, drawn from real life. Live drama anthology series were a showcase for young people looking for a break in television—such series as *Studio One, The U.S. Steel Hour, Kraft Television Theatre, The Alcoa Hour, Pulitzer Prize Playhouse,* and many others. Many producers and directors, including Fred Coe, Sidney Lumet, John Frankenheimer, Fred Zinnemann, and George Roy Hill got their first jobs working on these live dramas.

From this so-called Golden Age emerged also an extraordinary group of writers: Paddy Chayefsky (whose television drama *Marty* is a classic), Reginald Rose, Robert Alan Aurthur, William Gibson

GOOD?
IT'LL SIMPLY
KILL YOU.

HEAVY
CREAM

In 1956, Ed Wynn (below right) switched from comedy to a rare and moving dramatic role, appearing with his son Keenan (left) and Jack Palance in a Golden Age classic, Requiem for a Heavyweight, *written by Rod Serling.*

26

(The Miracle Worker), Rod Serling,* and Gore Vidal. "The Golden Age was golden largely in the sense of opportunity," Gore Vidal recalled. "There was an awful lot of drama. Television was still new and exciting. Everybody watched. You would walk down the street the next day and you would hear people talking about it. You had a sense of an audience, and you had a sense that what you did was needed."

Before The Twilight Zone *and* Night Gallery *anthologies, Serling wrote such distinguished television plays as* Requiem for a Heavyweight *and* Patterns, *a play about the pressures of big business that was so powerful and successful that the cast was reassembled four weeks later for another live performance.*

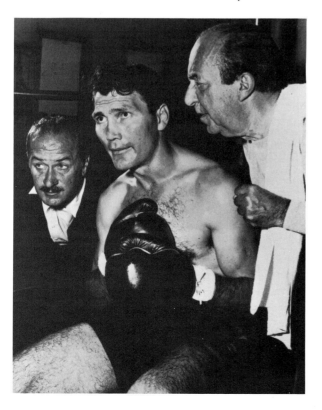

J. P. MILLER

J. P. Miller is another of the great writers, a regular contributor to two of the biggest live drama series: *Philco TV Playhouse* and *Playhouse 90.* Luck and timing got him started.

"I was starving to death, but trying to write for the theater," he said.

I didn't have a television set and my children were barefooted. I was writing ten-hour dramas that had to be done in five consecutive nights—that sort of thing—and I couldn't get anybody to read them. . . .

A friend of mine was a television repairman, and he brought me a TV tube—it was just a tube with controls—so one night I started tinkering with it and a show came on. It was a show called *Playhouse 90,* and there was a play by Horton Foote. I started watching it, and it was terrific. I thought, "Gee, if they're doing things like this on television, I might give them the benefit of me!" There's no arrogance like ignorance, right?

I made little notes about the characteristics of the plays that were on *Playhouse 90,* and I wrote one. I took it to NBC. I happened to know a guy who worked for producer Fred Coe. He was kind of an assistant. I took it up, and I handed it to him, and I said, "Can you give this to the script editor?" He said, "Yeah, I suppose so." He did me a great favor and put it on her desk. It was the kind of thing you're not supposed to do.

That night the script editor took it home with her in a stack of scripts and read it, and the next morning she called and said, "Who's your agent?"

I said, "I don't have an agent."

"Well, how did I get your script?"

I told her, and she said, "Good God, if I'd known that . . . We don't take unsolicited manuscripts, but now that I've read it, I want to buy it."

It was like magic, Cinderella, everything rolled into one. One day I was selling air conditioning—or rather, *not* selling air conditioning—and the next day, I was a member of Fred Coe's stable. . . .

Television was exciting just because it was new, and it was all live, which made it even more exciting. A few young,

Cliff Robertson and Piper Laurie starred in the 1958 Golden Age drama, The Days of Wine and Roses on Playhouse 90. A story of love beseiged by alcoholism, it was written by J. P. Miller, produced by Fred Coe, and directed by John Frankenheimer.

brilliant producers came into the medium and devised a way of doing shows in sets that were very cheap. They rehearsed them like plays, they treated writers like playwrights, the show went on, and it was an event. You got phone calls afterwards from all over the country. It was wonderful. . . .

The main thing was that we took ourselves seriously. We sat down and said, "I'm going to write something *good.*"

It was such a new medium and such a powerful medium and advertising was so incredibly successful on a successful show—the producers sensed their power. Fred Coe sensed *his* power; he insisted on total autonomy. If a man from the advertising agency walked into the control room and said, "That's kind of slow," Fred Coe would go into a screaming fit. He'd throw the man out. And the guy accepted it. Where else could they get that kind of attention for their money?

Miller was lured away to Hollywood, but luck stepped in once again, leading him to the creation of what is undoubtedly Miller's most famous and finest contribution to live television—*The Days of Wine and Roses,* the story of an alcoholic couple, written in 1958 for *Playhouse 90.* It starred Cliff Robertson and Piper Laurie.

That was kind of a minor miracle. It almost never happened because I was going to quit writing. . . . I was disgusted with Hollywood. I was walking down the street one day in New York, and I bumped into Fred Coe. He said, "You're just the guy I want to see. I thought you were in California. I've been trying to find you. I'm going to do three *Playhouse 90*s, and I want you to do one of them."

"No way," I said. "Forget it. I am not going to write anything for anybody for I don't know how long. I'm going to be a fisherman."

"Nonsense. Think about it. . . . If you change your mind, I want to do something really strong—alcohol or crazy—whatever. . . . If you get an idea, call me, you've got the slot."

I said, "Thanks a lot, Fred, but forget it." But somehow, the word *alcohol* stuck in my mind. And that night, I was lying in bed, and I started thinking about my uncle; we all lived together during the Depression. I thought of one particular scene in which he came home one Christmas Eve and tore up the Christmas tree. I had a thing about that, and somehow or other a story started coming to me.

At one o'clock in the morning, I picked up the phone. I knew Fred would still be up because it was a Saturday night. . . . He was smashed himself, half out of his gourd, and I said, "I've got an idea for a story."

He said, "What is it, Pappy? Tell me about it."

I said something like, "I want to do a story about a love affair between two people who drink a lot—a nice young man and a nice young woman. When they drink a lot, they fall in love, they have a lot of fun drinking, and slowly, slowly, the bottle becomes more important to each than each is to the other. The bottle that brought them together separates them."

And Coe said, "I love it, Pappy, write it. Have another drink."

I started researching. I started going to A.A. meetings. I didn't go and say "I'm a writer." I just went in, you know. I felt kind of guilty, because the people would pat you and say, "I hope you make it, pal."

And I wrote it.

The Days of Wine and Roses would be one of the last of the great live dramas. "It couldn't last," Miller said.

Paul Newman (left) played ball player Henry Wiggins in The U.S. Steel
Hour *adaptation of Mark Harris's novel* Bang the Drum Slowly *in 1956. The
live drama also starred Albert Salmi (center) and George Peppard (right).*

Fred Coe started getting older and weaker—so did all the others—started losing some of their power, and then tape came in. Lesser producers could do shows, they could do more good shows because if the show wasn't good they could change it around until it was better. And then they found that by doing tape, they could go outside. Car chases—that was the beginning of the end of television!

The shift of production to the West Coast was very important, because the symbol of the West Coast was the quickie movie. That's what they started making. They started making movies for television, and they started making them like a formula . . . a certain amount of spilling over the top of the gown, a certain amount of female pulchritude properly displayed, a few car chases, a few gunshots, and so forth. They learned by doing these things they could get more viewers and have a surer shot than they could with these little plays. A simple matter of the marketplace did us in.

JOHN FRANKENHEIMER

John Frankenheimer is best known today as a director of motion pictures such as *The Manchurian Candidate, Seven Days in May,* and *The Fixer,* but he too is an alumnus of the Golden Age. He started out as an assistant and was soon directing plays on *Playhouse 90* and *Studio One,* plays such as *The Rainmaker, The Turn of the Screw,* an elaborate two-part production of *For Whom the Bell Tolls,* and J. P. Miller's *The Days of Wine and Roses,* a particular favorite of Frankenheimer's.

"It was one of the best scripts I've ever had and the producer, Fred Coe, was one of the two best producers with whom I've ever worked," he said. "Fred had been a director—a good one—so he knew how to talk to directors. He was wonderful with writers. He just gave you the feeling that everything was going to be okay. He gave us a climate in which we could function creatively, and that cer-

tainly is the role of a producer. He was just a brilliant, wonderful man."

Ironically, he said, "Alcohol killed Fred Coe. I loved working with him and I mourn his death a great deal."

Alcoholism was just one of the side effects that afflicted those involved in the production of live television. The stress and tension were enormous.

I became a director when I was twenty-four years old, and I really didn't know any better. I think if I were to go back and try to do it now, it might be absolutely impossible. I remember that I developed a terrible lower-back problem, and I shared that problem with many of my fellow directors.

I remember during an air show—for instance, a *Playhouse 90*—I would lose four to five pounds in perspiration. I'd have to take my shirt off and just wring it out at the end of one of those things.

The time when the tension was at its highest was between dress rehearsal and air. After the notes were given out to the cast and crew, we had approximately fifty minutes before the air show. That's the time when people were really by themselves, and they get terribly nervous. I remember one show I did with Dennis O'Keefe—his first live television show. It was 1955, and he started walking behind the scenery, and he saw his leading lady there—Mary Sinclair, she was literally the queen of live television at that time.* She'd done about three hundred live television shows. Dennis went up to her and said, "Mary, how do you do it?"

She said, "Well, Dennis, there's absolutely nothing to it." Whereupon she turned around and vomited.

Sinclair's reaction is all the more understandable when you hear some of the horror stories related by Golden Age veterans like Frankenheimer. He remembered one particular incident in a show that starred Lee Marvin.

---

*Mary Sinclair was a major leading lady of the Golden Age. Among her many other roles, she was the star of over a dozen *Studio One* adaptations of such classics as *Jane Eyre* and *Wuthering Heights* (see interview with John Forsythe).

Andy Griffith starred in The U.S. Steel Hour's
No Time for Sergeants, *a live TV comedy that also became a successful Broadway play and Hollywood motion picture.*

I was still, thank goodness, an assistant director. The director was a fellow who had done hundreds of live television shows. He was a gentleman who really thought on his feet rather than planning it all out beforehand. . . . In this particular case, Lee Marvin was playing a private detective, and the director decided that he would end on a shot of Lee Marvin and begin on a shot of Lee Marvin in a phone booth for the next scene. I pointed out to the director that was highly improbable and impractical—Lee Marvin was already on the set. How was he going to get to the phone booth?

I was told to mind my own business. *He*—the director—would figure it out. Rather than cut to the lady who was playing the scene with Marvin, the director decided that he was going to save face and show me, this upstart, that he was able to do this. . . .

He said to Lee, "All right, what you do here at the end of this scene is put your cigarette out in that ashtray and we'll pan down to the cigarette, and you get out of the set and run over to the phone booth."

Lee said, "I can't make it."

The director said, "Look we'll fix it. We're gonna put the phone booth on a dolly with wheels on it and we're gonna put it right here next to the set, and you just get up from here, run into the phone booth, and that's that. You see, Frankenheimer? You see how I fix that?"

Well, it was great if you like shots of smoldering cigarettes in ashtrays, because we hung on it for about fifteen to twenty seconds in dress rehearsal until we got Lee in the phone booth.

The director forgot a couple of things: One, he forgot about the adrenaline of live television; and two, he forgot that the studio in which we were doing this show was at a slight incline and we were at the top of it. . . .

On the air, we panned down to the ashtray, the cigarette was sizzling, and Lee—because he was on the air—got this terrific burst of adrenaline and hit that phone booth at about twenty miles an hour. The phone booth proceeded to roll right across the studio very slowly.

It was like a Fellini movie—we panned this phone booth across the studio, past the cameras—we even panned past one actress who was completely naked, changing for her next scene! And of course, you couldn't hear anything that Lee was saying because the boom was still where we left it. Lee was talking a mile a minute, we were panning,

and it came to an end when the phone booth hit the wall at the end of the studio!

Frankenheimer told another war story that gives an indication of just how deeply into mayhem live TV drama could descend. He was still working as an assistant director.

The assistant director's job in live television in those days was to go in at the end of the rehearsal period and be the director of photography for the director. Only in this particular case, I was called the day beforehand and told that we were doing this show with [British character actor] Francis L. Sullivan and Eva Marie Saint. It was Francis L. Sullivan's live television debut. He was playing a British missionary who was flying with his assistant in a plane fifty thousand feet above sea level across the Himalaya Mountains. They were to crash-land and be rescued by a group of Chinese ski troops. . . .

The studio in which we were doing this show was terribly small and we were doing the commercials from the same studio.

I said to the director, "How are you going to do the Chinese ski troops?"

He said, "That's very easy. You're going down to Chinatown, and *you* are going to find the Chinese ski troops."

I went down to Chinatown, and I found that all of the Chinese actors I talked to couldn't speak English and couldn't ski. I finally found some who were able to ski but could not speak English. I got them back to the studio and put them in costumes, and I said to the director, "What are you going to do for skis?"

The director said, "Very simple. We're gonna put wheels on the bottom of the skis."

"Where are you going to position them?"

He said, "You tell them that when we come to the commercial man for the first time, they're to get into position." It was a really shaky operation—I don't have to tell you.

The show started, and we're in the cockpit. Two seats, that's all we had as a set, no budget. We were going along, and suddenly Francis L. Sullivan dried up. He just totally forgot his lines.

He looked at Eva Marie Saint, and he said, "Well, my dear, what have you got to say for yourself?"

And she looked at him and she said, "I think I'll just go to sleep." Whereupon she did. Whereupon Francis L. Sullivan said, "My stop, I think I'll get off," and he stepped up and walked out of the airplane.

The director panicked—as well he should have—and he screamed, "Take one!"

Well, camera one was on the commercial announcer, who was talking to his agency boss. The camera's on him, and suddenly he starts to say his commercial, except the audio boom was still over Francis L. Sullivan. So over the commercial man's mouth going, you heard "forty years in this goddamned business . . ." and so on. . . .

Finally, we got Francis L. Sullivan back in his plane. The audience must have been terribly confused, but we got him back, and he was saying his lines, and suddenly that glassy look came into his eyes again and we knew it was all over. . . .

This time, the director wasn't gonna wait for him to walk off the plane. He screamed, "Take one!"

Camera one was on the announcer again, and the commercial announcer is saying to the agency man, "The nerve of that son of a bitch. . . ." The light is on, he starts his commercial. . . . Suddenly, right across the screen, comes the Chinese ski troop, and the guy is trying to do his commercial. . . .

I called master control. I said, "Look, this thing's totally out of control—just cut us off. We're down in flames!" We were taken off the air.

In spite of all that, Frankenheimer has fond memories of that so-called Golden Age.

"We were not bothered by the pressures of huge budgets and ratings that television in the United States is bothered with today. We also had the best writers available. . . .

"It just happened to be a time when there was an awful lot of talent collected in one place, and that place was live television. It was the perfect place for that talent to be."

What was lost with the death of live television drama?

All sense of urgency. The directors had control for the simple reason that there was no time for temperamental actors in live television. If anybody started to argue with you or be late or something like that, what you did was just take them aside and say, "Look this is not very pleasant. I don't like it, but in the long run it's you who's going to be up there on Thursday night live at nine-thirty, not me." That was a bluff that worked quite often.

As soon as we went to tape, in the back of people's minds was the fact that if it really got bad, if the scenery fell down, if they forgot their lines, if the whole show went out the window, you could start again. A lot of things just did not have the same spontaneity, the same urgency on tape as they did live. . . . The invention of magnetic tape destroyed live television. . . .

Two, television became such a tremendous big business that the ratings took over, and our ratings were not commensurate with the ratings of the shows opposite us. . . .

Three, it was a new type of executive who took over, who was just in it for the short run and really just wanted the numbers for the ratings. . . .

And so ended the Golden Age. Frankenheimer misses the combination of excitement and agony.

"Someone once compared doing live television to doing summer stock in an iron lung," he said. "I think that about says it."

Walter Matthau (left) is just one of many Hollywood stars who got their start appearing in the live dramas of television's Golden Age.

IMERO FIORENTINO

Imero Fiorentino has gone from being a staff lighting director at ABC to running an eighty-employee company that is involved in virtually every aspect of production. Imero Fiorentino Associates works in television, concerts, and industrial shows and has designed for everything from Frank Sinatra appearances and Neil Diamond tours to bullfights.

He learned his trade during the Golden Age. "I first saw television when I was a kid growing up in Brooklyn, in my late teens, I guess," Fiorentino said.

We didn't own a television set—most people didn't. But the *Texaco Star Theater* with Milton Berle was on Tuesday nights. So we all stood on the street, and the people who had a television set on my block would put it in the window facing the street. Half the block would gather—maybe fifty people would watch the show.

Along with most people, I didn't know how it worked. Okay, so it's pictures through the air instead of sound only. I had no desire to become involved in television because I didn't know what it was.

I got out of college and lined myself up to be a teacher at Indiana State University. . . . I was waiting for the semester to start, and my father died. I was left with the problem of having to become the breadwinner and live in Brooklyn, because I couldn't afford to live in Indiana and send enough money home to pay for the bills.

I had no job, so I applied to various places in the city. Among them were the networks. A few weeks later, ABC called me in and said, "Would you like to come in and talk to us about a job as a television lighting engineer?"

I talked with them, and I told them I knew nothing about television. They said, "That's okay, kid. Nobody else does." That was in 1950. I said I knew theater lighting, but I did not know television. And they said, "We'll assign somebody to you to help you learn it."

They assigned a guy to me. He was a light-direction engineer. They just poured light on in those days. It was really floodlighting.

After not even two weeks of following this guy around, one morning he said to me, "Okay, you light it." This was two o'clock in the morning because we went on live in those days.

It was *Pulitzer Prize Playhouse.* An hour-and-a-half drama, live. I'll never forget it. The name of the play was *Mrs. January and Mr. X,* with Spring Byington and Douglas Fairbanks, Jr.

The guy went home, and I had no idea what to do. I knew how to light things for the theater. I used a minimal amount of light, even though I was told you had to use a lot of light. I used less, because I just didn't know, and I didn't have the time. Amazingly enough, the picture looked pretty good.

So, since it looked good, people started to say, "This kid's very artistic." The shows came out looking good, and everybody wanted me to do them. And I became known as the artistic lighting designer.

At the same time, there were other lighting designers on the scene who were doing the same thing. We were pioneers. The television industry is such a baby that some of us are still alive. My colleagues like Bob Barrie and Ralph Holmes, they were doing the same thing at their networks. We started achieving reputations for doing creative, artistic things.

We had something going for us, too. Technology was changing. Cameras got smaller, better; they needed lower light levels. We could do more with less.

We could use shadow. Before, shadow was taboo. Now we could use shadow to our advantage. We could create a third dimension. The engineers became more adept at utilizing shadow, making pictures happen. A lot of cajoling went on, but we all were in the same boat together, you see. We were growing and learning.

They built from the ground up.

It was twenty-two hours a day, every day, filled with great excitement. There were no days off. . . .

You did things and somebody would say, "Isn't that wonderful? How'd you do that?" So we tried to remember how we did it, and we tried to do it again. That's how we set standards, rules, and goals. We talked to each other.

Whether the Golden Age produced shows of great substance, I don't know. It produced a lot of people with a lot of substance, that's for sure. Especially in the writing and directing area. Sitting next to you would be Rod Serling, Reginald Rose, Tad Mosel. We didn't know they were great writers then—neither did they. Also directors like John Frankenheimer, George Schaefer, Sidney Lumet, Alex Segal, Charles Dubin.

There were always disasters. There were many shows where scenery fell down; it just fell down on camera. On *Paul Whiteman's Goodyear Revue* a series of columns came in from both sides on two dollies. The two dollies hit, and all the columns fell down, right on camera, live. There was nothing you could do about it.

I remember one show called *Tales of Tomorrow*. The opening shot was a big pull switch. The camera zooms in on this, and a gloved hand, black with lightning on it, would come in. It was a little stagehand named Danny Terrill, a little jockey, his hand was like his whole head size. The hand would reach in and pull the switch. Right underneath was a flashpot that would go off on cue, and out of the smoke from the flash powder would grow the words *Tales of Tomorrow*.

So we were in rehearsal, he pulls the switch, and the flashpot goes *psstt*—just a little puff. So somebody says, "Tell the prop man we'll need more flashpowder."

Everybody heard that, so everybody went out on the studio floor; different people told every prop man they could find to put more flash power in. Six people put another spoon or two of flash powder in there, unbeknownst to the other guys—now we have dynamite. I mean, we have a bomb!

We go on the air, the guy pulls the switch and *boom*! The little guy went to the hospital with burns on his face and his clothes on fire. Blew the camera right off the air. Completely destroyed it.

Another time, same series, *Tales of Tomorrow*, Lon Chaney, Jr., was on the show. He's supposed to go crazy. He picks up furniture and hits people over the head with it, cracks chairs. Of course, the furniture was all made out of balsa and stuck together with toothpicks.

We're rehearsing that scene. It was live TV, but we're rehearsing beforehand. In the early rehearsals, he doesn't break the chair because it's the prop. He picks it up and he says, "Then she sits, and then I hit her over the head, and then I put it back down."

So now we're on the air live. He goes to pick up the chair,

but for some reason, he thought it was still a rehearsal. He looks right to the camera and says, "Here's where I hit her over the head with the chair." And he puts the chair down! The whole control room died. Died! . . .

Another one: It was a show called *Fearful Decision*. Alex Segal directed it. It was a kidnapping story with Ralph Bellamy, Meg Mundy, and a little boy. Ralph Bellamy is a wealthy doctor. They live in Connecticut somewhere. The boy gets kidnapped. Bellamy can afford the ransom, but he decides he's going to go on television instead, address the kidnappers and tell them, "I'm not going to give you the money, but I'll double it to anyone who turns you in. . . . Therefore, everybody who's around you, you don't know who will turn you in."

It's an interesting concept. In rehearsal, Alex said to me,

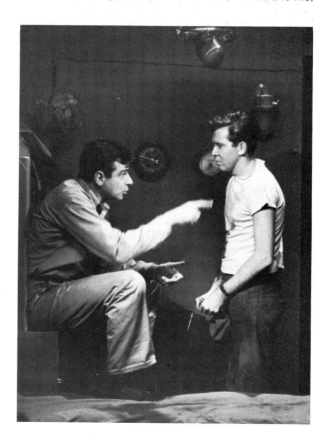

The brash and talented Ethel Merman was one of the Broadway and Hollywood stars who appeared with "Mr. Television," Milton Berle, on one of the Golden Age's comedy-variety hits, Texaco Star Theater.

"I got this guy who's bugging me. He's a friend of a friend, a bit-part actor." He tells me that, reluctantly, he's given this guy a bit part in the show. He plays a state trooper. You see him in the first act, and that's it. You don't see him again.

The play goes on. . . . Everybody's down on the doctor, Ralph Bellamy—"Give them the money, forget the principle, pay the dollars, get the kid." The father sticks to his guns.

Now comes the deadline. This is the last act of the play, a very emotional moment. We start to realize that the kid has probably been killed. Too much time has gone by. The father is now alone, he feels that he's been wrong, he has lost his son, how will he face his wife? He's out in the yard, sitting on a tree stump or something, desolate and alone.

It's twilight. There's a backdrop with painted trees on it, so it looks like the forest when it's dark. The father starts to cry. People in the control room are crying. Alex is crying. He's got his shirt off, he's crying. . . .

And I see something move. The backdrop. You know, when you walk between a backdrop and the studio wall, it creates an air pocket, makes a wave ahead of you as your body pushes the air.

Alex hasn't seen it yet. He's concentrating—"Take two!" Somebody's walking back there. He gets to the split in the two drops, where a tree is painted. He opens it. The father, Ralph Bellamy, looks up. It's this bit-part actor! Dressed in street clothes, he's going home. He walks right through the scene, says to Bellamy, "Good night, Ralph!"

I thought Alex was going to have an apoplectic fit. He starts to rave, "I'll kill him! I'll kill him!"

Alex runs out of the control room and is about to run onto the set, live. He doesn't care. He's going to kill that actor!

They got the actor off and onto the street. They said, "Grab a cab, and get out of here!" They stopped Alex from running onto the set. He's screaming at the top of his lungs, "I'll kill him! I'll kill him!" He's going crazy.

Meanwhile, on camera, the kid comes in, there's a reunion with the father. But you couldn't stop tape and do it again. Done. Done!*

*As is so often the case with history, there are conflicting accounts of this incident. Jack Sameth, the executive producer of *Television*, was the assistant director on *Fearful Decision*. He maintains that Segal actually did get hold of the actor in question, and clobbered him.

In those days, I never lit a news show or a cooking show. I was lucky. I got the big ones: *U.S. Steel Hour*, Leonard Bernstein, Martha Graham, *Omnibus* . . .

Omnibus—Alistair Cooke, produced by Bob Saudek . . . We didn't have electronic boards or anything like memory systems. Forget it. This was all done by hand. I had two men operating thirty-six dimmers by hand. . . . Everything had to be on paper and done manually, so the cues could only be as fast as a man could work. . . .

So whenever anything got transposed, it was chaos, because every cue worked on the cue before it. It depended on the sequence. Today, you can go backwards, forwards, whatever you want. Just push the button. No problem.

But imagine a live show like *Omnibus,* an hour and a half, with many segments in it, maybe three or five per show. We would rehearse them—we're set—it's half an hour to air time. I'm making my final changes and notes and cleaning up things. Saudek would come in and say, "The third segment is now first. The first segment is fifth. The second segment is fourth." I'd say, "Jesus, how can we do that?"

So the last half hour was spent with me and the electricians, on the floor, in the middle of the studio, with all the papers spread out, changing it, but never seeing it changed, and hoping that the brain remembered. . . . I guess it's an experience that most people today don't have, because they rely on systems to do the thinking. The brain was the only computer I had. . . .

I used to go home—I lived in Forest Hills. Every night, I'd go home, I'd shut the car doors and then scream all the way home, at the top of my lungs. I'd get into bed, I'd take four Empirin with codeine. I couldn't get out of bed until I took four more. And that went on daily. The pressure was great.

Still, there was a certain thrill in those early days at a job well done. That becomes obvious when Fiorentino talks about a specific job: the lighting of an American Ballet Theatre production of *Les Sylphides* for *Omnibus.* "The dancing was so beautiful and so simple. Everybody was on, everybody was right, and I was enjoying it to death. The whole control room was just loving it. . . .

"But the crowning moment of it was at the very

Two of the biggest stars of the Golden Age of television: puppets Kukla and Oliver J. Dragon, minus their human sidekick, Fran Allison. Kukla, Fran and Ollie *was a children's show that was almost as popular with adults because of its good-natured yet knowing wit, a style largely attributable to the creative magic between Fran Allison and puppeteer Burr Tillstrom.*

end. . . . Everybody takes their final pose, and there's a slow light change that occurs, that is supposed to end exactly at that moment, that magic moment. I get my electricians on the other end of the headset, and I say, 'No, no, easy, slow, go ahead, right, slow, a little more, a little more, slowly . . .' and then—'Aaaahhh! Look at that!'

"You hit a home run; you won the Super Bowl; you did all that, all on one lousy light cue. Once in a while it all comes together, and you say, 'Wow, we did that! Son of a bitch!' "

FRAN ALLISON

Fran Allison was one of the first of television's first surrogate mothers. *Kukla, Fran and Ollie*, one of the gentlest, cleverest, and funniest children's shows ever, was "hip" in a special way, never smug or patronizing, filled with adult humor, but always retaining an essential sweetness. One boring afternoon after school, when there was nothing on TV but a United Nations Security Council debate, NBC's UN correspondent, Pauline Frederick, signed off, and on came *Kukla, Fran and Ollie*'s Beulah Witch, who announced that she had just flown on her broomstick smack through the United Nations Secretariat.

Fran Allison began as a teacher in Iowa, then went to work at a radio station in Waterloo, Iowa, where she first made a splash playing a character named Aunt Fannie, a regular fixture on Don McNeill's *Breakfast Club*. Aunt Fannie would follow her throughout her radio and television career.

"The program director [in Waterloo] had a noon show called *The Cornhuskers*," Allison said.

He was a man of many voices, and there was a violinist and a man who played the accordion. They'd do these little skits. They were so entertaining that I'd hurry out and grab a sandwich and then run back to the studio to listen to the rest of it.

One day, I was right outside the studio door and the program director said, "Well, look who's coming up the hill. Is that Aunt Fannie on her bicycle? The poor soul looks winded. Let's ask her to come in and sit a spell."

I thought, "Now what kind of voice will he do for her?" The next thing I knew, the door opened, they snatched me in, and I was Aunt Fannie. So I huffed and puffed a little bit, we exchanged a few pleasantries, and that was it. I forgot about her.

There was a big farm implement company in Waterloo, which sold directly to the customer. The radio sales people had been trying to interest them in radio, but they couldn't suggest anything that appealed to them. One of the announcers said, "You know, Fran, I'll bet you we could sell them Aunt Fannie."

I said, "Who's that?"

"Well, you are. Don't you remember?"

So we did a five-minute program in which I sold cream separators, tractors, manure spreaders, pump jacks—I wouldn't know a pump jack if I fell over it, you know, but I put their copy into Aunt Fannie lingo. And for that I got the magnificent sum of two dollars a program. I thought I was doing just great.

Within three years of the beginning of her radio career, she was in Chicago, starring on NBC radio programs such as *K. C. Jamboree* and *Meet the Meeks* and acting as a participant in early TV experiments.

Allison's experience with early TV would come in handy. Chicago became an important production center for RCA and the NBC television network, giving rise to what became known as "the Chicago school of broadcasting." With no money, but enormous imagination and resourcefulness, such programs were produced as Dave Garroway's *Garroway at Large, Studs' Place* with Studs Terkel, and of

Members of Howdy Doody's *Peanut Gallery get to visit with the stars of their favorite show during a personal appearance at New York's Macy's Department Store in 1949: Buffalo Bob Smith (left), puppet star Howdy Doody, and Clarabell the Clown, played by Bob Keeshan, the once and future star of* Captain Kangaroo.

course, *Kukla, Fran and Ollie.* Among the people approached to provide programming was a young puppeteer who himself had participated in television experiments, Burr Tillstrom. RCA realized that one of the most effective sales tools for television was television itself. Not only would programs persuade people to buy, commercials selling the new sets could be broadcast as well.

"They thought that a wonderful avenue of approach would be one which was directed toward children," Allison said,

because if children want something, and it's possible for the parents to get that something for them, they will do it."
So they wanted to do a show five days a week, an hour each day. Burr was supposed to sell televisions, records,

Lassie went on the air in 1954 and can still be seen on TV today, although the production of new episodes ended in 1971. Tommy Rettig, playing Jeff Miller, was the first of a succession of owners who would marvel each week at Lassie's canine smarts.

George Burns and Gracie Allen were one of the first comedy teams to make the transition from radio to television, just as they had made the transition from vaudeville to radio. After Gracie retired in 1958, George was one of the many performers who took a turn hosting ABC's Hollywood Palace, *one of the last of the old-style variety shows. It ran on ABC from 1964 until 1970.*

phonographs, all that sort of thing, and he felt that it would be a rather heavy assignment. If he could find someone to work with in front of the stage, it would be ever so much easier.

So the head of the station at that time remembered that when he had asked me to come over [for the earlier experiments], I had come, and I had stood where I was supposed to stand and spoken when I was spoken to. So he suggested I might be just such a person.

They called me on Thursday and asked me if I could come to a meeting on Friday. After the meeting, Burr and I both agreed that it would be fun to try. And on Monday afternoon, I went down to the station at two o'clock. Burr and I went down to the drugstore, had some coffee and talked about what we might do. Went on the air at four that afternoon and worked for ten years.

Tillstrom developed a marvelous, disparate cast of characters. "Oliver J. Dragon was the kind of person I think Burr might have wanted to be," Allison said. "He was so flamboyant. He just thought that all that came to him was due him. Kukla was more near Burr's personality: kind and sensible.

"Beulah Witch, I loved her. I thought she was the most resourceful woman I had ever met. She was a graduate of Witch Normal in North Carolina. She left there and went with a traveling troupe of *Hansel and Gretel,* but she quit that because she was afraid of being typecast."

Among Beulah's duties was patrolling the NBC network's coaxial cable on her broomstick. Other characters included Fletcher Rabbit, Cecil Bill— "our union representative"—Colonel Crackie, a southern gentleman; and the redoubtable Madame Ophelia Oglepuss. Allison said, "The characters grew as we'd talk back and forth, asking questions and finding that some of the things we liked were very much the same as the things the different characters liked. We grew that way. We were so fortu-

A master of comic timing, Jack Benny could get bigger laughs with a single gesture, look, or line than anyone. Benny, with a supporting cast that included Mel Blanc, wife Mary Livingston, Dennis Day, Don Wilson, and Eddie "Rochester" Anderson, fronted one of the funniest shows on television.

nate to begin in television in the covered wagon. We grew along with the industry itself."

The makeup, in those early days, she said, was "a little startling, I think, and the lights were so hot!" That heat led to a moment that reveals how completely Fran Allison had become a member of Kuklapolitan society. "At the end of the first season, we were to have eight weeks off. The way we closed was that Beulah Witch was going to fly us all off to Vermont, where Ollie's parents had a summer home. We had a letter from Ollie's mother, and she said to be very careful and see that Ollie was bundled up because his throat was very susceptible to night air.

"I had brought a scarf to Ollie from his mother. So we had it around his throat, and Kukla had a little stocking cap on and a sweater. And I had on a sweater and a babushka around my head. When they faded from us, we had to stay there, but our mikes weren't on. I turned to Ollie [the dragon], and I said, 'Aren't you dying in that scarf?'

"Burr broke up. He said, 'You *are* a believer.'"

There were never scripts, just "an idea," Allison said. "Maybe it would be built around a particular piece of music we wanted to use; maybe the plot would grow out of something that had happened either to Burr or to me or maybe to one of the girls in the office." Music was always a specialty. "We did *The Mikado* seven times—different version every time, always a disaster." They performed with Arthur Fiedler and made up parodies of other TV shows. "We did an amateur show when Ted Mack and Arthur Godfrey were in their heyday. We did detective shows, too."

When *Kukla, Fran and Ollie* became a national show, they were a hit across the country and not only with kids. "The greatest following we had was among people in the arts," Allison said. "Tallulah

Amos 'n' Andy was the first television comedy series with an all-black cast, but it drew fire from critics who attacked the show for perpetuating racial stereotypes. Only two seasons of episodes were filmed, but it was seen in syndication until 1966, when CBS withdrew the series after protests from civil rights organizations.

Gertrude Berg was the matriarch of the Golden Age sitcom The Goldbergs *in more ways than one. Not only did she star as Mrs. Goldberg, she wrote and produced every episode. Despite Berg's efforts in his behalf, Philip Loeb (left), who played her husband, was forced off the program by the blacklist. He committed suicide in 1955.*

Bankhead used to call us every night after the show. I remember Bea Lillie visited the set one day. We had a wonderful young man who did costumes and things for the little people, and within five minutes, he had Beulah decked out in a pillbox hat and a long double string of pearls."

Allison said that at its height, the series received some fifteen thousand letters a week, many from children who were just as captivated by the Kuklapolitan world as she was.

At the very beginning, children were attracted to the fact that there was a dragon who spoke, a rabbit who spoke. They weren't quite sure about Kukla. . . .

One day Kukla seemed rather sad, and I said, "You're not your usually happy self. Is something wrong?" And he said, "No I'm just bothered, Fran. You know who you are. Ollie knows he's a dragon, and Fletcher knows he's a rabbit. Some people write to me and say, 'What is Kukla?' I just don't really know."

I said, "Just as long as you're here, that's all I need to know." But several days later, he was so happy. He said, "Fran I have a letter. You must read this letter."

He gave it to me. A little girl had written, and she said, "We love you, Kukla, and we don't want you ever to be unhappy. We certainly don't want you to worry about who you are, or what you are, because my mother says you're a blessing."

There have been other shows for Fran Allison, television specials and commercials, but she will never forget the live days when she and a dragon and a puppet named Kukla (Russian for "doll") were three of television's first stars. "I never thought of it as being a television thing," she said. "I just thought of what we were doing as a happy meeting with people I loved and whom I enjoyed so much. I never really had the feeling that we were doing a show, per se. Each day was just a new wonderful experience.

"When I see some of the old kinescopes and see some of the hairdos and getups that I had, I certainly didn't think of it being a show, or I would have mended my ways!

"Television is wonderful now; they do things so well. But it's also kind of cut-and-dried. It would be great to see something like it used to be. . . ."

Fran Allison is still a believer.

Phil Silvers, who played wily army con man Sergeant Bilko on the situation comedy, You'll Never Get Rich, *introduces cast members after the filming of one of the series' first episodes in 1955. The series was at first shot before a live audience at the old Du Mont Network studios in New York City. Note Fred Gwynne (fourth from the right), who would go on to star in sitcoms* Car 54, Where Are You? *and* The Munsters.

JOHN FORSYTHE

A 1953 biography from Universal International's publicity department says his legal name is John Lincoln Freund. John Forsythe, in many respects, is the quintessential television actor: the kind of personable character actor who has always been welcome on the home screen in a variety of roles.

As a Broadway leading man, he starred in *Teahouse of the August Moon* and replaced Arthur Kennedy in Arthur Miller's *All My Sons* and Henry Fonda in the title role of *Mister Roberts.* He worked in radio as an actor, director, and sportscaster. He has also made movies, most notably Alfred Hitchcock's *The Trouble with Harry.*

But it's because of TV that John Forsythe is a household word. He has performed on television since the very first days of live TV. He was Uncle Bentley on the long-running *Bachelor Father,* star of *The John Forsythe Show,* the voice of Charlie on *Charlie's Angels,* the unseen spokesman for Michelob beer and now the television hero of the Reagan era: handsome, wealthy, faithful Blake Carrington on *Dynasty.*

"We did a production of Ben Hecht's play *Miracle in the Rain* on NBC in 1948," Forsythe said.

We did it in a radio studio with about sixteen or twenty sets, and it all took place in the rain. I was a soldier, and there was some miracle that happened. I can't quite remember what it was, but it was a very romantic, if somewhat soggy, piece. . . .

My mother went to see this thing in one of the bars on Third Avenue in New York. I tried to get her into the projection room, but they didn't have enough room.

So here's this rather well-dressed, somewhat elegant lady in a Third Avenue saloon by herself. She ordered a pink lady or something, and they were watching the wrestling matches. After a while she said to the bartender, "Would

TV GUIDE

15¢

THE ZANY EXPERIENCES OF A LADY COMIC

see page 20

LOCAL LISTINGS • JUNE 11-17

NOREEN CORCORAN,
JOHN FORSYTHE,
SAMMEE TONG OF
'BACHELOR FATHER'

The sitcom Bachelor Father, *starring John Forsythe, was a family comedy with a twist. Forsythe played wealthy Beverly Hills attorney Bentley Gregg, raising his niece, Noreen Corcoran, with the help of servant Sammee Tong. Among the young actresses who appeared on the series was a teenage Linda Evans, later to become Forsythe's TV wife on* Dynasty.

you gentlemen mind if we switched that? My son is going to be on Channel 4, on NBC, on a dramatic show."

They said, "Well, lady, we can't do that; we've got all these guys down the bar."

And she said, "Well, I'd be very happy if you would."

I don't know how she did it, but she charmed them. They all watched the show. Pretty soon, they were all gathered around, didn't miss the wrestling at all. When the show finished, they congratulated my mother on her son's performance!

Forsythe remembered some of his other appearances in the days of live TV. "I was on the first *Studio One* show, *The Storm*. Margaret Sullavan, Dean Jagger, and I starred in it. I played Dean Jagger's younger brother, who had some kind of relationship with Margaret Sullavan. Worthington Miner was the producer and director of it. . . . I also did *Wuthering Heights* with Mary Sinclair. Good actress—but I was probably the most American Heathcliff ever. My English accent leaves something to be desired. They spread some dirt around and called it the 'NBC moors.'

"They were rehearsed as plays," he explained. "The dramatic movements were all put together, and then camera people came in and put tapes on the floor—the marks that you had to hit." Rehearsals went for

about two weeks, or two and a half weeks. Rarely did it go to three weeks. . . . And then we would move into the studio. The same marks that had existed in the rehearsal hall had been transferred to the studio, and we adapted to that.

The camera people came in and you just walked through the thing. You didn't act it. You walked through the positions for them, because it was a very tricky affair. You didn't have the luxury of stopping and starting again [once on the air]. Once you started, you were hooked.

The difficult thing that I remember most from live television was the transitions that had to be made. You were always running somewhere, tripping over cables, people tearing your clothes off to put other clothes on. I remember one thing I did in which I had to change from a baseball uniform into a tuxedo in the space of—it couldn't have been more than thirty-five or forty seconds. I had three people tearing my clothes off, three people putting clothes on, and I made it—breathing hard all the way!

That kind of chaos and nervousness brought about exciting performances, because it was totally different than in motion pictures, where you could stop. The element of chance and error are completely taken out of it. . . .

Some very interesting and stimulating things happened for just the reason that you *had* to do it. You couldn't stop and ask, "Would you give me that line again, please?" It just didn't work.

One famous stage actor tried to find an alternative solution. "Paul Muni did a show once, and he had difficulty with lines. He was a great actor of course, and they were delighted to get him on one of those early shows. He had a device tucked into his ear. Every time he stopped—he was such a good actor, the audience never knew that he had gone up—he would get the line in his earpiece from somebody who cued him. He played the whole performance that way, and it was a wonderful performance. We thought about the possibility of doing it ourselves. It would have relieved a little nervousness. . . .

"It was such an experimental thing. It had not become the great advertising medium that it is today. Today, my feeling is that when something good happens on television, it's extraordinary."

3. SITCOMS

The Ricardos and the Mertzes of I Love Lucy *spent each week becoming ensnared in and then unentangled from one harebrained scheme after another. With the help of "unseen spirits" Lucy and Fred, Madame Ethel "Mertzola" conducts a seance with Ricky and actor Jay Novello, trying to contact his dear, departed cocker spaniel, Tillie.*

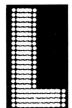ike the vaudeville and burlesque houses of the not-so-distant past, early TV was filled with sight gags, slapstick, stand-up comics, and sketch comedy—mixing moments of lowbrow corn with high hilarity. If Milton Berle called for "Makeup!," we knew that an enormous powder puff would smack him right in the kisser. Jerry Lewis tumbled into orchestra pits; Bob Hope tossed off one-liners; Sid Caesar and Imogene Coca performed hilarious husband-and-wife routines.

There was another type of television comedy, too, right from the beginning, a transplant from radio: the situation comedy or sitcom. The format has varied little over the years; week after week the same basic cast plays the same characters—families, neighbors, or co-workers getting stuck in various and sundry small-scale crises. Many of the first were transferred direct from radio—Burns and Allen and Jack Benny, for example, *Amos 'n' Andy,* and *The Goldbergs.*

But soon, sitcoms written especially for television were on the air. One of the first and most successful was NBC's *Mister Peepers,* starring Wally Cox as mild-mannered science teacher Robinson Peepers. Another began as a sketch on Jackie Gleason's variety show and became a series of its own—*The Honeymooners.* Gleason's Ralph Kramden was the classic little big man, full of bravado, hot air, and dreams that exceeded his grasp every week. His friendship with pal Ed Norton, played by Art Carney, was as warm and hilarious as the link of ineptitude that graced Laurel and Hardy, and his relationship with his wife, Alice, played by Audrey Meadows, was filled with high-volume insults and gibes that failed to hide real affection. "I call you 'Killer' 'cause you slay me," Alice might say, trying to vamp Ralph. "And I'm callin' Bellevue 'cause

What may have been the greatest comic duo since Laurel and Hardy: Art Carney and Jackie Gleason as Ed Norton and Ralph Kramden in the classic situation comedy, The Honeymooners.

A "modern Stone Age family," The Flintstones *was a cartoon near-clone of the Kramdens and Nortons of Jackie Gleason's* The Honeymooners. *It was the first animated series created for television to make it onto the prime-time schedule.*

you're nuts!" Ralph would roar back, but in the end, he was bound to tell her, "Baby, you're the greatest!"

Another great schemer was Sergeant Ernest Bilko, played by Phil Silvers on *The Phil Silvers Show*, originally titled *You'll Never Get Rich* and known in syndication as *Sergeant Bilko*. Ernie Bilko was the con man *extraordinaire* of the peacetime army, and CBS had the temerity to put him on against Milton Berle. With a little help from Bishop Fulton J. Sheen on the Du Mont Network, Bilko knocked Berle out of the top of the ratings.

But the classic sitcom of this period was and is *I Love Lucy*. Lucille Ball's brand of humor transcends time and national boundaries. Turn on a TV in virtually any country in the world, and chances are you'll still be able to see Lucy—knee-deep in grapes at an Italian vineyard, stuffing chocolates as they stream down a conveyor belt, becoming drunker and drunker as she flubs take after take of a commercial for an elixir called "Vita-meatavegamin."

In the fifties, few sitcom families were as zany as Lucy and Ricky Ricardo's—they were, after all, in *show business*, as were Danny Thomas and his clan on *Make Room for Daddy*. In the Eisenhower era of prosperity and alleged good feeling (never mind blacklists and the Cold War), a half hour visiting the homes of most TV families was like taking a combined dose of Valium and jelly beans. All was calm; all was sweet. Dad went off to some kind of job somewhere and returned to shout, "Hi, honey, I'm home!" as he came in the front door to the delighted squeals and wreathed smiles of his beloved wife and kids.

"It was a different period of time then," John Forsythe recalled, "because everything was much more innocent. Family-oriented shows were the

shows of the day: *Father Knows Best*, with Robert Young and Jane Wyatt, [*The Adventures of*] *Ozzie and Harriet, Leave It to Beaver.*" Forsythe, too, had his domestic sitcom in those days: *Bachelor Father*. A single, unmarried father? Of course not. Forsythe played a Beverly Hills attorney raising his niece—with all the proper values, of course.

Just as the national mood swung toward a bit more youth and sophistication with the Kennedy administration, so did some situation comedies. The most notable example was *The Dick Van Dyke Show*. Once again, this was a show about a family in show business. Van Dyke's character, Rob Petrie, was the head writer of a comedy-variety show. His wife Laura, played by Mary Tyler Moore, was a former dancer. The family was as all-American and New

Over the course of his army sitcom, You'll Never Get Rich *(known in syndication as* Sergeant Bilko*), comedian Phil Silvers took the opportunity to exchange his uniform for that of an irascible Santa Claus and a camp counselor (with one of the most popular cast members of his show, Maurice Gosfield, who played Private Duane Doberman).*

Frontier as it could be, but the scripts had a genuine wit and style. Although not as frequently, *The Many Loves of Dobie Gillis,* based on short stories by Max Shulman, was also a series that went beyond the boundaries of the standard family sitcom. Dobie's best friend, beatnik Maynard G. Krebs, even made jokes about Dizzy Gillespie.

Soon, however, comedy took a backslide into silliness that made the domestic sitcoms of the fifties seem like high art. All right, the reasoning may have went behind the closed doors of the networks, people are getting a little tired of these family shows. Let's make the families really strange. We were inundated with monster families *(The Munsters* and *The Addams Family)* Martians *(My Favorite Martian),* genies *(I Dream of Jeannie),* talking horses *(Mister Ed),* flying nuns, hillbillies living in Beverly Hills mansions, and perhaps what represents the true nadir of this entire era, the heartwarming saga of a man whose mother returns from the dead reincarnated as an antique automobile— *My Mother the Car.*

Then, as the seventies got under way, a remarkable change took place. "The genre was burned out and people were ready for something different," former CBS-TV programming head Michael Dann said. "That something different was the truth in comedy, the satire of making fun of bigotry and hate and racial discrimination."

There was a three-pronged attack on the inane sitcoms of the past. The main assault came from Norman Lear and his breakthrough sitcom, *All in the Family,* based on the successful British series *Till Death Us Do Part.* The outrageous prejudices of Archie Bunker and his constant confrontations with liberal son-in-law Mike mirrored what was happening in an America embroiled in struggles over civil rights, poverty, sexual equality, and the Vietnam

The George Burns and Gracie Allen Show *was part situation comedy, part variety show. Each episode ended with George and Gracie performing one of their "in-one" vaudeville routines. Burns enjoyed making fun of television's conventions by making asides to the audience, often while observing the action from a TV set in his study. The Burns' next-door neighbors, Blanche and Harry Morton, were played by Bea Benaderet and Larry Keating.*

Real life and sitcom fiction collided on The Adventures of Ozzie and Harriet.
Ozzie Nelson (center), his wife Harriet, and sons Ricky (left) and David played
themselves on the series, which ran on television from 1952 until 1966.

War. "The shows reflected what all of us who wrote and directed and produced were feeling," Norman Lear said. "What we were observing in our society, what we were learning from our kids and our wives and our husbands. We were reflecting on our times—but funny."

It took Norman Lear three years to convince the nervous networks that America was ready for Archie Bunker. "CBS did get a lot of phone calls, but they were surprised that many of the calls were positive and that no states seceded from the Union," Lear said. "Their worst fears were not realized, and I think we all learned together—not to the point where they never harassed again and didn't fight again about content, but they learned that America was far more grown up than they had thought."

All in the Family begat *Maude* and *Good Times*

One of The Many Loves of Dobie Gillis, *starring Dwayne Hickman (right) in the title role, was a young Tuesday Weld, who played Dobie's unrequited love, Thalia Menninger. Also featured on the sitcom, based on Max Shulman's short stories, was Dobie's beatnik pal Maynard G. Krebs, played by Bob Denver, who would go on to play the bumbling Gilligan of* Gilligan's Island.

Perhaps the ultimate hi-honey-I'm-home show of the fifties was Father Knows
Best, *a family sitcom that depicted the idyllic life of the Anderson family: (left
to right) daughter Betty (Elinor Donahue), father Jim (Robert Young), mother
Margaret (Jane Wyatt), daughter Kathy (Lauren Chapin), and son Bud
(Billy Gray).*

and *The Jeffersons*—Norman Lear situation comedies that took an until-then-unheard-of look at social issues, real family problems (beyond who has
the car keys), and politics. Lear also took another
British sitcom, *Steptoe and Son,* changed the characters from white to black, and generated another hit
with *Sanford and Son.* He even dared to take on the
sacred soap-opera format with the totally off-the-
wall story of *Mary Hartman, Mary Hartman,* a show
that would help prepare an unsuspecting world for
the unrestrained lunacy of Susan Harris's ABC series, *Soap.*

The second prong of the attack on sitcoms of the
past came from a series based on a hit movie.
M*A*S*H used the Korean War for a thinly dis-
guised assault on the madness of all wars in general

Fred MacMurray was all-knowing patriarch and widower Steve Douglas in the family situation comedy My Three Sons, *doling out advice to everyone from son Chip (Stanley Livingston, left) to live-in grandpa Bub O'Casey, played for the first four seasons by William Frawley, the former Fred Mertz of* I Love Lucy.

Jerry Mathers was Beaver Cleaver on one of the most popular family situation comedies of the fifties and sixties, Leave It to Beaver. *Beaver spent each week's episode falling into a minor jam from which he would always be extracted by his astoundingly understanding parents or older brother Wally.*

and Vietnam in particular. It was a long way from the world of Sergeant Bilko, but it never became overly preachy. The stories were real, and in the course of its run, *M*A*S*H* managed to change many of our notions about how a sitcom can be structured and written.

Finally, the sitcom form was forever changed by a group of programs produced by MTM Enterprises,

the company founded by Grant Tinker to create a sitcom for his wife, Mary Tyler Moore. *The Mary Tyler Moore Show* and such other MTM products as *Rhoda* and *The Bob Newhart Show* didn't tackle the big issues, like Norman Lear or *M*A*S*H* did, but they perfected a form of the family situation comedy that brought to television intelligence, wit, and a far more open look at personal relationships. They may

A bright spot in the sitcom doldrums of the early sixties was The Dick Van Dyke Show, *a sophisticated family sitcom that followed the lives of television comedy writer Rob Petrie (Van Dyke, second from right) and his wife Laura (Mary Tyler Moore, third from right). Among their friends were fellow writers Buddy Sorrell (Morey Amsterdam, left) and Sally Rogers (Rose Marie, right) and neighbor Millie Helper (Ann Morgan Guilbert).*

not have been addressing themselves to Watergate or sexual confusion, but they were genuine, and that was something very fine and rare for the situation comedy.

Of the three-pronged attack, it is the MTM school that has survived today more strongly than the others. Maybe that's because the issues don't seem as burning these days; we are not directly swamped in a shooting war, and although poverty, racism, and sexism still exist, they are finally recognized as very real problems—even if we are far from eradicating them. Sitcoms today are still preaching a gospel, albeit a more subtle one, of acceptance and equality.

And so, the family situation comedy is back—written with flair, openness, and genuine humor. Many of them have been concocted by MTM alumni: *Taxi, Cheers, Family Ties.* Even *The Cosby Show* took its first steps with the help of people who

once worked at MTM. They may not be the Mom, Dad, and kids nuclear family of the fifties—witness the two divorced mothers of *Kate and Allie* or the four older women of *The Golden Girls*—but they are families nonetheless.

If there is another change, it may be in the increased self-awareness that television comedies have of the medium itself: the knowing jokes that let all of us know that, Hey, this is a TV show—you know it and I know it. *It's the Garry Shandling Show,* the sitcom telecast by the Showtime cable network, is a prime example. Characters make jokes about the show's theme song, special effects, and closing credits, and Shandling thinks nothing about breaking away from a scene and suddenly addressing the audience.

But wait a minute. George Burns was doing that on *The George Burns and Gracie Allen Show*—in 1951.

PAUL HENNING

At the height of Paul Henning's success in the 1960s, his name was synonymous with a certain type of unsophisticated sitcom—rural comedies that were hits for CBS in the ratings, but often scorned by critics as a lowbrow tarnishing of CBS's "Tiffany network" image: *The Beverly Hillbillies, Petticoat Junction, Green Acres*—down-home shows created by a kid from the Midwest who fell in love with the Southern California life-style.

Henning is a television old-timer, a radio veteran who made the transition to television with relative ease. In fact, Henning was familiar with television before a lot of people even knew it existed. "I was on television in 1929," he said. "I was still in high school, but I loved to sing, and a fellow that I went

to high school with played piano. We'd appear anywhere, anytime, just for practice and to try to get into radio. At that time, the power and light company in Kansas City had an experimental television set-up. Somewhere, in one of my wife's scrapbooks, there's a picture of us in a little room in the power and light building, with the spinning lights and all the paraphernalia they had in those days. It didn't telecast outside the building, but somewhere, someone was sitting there watching television.

"They painted you all kinds of crazy colors to get you to appear on the screen. Nineteen twenty-nine —it was hard to believe."

Henning succeeded in getting into radio, at station KMBC in Kansas City. He began as a singer and became a radio writer out of necessity. "I went to the program director, and I told him I had an idea for a program for the Associated Grocers. He said, 'Fine—write it.'

"I said, 'I'm a singer.'

"He said, 'Well, we don't have any writers, so if you want to do it, you have to write it.'

"I wrote it. Another fellow and I sang. We were the Associated Grocers, and we would sing parodies of popular songs, which I didn't know was against the law. That was breaking into radio writing the hard way!"

Henning heard that the popular radio series *Fibber McGee and Molly* was in need of writers. He wrote a script on spec and was hired. After a year with the show in Chicago, he moved to California. He worked for radio shows starring Joe E. Brown and Rudy Vallee and then landed a job with George Burns and Gracie Allen. He wrote for them for ten years—1942 to 1952—a period that saw Burns and Allen make the transition from radio to television. "Radio was a breeze," Henning said. "You could write a script in a couple of days, if you had the

"American Gothic" Ozark-style moved west to live the high life in Southern California on the CBS sitcom The Beverly Hillbillies *in 1962. Created by Paul Henning, the series vaulted to the top of the ratings and spawned a string of "rustic" TV shows.*

right idea. Television was really an education. It's a lot more work. You have to understand other things, such as stage dressing and set dressing, all of the various things that we had never bothered with."

One who took to television immediately was George Burns.

In radio, George really didn't have that much interest. He was the straight man, and if we had a good idea that he liked, he'd say, "Write it," and go off to Hillcrest to play golf.

Television was an altogether different thing. George was in a medium that he understood, because he'd been in vaudeville since he was born, practically. He really took an active interest, and just blossomed when we got into television, because the visual medium appealed to him, and his vaudeville training came into good stead.

We went to New York to begin the television series, because in those days, in 1950, it was considered wise to originate your show in New York. That's where the publicity originated. The West Coast was out of it.

"We were broadcast live out of New York for about six months, but when George decided to go to film, then we could originate out here.

Henning left Burns and Allen when he was offered a show with Dennis Day. "Dennis said, 'You can produce it. You can write it. You can do everything. You're the head man.' George couldn't match that, because he and his brother produced the show themselves.

"Every writer dreams of becoming a producer, because you get so infuriated by the fact that your script—which you poured your heart and blood into—is changed arbitrarily by the producer. So I said, 'Someday I'm going to be a producer.' Dennis Day was the opportunity."

Henning also wrote scripts for a Ray Bolger television series and created *The Bob Cummings Show* (known in syndication as *Love That Bob*), which ran

for five years. Then Stan Shapiro, a friend from Burns and Allen days who had gone into the movie business, gave him a call. "He said, 'Television is too difficult. Join me at Universal. I'll show you what fun it is to do movies. This is leisure. You just write a couple of pages a day. It's not like that glass furnace.'

"Ed Wynn called television 'the glass furnace,' which I thought was the most apt description, because it burns up scripts; it burns up talent. It's just a fierce thing."

Henning joined Shapiro at Universal, but one day he got a call from another friend, Al Simon, who was working for Martin Ransohoff's production company. "He said, 'We need a television show. Come back to television,'" Henning remembered.

I said, "Al, I want no part of it. It's too hard, and I'm really enjoying movie writing."

Finally, there was a kind of lull between pictures and Al said, "Anything you want to do, just come up with an idea." I had lunch with Al and Marty Ransohoff, and Marty said, "I know you like hillbilly humor."

I've always been a sucker for hillbilly humor. My favorite portion of the old *Kraft Music Hall* on radio was Bob Burns, the "Arkansas Traveler." I loved his stories about the hillbillies. Having been born and raised in Independence, Missouri, my scout camp was in the Ozarks.

Marty said, "I'll buy the television rights to *Ma and Pa Kettle.*"

I said, "Marty, if you want a hillbilly show, let me write my own. I don't need *Ma and Pa Kettle.*"

The inspiration, if that's the right word, came during a motor trip through the South in 1959, visiting Civil War sites with his mother-in-law.

We were driving along one day, and I said, "Wouldn't it be interesting to transpose someone from that era into this modern situation, speeding along a highway at sixty miles

From the creators of The Beverly Hillbillies *came* Green Acres, *a mildly off-the-wall situation comedy that pulled a reverse on the* Hillbillies *plot premise. On* Green Acres, *rich city folk Oliver Wendell Douglas (Eddie Albert) and his ditzy wife Lisa (Eva Gabor) bought a farm and moved to the country, facing an endless variety of rural crises and eccentric natives.*

per hour in an air-conditioned car—take someone who has never been exposed to modern life and suddenly put them down in a sophisticated community." I think that was really the germ of the idea.

First, I thought of New York, and then I thought, "That's foolish. We'd have to go to New York, and it would be a very expensive location." Beverly Hills would serve the same purpose.

I wrote a pilot script, which ran about an hour. In fact, at one time, I was so enthusiastic about the idea, I said, "Let's make it an hour show." I soon got over that.

I took the pilot script to Marty and Al. Marty was as enthusiastic as I was. He said, "Let's go to the Ozarks and film it there." I said, "There's no need. We can duplicate the Ozarks right up in the hills."

Then, casting: I always had Buddy Ebsen in mind, because I had seen him do *Davy Crockett.* To me, he was the perfect hillbilly. Being a dancer, he was a big man, but he moved with such grace and ease that you felt that he could have roamed the woods all his life. Buddy was the character I had in mind when I wrote the pilot script.

Irene Ryan, who had been on some of the Ray Bolger shows, just happened to come by the office at Universal. I sort of looked at her and thought, "Gee, she could be Granny." She's little and wiry and had a great, great sense of comedy. A fine performer.

I said to Irene, "Could you play a hillbilly character?"

She said, "Why, sure! I remember playing a little town in Arkansas when I was in tab shows." She was in this traveling group, and they went to this town in Arkansas. They were going to appear in the theater. They were ready to raise the curtain, but there was no one in the audience. She said, "We had seen people standing out in front, so we knew that we should have an audience. So we said to the fellow who owned the theater, 'Why don't you let the people in?' He says, 'I won't let the people in until you're ready to raise the curtain, because if I do, they'll whittle away the seats!' "

After shooting the pilot, Henning said, "I took the pilot film, rented a sixteen-millimeter projector, and gathered the family in the house where my mother was living in Independence. When it was over, Mother said, 'They pay you for this?' "

In spite of her opinion and that of many critics, *The Beverly Hillbillies* was the fastest success in the history of American television, shooting to the top of the ratings in record time. It lasted nine seasons.

CBS Television President James Aubrey wanted more. He got it in *Petticoat Junction,* a show set in a rural boarding house along the railroad tracks, starring a Henning favorite, Bea Benaderet. Included in the cast was Henning's own daughter, Linda Kaye Henning, who played Betty Jo. Once again, the idea came from within Henning's own family. "My wife used to tell me about her days as

During the phase of bizarre sixties sitcoms, audiences were confronted with comedy series that featured talking horses, Martians, genies, and the antics of supernatural folk like The Addams Family, *a show based on the macabre, sophisticated* New Yorker *cartoons of Charles Addams. The series starred John Astin (Gomez) and Carolyn Jones (Morticia).*

a child, when she would go to a little town in Missouri—Eldon, Missouri—where her grandmother and grandfather ran a hotel that set right beside the railroad tracks. All of the traveling salesmen—drummers, as they were called—would stop at the hotel. She and several of her cousins would spend the summer there, and they were always warned, 'Don't get involved with the drummers!' "

Although it was not as big a hit as *Hillbillies,* *Petticoat Junction* ran for seven seasons and begat yet another show, *Green Acres,* based on an old radio series. "Jim Aubrey said, 'I want a third show.' And I said, 'I can't. I just can't.' He said, 'You don't even have to make a pilot. If you're connected with it, I'll commit to it.' "

Jay Sommers, who had written several episodes of *Petticoat Junction,* came to Henning with the scripts of *Granby's Green Acres,* a radio show he had done with Bea Benaderet and Gale Gordon. The premise was the mirror image of *Hillbillies:* This time, rich urbanites found themselves in the sticks. Henning and Aubrey said yes.

Part of the charm of *Green Acres*—and the reason it still has a cult following—was its somewhat loopy, almost surreal sense of humor. What other show featured a pig, let alone one named Arnold Ziffel? "I used to be summoned to CBS meetings, and they would say, 'Can you tone it down?' " Henning said, "Jay Sommers and Dick Chevillat were writing the show, and I said, 'Listen, as long as the ratings stay up, leave it alone.' "

Petticoat Junction was canceled in 1970. The next year, both *The Beverly Hillbillies* and *Green Acres* died. There was a new president at CBS-TV, Bob Wood. "He thought that rural shows were not getting a rating in the cities," Henning said, "and I guess they weren't. I don't know."

A colleague of Henning's said, "When Bob Wood became president of CBS, he canceled every show with a tree in it."

It's a cyclical business; everybody says so.

TONY THOMAS

Tony Thomas is a child of television and a child of Hollywood. He's the son of Danny Thomas and the brother of Marlo. But on his own, he's an accomplished executive producer, one of the partners in Witt-Thomas-Harris. Working with Paul Junger Witt and Susan Harris, he was one of the creators of *Soap,* the soap-opera parody that tried to offend virtually everyone, and *The Golden Girls,* coproduced with Disney's Touchstone Films—four older women doing their best to prove that advancing age is no reason to slide into senility—or gentility, for that matter—without putting up a fight.

Tony Thomas started as an assistant at Columbia Pictures' television division—Screen Gems, as it was known then—in the late sixties. He was the associate producer of *Brian's Song,* starring James Caan and Billy Dee Williams. It was one of the first

Two TV families met head-on when Danny Thomas and his costar, Marjorie Lord, appeared on The Lucy-Desi Comedy Hour. *Produced from 1957 to 1960, the thirteen hour-long shows featured such guest stars as Tallulah Bankhead, Fred MacMurray, and Harry James and Betty Grable. The last, with Ernie Kovacs and Edie Adams, was filmed while Lucy and Desi were getting divorced.*

Danny Thomas used his own experiences as an entertainer, husband, and father to create the role of nightclub performer Danny Williams on Make Room for Daddy, *later to become* The Danny Thomas Show.

really successful TV movies—chronicling football star Brian Piccolo's fight against cancer and his friendship with Gayle Sayers—a show that opened the floodgates for a series of TV films detailing the heroic struggles of people against fatal diseases. It was while working on *Brian's Song* that Thomas met Paul Witt.

"I was raised in the business," Thomas said, "My family has been in television ever since I can remember. There's never been any other option."

How could there have been? As a child, Tony Thomas's daily life was providing material for his father's sitcom, *Make Room for Daddy,* later called *The Danny Thomas Show.* "We used to see our lives flashed on the screen all the time," Tony Thomas remembered. "There would be a dinner, a fight, a happy moment, something in the kitchen, and the next thing you know, my father was fleshing it out into a story. He and Sheldon Leonard were making it into an entire episode. From four lines that one of us said would come an episode.

"The names were changed to protect the innocent, but you know, everything from the classic punishment go-to-your-room stories to dating stories to sticking-shoes-down-the-garbage-disposal stories—all those family things were on television."

Being Danny Thomas's son was more a joy than a hindrance. "The only tough time I really had with it was trying to prove myself," Thomas said. "I knew that I had to do a little bit more than everybody else so people would take me seriously. When I just did my job, it wasn't good enough because people just assumed I had it because of my connections and my family."

Dad still calls with advice, though. "He'll tell me what he thinks is good, what's working, what isn't working. It's up to me to pick and choose when I think he's right," Thomas said, laughing.

When Thomas and partners Witt and Harris created *Soap* in 1977, many thought characters were "crossing the line." "We wanted to do something outrageous," Thomas said. "Susan Harris wanted to write something in a serialized comedy form on soap operas. We came up with these two families. We went to ABC and [then ABC programming chief] Fred Silverman, and they went for it."

It was a series that enjoyed quick notoriety, even before it aired:

For some reason, everyone got threatened by it. We were stunned at the amount of negative reaction we were getting on a show no one had seen.

Someone had heard that one of the characters seduced

Family sitcoms are back, but they don't always have to be the Mom-Dad-and-kids nuclear family of the fifties and sixties. Bea Arthur (left) and Rue McClanahan (right) star with Betty White and Estelle Getty as four older women living together in Miami on The Golden Girls.

a priest in the confessional, and everyone chose to accept that as what was actually going to happen—or had happened and had yet to be seen by America. The Catholic Church condemned us. Priests were praying for our cancellation. People are starving all over the world and priests are praying for our cancellation. It was really a bizarre situation.

There was nothing on that show that wasn't done constantly on daytime television all the time. So we were shocked at who was being offended.... A lot of people got on a lot of soapboxes and started screaming and yelling. There was a good deal of pressure. But ABC defended us and stuck with us.

We dealt with homosexuality, mothers and daughters having affairs with the same people, mental illness—everything. We managed to offend everybody, judging by the amount of mail we got. But it was all in good fun.

The original idea for *The Golden Girls* came from the network. "We were talking to NBC about a couple of projects, and one of the executives there mentioned to us that they would love to do something about older women living together.

"They had done a network presentation about a year before in which Selma Diamond and another lady were introducing *Miami Vice*. They did some sort of sketch in which they kept referring to it as 'Miami Nice.' From that sketch, I guess, some of the guys looked at this and said, 'There's something here with these ladies of this age relating to each other.'

"Paul and I knew that Susan Harris would love to write it. She has the most fun writing about people with longer stories and more mature outlooks on life."

To Thomas, *The Golden Girls* works because "people had been talking about the aging of America, and the audiences were ready for this kind of show. But that isn't why we did it. These ladies are funny, and that's why it's a hit.

"Everybody's got a mother; everybody recognizes these ladies. They are a touch exaggerated, but not by much. I certainly know a few of them in my family. But again, I go back to the fact that it's entertaining. If you laugh, you come back every week."

Thomas does not think that a series like *The Golden Girls* could have gotten on the air ten years ago, but not because the audience wasn't ready for it. "I think the toughest thing would have been to sell it," he said. "There was such a taboo about putting older people on television, especially in the sixties and the early seventies. If you mentioned characters of that age, the network usually asked right away, 'Where are the kids? Who are the other people? Will there be neighbors who are younger?'"

But now, he says, "We haven't gotten any feedback other than positive feedback, saying, 'Thank you so much for portraying us as we really are, which is as vital people interested in a lot of things.'"

Thomas denies any problems with the network's censors over the program's forays into double-entendre. "NBC has been extremely good with us. One of the reasons they allow us to function the way we do is because it is humorous and in good taste. I know some of our stuff on occasion—if looked at without a sense of humor—people would be offended. But we ask you to look at it with a sense of humor, and it's not offensive.

"I guess the lesbian show would be the most controversial show we've done to date. That was a show in which one of Bea Arthur's school friends came to visit. The rest of the ladies aren't aware of the fact that she is gay and that the mate she has just lost is another woman. We received a good deal of mail on that subject, but the censors were great.

The Hickenloopers, played by Sid Caesar and Imogene Coca, were familiar characters to viewers of one of the classic comedy-variety series of the Golden Age, Your Show of Shows. *Superb writing and the chemistry of Caesar and Coca resulted in many memorable performances, from sketches like this one, "The Birthday Party," to brilliant parodies of movies and other television shows.*

We dealt with it honestly, yet humorously, and they were fine with it."

Thomas believes that sitcom forms are cyclical.

I think it's coming back to where it started. The sitcom age that I grew up in, the fifties, was obviously family oriented, and we all know about Mr. Cosby and his triumph. . . .

It was more character-oriented in those days. Then it got into the sixties and early seventies and it got to be one-liners, a lot of youth-oriented schtick. Now, most of it is back to character comedy. So it has come around again.

Right now, comedy is in. Two years ago, as we all know, comedy was dead. A friend of mine said that if comedy was dead, he knew a few television executives who had better have very good alibis. . . .

Comedy was never dead. Good comedy shows will always be in fashion, just as good dramatic shows will always be in fashion. Likable characters are the key. From likable characters, you get funny. If the audience doesn't like the people, there's no getting them to come back.

LARRY GELBART

Larry Gelbart is a very funny man, a writer not only of wit and style, but great intelligence and warmth as well. Television is only one card in his deck: He has written some wonderfully funny movies, including *The Wrong Box, Oh, God,* and *Tootsie* (with Murray Schisgal), and for Broadway, *A Funny Thing Happened on the Way to the Forum* and *Sly Fox.*

As a television writer, his main achievements are three: He was a writer on *Caesar's Hour;* he developed, coproduced, and wrote the first ninety-seven episodes of the TV version of *M*A*S*H;* and he was the man behind an offbeat situation comedy called *United States,* a show that attempted to bring a new sense and reality to the sitcom form, albeit not for long.

Gelbart is a native Californian whose father was Danny Thomas's barber. A few well-placed words between trims got Gelbart the Younger a job writing for Thomas on Fanny Brice's *Maxwell House Coffee Time* radio show. That led to work on *Duffy's Tavern* and gag writing for Eddie Cantor and Bob Hope, among others.

Gelbart made the transition to television with Bob Hope; in fact, it was with Hope that he first saw television. "It was in New York," Gelbart said. "We were doing his first television special. The first thing I saw was Milton Berle, which is an awesome thing to see for the first time. . . .

"Bob Hope's reaction to television was pretty much the same as all of us. He was watching it as a student, thinking how he would adapt himself to it and it to him. Television gave Bob something to do that he had never done before. He had done, of course, the monologues in every medium—and in every war zone. And while he had done stand-up spots with people and certainly song-and-dance variety, I don't think he had ever done sketches—even on Broadway, even in vaudeville. So that was a challenge to him, to all of us.

"Early TV was a good deal like vaudeville—it was the box they buried vaudeville in after it died."

That began to change, as television performers began to use the medium, taking advantage of its unique properties. Ernie Kovacs was one of the first. "He didn't come from vaudeville, he didn't come from radio," Gelbart said. "He treated television as a new entity and tried to work out what would do well in that entity. He was very aware of the camera as an instrument for providing new entertainment rather than photographing the old."

Gelbart worked for Sid Caesar, another of TV's early geniuses, not on the fabled *Your Show of Shows,* but on the Sid Caesar–Imogene Coca series that followed it, *Caesar's Hour.* "It was a remarkable happening," he said, "a daily happening for those of us who were lucky enough to be part of it. It was a huge writing staff. There would be seven or eight writers in the room at any time, not counting Sid, who sat with us, and Carl Reiner, who sat with us, and Howie Morris. I suppose most people know who was in that room by now—there was Mel Brooks, of course, Neil Simon, Mel Tolkin, Mike Stewart, who went on to write a lot of musical comedy [*Bye, Bye, Birdie; Hello, Dolly!*].

"It was a mad environment in the best sense of the word. I mean, it was cooking. We often compared it to jazz, because it really had that kind of improvisational back-and-forth rhythm. It was exciting. It was wonderful—even then, not just in retrospect. . . ."

It could also be harrowing.

It was a live program. We did go on every seven days, which meant that every time we finished one we had to start from scratch again. It made you feel you were working and living without a net most of the time, but it was fun. We always got on the air; we always got off the air. Some of the shows were disasters, creatively. The nice thing about *Caesar's Hour* was that in any given hour there would be probably half a dozen memorable moments. If we didn't bat a thousand every week, we were able to come back the next week and redeem ourselves and top ourselves. It had that virtue. We did thirty-nine shows a year then.

It enriched my life in several ways. We all felt we were part of a very good team. We liked each other. We socialized with one another, which is a rare thing for people who usually can't wait until it's six o'clock to say goodbye, no matter how much fun they've had all day long.

Caesar's Hour also reflected a certain part of everyone's private life, in that I think at least five sixths—I don't know why I pick that particular fraction—of the people involved in the show creatively were or had been in analysis. So they were bringing a lot of their personal reflections and reactions to the show. I know Sid's mostly remembered for the professor and the movie takeoffs, but we did an awful lot of I guess what today would be called sitcom. We did a lot of domestic comedy, but I think on a very high level.

Caesar was known for his ability to think on his feet. In one famous incident, he was playing a *Pagliacci*-like clown,

sitting in front of a mirror with a mascara stick. He had to draw a teardrop, and the pencil broke. This was not prepared. He just continued, drew a line, then another one, two this way, and started playing tic-tac-toe on his face. It was really inspired. You didn't laugh so much as you admired the courage and faith in himself—the confidence and the abandon. When you think of improvising on a large show in front of thirty to forty million people, you can only admire the matador in him.

America was his room. He felt very free to do whatever occurred to him at the moment. Not that he did a lot of it, because you can't wing it for an hour—although Art Carney tells stories of Jackie Gleason saying between the second and third act of a *Honeymooners,* 'Forget the script in the third act. Don't worry about it. Just wing it. Follow me.' Ad-libbing for twelve or thirteen minutes, which is really scary.

When M*A*S*H began airing on CBS in 1972, the United States was still embroiled in the Vietnam War. Using the Korean conflict as a thinly veiled substitute for Vietnam, producers Larry Gelbart and Gene Reynolds used sharply written comedy to provide a biting commentary on the horrors of war.

Variety shows like Caesar's no longer exist on American television. "To everyone's great loss," Gelbart said. "The linchpin of variety used to be the comic, surrounded of course, by other elements—dance, song. . . .

"Variety took a strange turn a number of years ago. Suddenly the Captain and Tennille had their own variety show. Sonny and Cher. Cher without Sonny. I don't think we ever had Sonny without Cher, though. . . . The comic suddenly was sort of written out. I don't know why. I think Carol Burnett was the last successful performer to have a variety show. But this is a very cyclical business. I expect it will come back one day."

When his Broadway musical, *A Funny Thing Happened on the Way to the Forum*, coauthored with Burt Shevelove, starring Zero Mostel, and with music and lyrics by Stephen Sondheim, was a hit, Gelbart decided to move his family to England—"to escape religious tolerance. I lived there almost nine years. The Swinging Sixties, as they were called, although it must have been happening somewhere other than where I was in London."

He watched a lot of British television, and it had a decided impact on his ideas about television writing. "British television has its share of garbage—rubbish, to use the British word. But the best of it is very fine indeed, as we know from the samples we see here. I think what I learned mostly was that you could use language—not in the new sense: four-letter words—I mean *language*. I mean English. They're much more playful with words. They have a much better time with words than we do; their ideas are bolder. There are very few Don'ts."

Gelbart's sojourn in England ended with a phone call from producer-director Gene Reynolds. CBS had agreed to bankroll a pilot script for a series based on the movie *M*A*S*H*. All his British TV

watching had an effect. "The British influence in *M*A*S*H* is evident in the nature of the themes, the dialogue, and the departure from what was then conventional for half-hour shows," he said.

Gelbart divides television comedy into shows written in major and minor keys. "If we were looking for a major, I would think about Bob Hope, I would think about comics without any shading, where fun is fun, and you laugh but you don't feel. I have no quarrel with that. I'm proud to have been the coauthor of a show [*A Funny Thing . . .*] which is two hours of sliding on a banana skin, so I don't mean to slip into my pretentious mode."

Minor-key comedy, like *M*A*S*H*, is the kind that "suddenly catches you feeling something other than the fun in any given line or situation or character. You feel a little more; it's bittersweet. It doesn't make you stop laughing, but it's a warmer kind of laugh. . . .

"Unfortunately, I think it's true that, with most television, the only way you get a feeling out of it is if you touch it while you're wet. People aren't encouraged to go for the feeling. They're encouraged to go for the broader show-business values. . . . By and large I think people are looking for success rather than for quality. If you can combine the two, you're in a very happy situation."

M*A*S*H was that happy situation, a show that combined humor with pathos, slapstick hilarity with reality. It came at a time when the United States was still bogged down in the Vietnam War. "By now it's no secret that a lot of the attitudes that *M*A*S*H* put forth as fifties–Korean War–type attitudes was really based more on what was happening in the seventies and in Vietnam," Gelbart admitted. "There wasn't as great an antiwar feeling in the Korean period, at least on the American side. It was, after all, a UN effort. We weren't quite as exposed as we were in Vietnam. But certain verities prevail in every war."

However, according to Gelbart, CBS never put any pressure on *M*A*S*H* to tone down the message. "I'd like to talk about censorship," he joked, "but I'm really not allowed to."

The best thing about censorship in *M*A*S*H* is that we didn't have any when it came to political matters. We were allowed to be as anti or pro anything we wanted to be. There was absolutely no interference on that level.

Censorship took the usual form that it takes with a network. Incidentally, they deplore the word *censorship*. There are many euphemisms—*program practices, continuity*—they censor the word *censor* very heavily.

We would be told to cut down on the number of *hell*s, *damn*s, what have you. They always wanted us to be very careful about any nudity. There is one shot of Radar in an episode called "The Sniper" in which, if you look very fast, you can see his bare bum. It goes by in an instant, but we got away with that.

Not that you *try* to get away with things; except you do find yourselves playing games. When the family hour was initiated, we weren't supposed to talk about anything that the whole family couldn't share before nine o'clock. We had a soldier saying to Radar—a very nervous young GI on guard duty for the first time, he didn't know the password—he apologized by saying he was a virgin—at being a sentry. I mean, we didn't even use virgin in a sexual sense.

They wouldn't let us say virgin, their explanation being that the family hour was meant to protect families from having to discuss things like virginity. The next week we got back by having a wounded soldier say that he was from the Virgin Islands. Virgin's okay if it's a capital V.

It was a running battle. It always is. But the acceptance of what we were doing by the program practices people varied with our success. The more successful we got, the less naughty we seemed. In the first year, we were not able to use the word *circumcision*. By the third year, when we were the first or second show in the ratings, we not only used the word, we did a whole episode based on the fact that a Korean woman and a Jewish GI had had a child and they wanted the baby circumcised.

there was no happy ending, because there are not too many in an army hospital. We would show a popular character, Hawkeye or Trapper John or any of the others, doing very unpopular things. We felt that it was important to show a well-rounded person rather than a predictable sort of character.

Half-hour forms—and hours for that matter—I think are a form of adult fairy tales. Audiences like to hear the same story told over and over and over. That's all right for the audience, but not if you're the teller. Even with my own children, I would tell them about the three bears, then the four bears, or there would be two bears; one would be off on vacation or in a story visiting some other character. I get very easily bored, and I can be very easily boring—as you're learning. So I keep trying to mix things up. It was a wonderful cast and production company and my coproducer Gene Reynolds was very willing to throw the whole thing up in the air every week and see how it came down differently.

The urge to be different even included killing off a favorite character—Lieutenant Colonel Henry Blake, played by McLean Stevenson—an action that shocked a lot of people. "I think the one we shocked the most was McLean Stevenson," Gelbart said, "who really didn't expect it. . . . He wanted to leave the series, and we thought that rather than just write him out in a very sort of simple way, we would take advantage of his leaving to make a point: It's not just extras or walk-ons or day players that get killed. Sometimes people you like and love very much are killed. . . .

"The network was not too sure they wanted to do that, nor was Twentieth Century–Fox. We shot it as a provisional ending, and when they saw it, to their credit, they went along with it."

Gelbart too departed *M*A*S*H*, and in 1980 he produced a series that was even more experimental than some of the things *M*A*S*H* had attempted—*United States*.

Success allowed *M*A*S*H* to turn the traditional sitcom format upside down. "We did a lot of experimenting, for several reasons," Gelbart said.

One, just a natural kind of restlessness, not wanting to make everything the same every week. Also, recognizing the fact that in any half hour in anyone's life, we are not just pursuing one subject to one conclusion—certainly not in a place as busy as a mobile hospital a few miles from the front lines. So we would do multiple stories. We would do up to seven stories, different tiers, not giving them all equal weight and trying to make as many of them cross one another as possible.

We did a show in black-and-white, which was very unusual, a show in which the actors practically improvised. It was called "The Interview." We would do shows in which

The many faces of Archie Bunker: Over twelve seasons, from 1971 until 1983, the comic character played by Carroll O'Connor on All in the Family *reflected a turbulent period in America's social history: the fights for racial and sexual equality, Vietnam, Watergate, the sexual revolution.* All in the Family *was a breakthrough—for the first time, a television situation comedy dealt with the issues of real life.*

United States referred to the state of being united, to being married. I know a lot of people probably thought it was something the National Geographic Society was putting out. In Europe, it was called *Married,* which gave people a better idea.

We tried to do something much more realistic in terms of a family. One out of every two American marriages ends in divorce, and we wanted to show the one that doesn't, not because it was so blessed and happy but because of what the people did to keep the marriage going.

They had two children, and again it wasn't a conventional kind of central-casting kiddies. We gave one of them a problem with dyslexia. We didn't want to just do a hello-honey-I'm-home show.

NBC-TV, which was then run by Fred Silverman, went along with the idea that nothing could be done until we

had written twenty-two scripts, which I think was a courageous and a very helpful thing to us. We did write twenty-two. We then shot thirteen.

The result?

We were taken off the air after the eighth episode. Our ratings were pretty dismal. I remember one week, *M*A*S*H* was number one in the ratings and *United States* was number six hundred and seventy, or whatever the last show was. The following week, in which we put on two episodes of *United States,* we were then last and next to last, which is probably another record low.

I don't consider the show a failure. I consider it a success in terms of being able to do what we attempted to do. Certainly as a business venture it was not a success. People said it was too tough, too unrelenting, too funny, too unfunny, too brittle, too soft, too sharp. . . .

At NBC, they said it was too "visceral." I guess anything having to do with guts was just a little too tough for them.

We used no laugh track; we used no happy theme music. We came on cold. We went off with a little music at the end. We just tried a lot of things. Some people said we tried too many things.

It had a second life, a little bit of a second life, on cable television, Arts and Entertainment. Now it's back in the vaults.

I guess I'll bring it out every few years like some crazy uncle you keep in a closet.

Gelbart has been quoted as saying that television spoils life for us because we're not as "good" as it is. "It's very hard for us to compete in our everyday lives with television," he said. "We're not as well made-up, we're not as in focus, we're not as glamorous.

"If you ever see a real fistfight in a restaurant, it's shattering. You shake for half an hour—it's so violent, so ugly. We watch people getting knocked around in commercials and cartoons, where violence is a joke or it really doesn't matter. But real violence really matters, and the first time you find yourself in a hospital, and you can't write the doctors' parts, and they tell you you have something serious, and it's not Alan Alda telling you—that's life. I don't think television should become one great sort of soapbox, but I think there's something wrong about escaping so far into it that we really aren't prepared to deal with reality when we meet it on very serious levels."

Gelbart believes that TV comedy reflects society more accurately than TV drama. "There's very little or no TV drama—there's a lot of TV melodrama. We really can't talk about the nighttime soaps as drama. We really can't talk about cop shows as drama. There are occasional dramas, but they tend to fall into their own sort of clichés—the disease of the month or the triumph of some athlete or performer or whatever over some particular hardship. Sadly, we've come a long way from real drama— *Playhouse 90* and *Studio One* and people writing directly for television."

But there is much that television does well, he feels, such as news.

It certainly can make us the global village that we're told we are and can be. It can put you in touch with everyplace in the world, which has its drawbacks, too. The more I know, the more helpless I feel. I know I can't do much about so many desperate situations in so many places. . . . I think, though, that when a subject is dealt with not merely as a headline, I think that when there's a discussion, I can begin to understand a little better what's happening in the world, and feel part of it and not just feel victimized by it.

After all this time, I don't really know what real television is. Real television might have been the early *Today* show, with Dave Garroway standing in a window doing a show that no one had ever seen before, something that wasn't borrowed from radio or the stage or motion pictures or newspapers. Most of what we see are these kind of bastardized versions of other things. You have to be selective.

Nostalgia for the fifties and the movie American Grafitti *inspired the hit seventies sitcom,* Happy Days, *the adventures of teenaged buddies (left to right) Ralph Malph (Donny Most), Arthur "the Fonz" Fonzarelli (Henry Winkler), Potsie Webber (Anson Williams), and Richie Cunningham (Ron Howard).*

I think if you watch it all the time, you can't tell the good from the bad. . . .

The best thing about television is you can write it and get it on with a minimum of fuss. But that fuss is pretty daunting, too.

Everything is daunting for a writer. It's all uphill.

GRANT TINKER

Grant Tinker is the hero of commercial television's new generation of writers and producers, a man who combines good taste and vast broadcasting experi-ence—at the networks, on Madison Avenue, and in the Hollywood studios. He has the sense and self-assuredness to leave good, creative people alone—unless they need help.

As the president of MTM Enterprises, a company that was started to create a vehicle for his then wife, Mary Tyler Moore, Tinker oversaw a studio that has turned out—and continues to turn out—much of the best of television: *The Mary Tyler Moore Show, The Bob Newhart Show, Rhoda, Lou Grant, The White Shadow, Hill Street Blues, Newhart,* and *St. Else-where.* As chairman and chief executive officer of

Sisters Jessica Tate (Katherine Helmond, left) and Mary Campbell (Cathryn Damon, right), their husbands, lovers, and families made for comic madness on Soap, *a soap opera/sitcom for which almost no subject was taboo. The only voice of sanity was the Tate family cook, Benson (Robert Guillaume, standing), who was rewarded with a series all his own.*

NBC, he took a network that was in the ratings-and-morale basement and helped make it number one, with such hits as *The Cosby Show, Cheers, Family Ties, Miami Vice,* and *The Golden Girls.* Today, in partnership with the Gannett Company, he has begun a new production venture, GTG Entertainment.

He began his career in broadcasting in 1949. The appeal of broadcasting was simply "a living," he said. "I had just gotten out of Dartmouth, and I was looking for a job in publishing. Publishing didn't have a great deal of interest in me, so while I was schlepping around New York, trying to get a job, a

friend said that NBC might be hiring. So I went over there and just knocked on the door of the personnel department. They were beginning to think about this management training program. I had several interviews, and a few weeks later, I was taken aboard. They hired about seventy-five employees, and most of them are still in the business, in one way or another.

"My first two years in the management program were very informal—they just pushed you around the building. Two weeks here and two weeks there. You learned what you could and did what you could, if anybody let you do anything. Finally, they gave you a real job. My next two years were in radio operations."

Television was "somewhere in a back room," Tinker said. "We were caught up in trying to keep radio from dying. These were the last gasps that finally ended that form of radio. Now, of course, it is something else.

"Radio, as we knew it when I was growing up, is what television is today. Some of the same formats, the same program lengths, the same categories of drama, comedy, and so on. Television just kind of put a camera on what was the network radio schedule."

Tinker left NBC to join Radio Free Europe in 1952. "Then I did a couple of years of local packaging in television and some personal management. [Television executive and game-show host] Allen Ludden and I started a network radio show called *College Quiz Bowl,* which later became *College Bowl* on television."

In 1954, he joined the advertising agency of McCann-Erickson as director of program development for television. Then he went to Benton and Bowles as vice president for television programming. This was at a time when many television

Lou Grant (Ed Asner), the gruff boss of the TV newsroom on The Mary Tyler
Moore Show *knew that a sudden show of vulnerability could get him just
about anything he wanted, much to the discomfort of newswriter Murray
Slaughter (Gavin MacLeod, left) and the long suffering patience of his associate
producer, Mary Richards (Moore).*

programs were often produced by an advertising agency for a single sponsor such as General Foods or Johnson's Wax.

Tinker returned to NBC in 1961 and stayed until 1967, at which point he was vice president of programs. He worked in Hollywood for Universal Television and Twentieth Century–Fox, leaving in 1970 to start MTM. Its initial project was *The Mary Tyler Moore Show.*

"My contribution was asking Jim Brooks and Allan Burns, two writers with whom I had worked, to become a team and create a show for Mary." The notion of a series revolving around a single woman, out on her own, even in 1970, was regarded as "if not revolutionary, a little more avant-garde for that time than it would seem today," Tinker recalled.

Originally, Tinker said, "Mary was to have been divorced, arriving in Minneapolis, coming off a

failed marriage. CBS had a problem with that, which they certainly wouldn't have today. But they preferred that she not be divorced. It seems ironic. The network preferred a story line that had Mary coming out of a failed affair. The pilot was about the guy who followed her out to Minneapolis and expected her to return to him.

"The pilot, in a way, is my favorite [show in the series], because they got so much done in that twenty-two minutes—the back story [the events that led the character to the beginning of a movie or a TV series] established her getting her the job—that famous scene with Ed Asner . . ." Mary worked at television station WJM in Minneapolis; Asner played Lou Grant, the news director. The scene Tinker is referring to is the one in which this exchange takes place:

> LOU: You got spunk.
> MARY: Well . . . yes.
> LOU: I hate spunk.

"I remember very well when Ed hired her as associate producer, and said, 'If you can get by on fifteen dollars less a week, I'll make you a producer.' It was an exquisitely made pilot."

Why was *Mary Tyler Moore* such a hit? "There's really a simple answer," Tinker said. "It was a very good television show—the characters were very well conceived, and the writing . . . not the stories so much, because you know, in twenty-two minutes of situation comedy, that isn't important. The words given those characters to speak to each other were better words than characters were getting on other shows.

"It was beautifully cast, as it turned out," he added. "Not everybody was up to speed from the very first episode, but as the series progressed, ev-erybody made a major contribution. It was just a damn good television show. This is going to sound a little parochial, but I never saw a *Mary Tyler Moore* half hour I didn't like."

Asked what encouraged the creative atmosphere at MTM, Tinker said, "Part of it is a phenomenon that occurs when good creative people come together—others, on the outside, watching, tend to want to join them."

I asked Tinker how the MTM comedies of the seventies compared to the kind of shows being produced at the same time by Norman Lear *(All in the Family, Maude, Good Times)*. "I preferred ours—that might not surprise you to hear," he said. "His were harder hitting, had a lot more impact, and were more daring, in many ways. But I also think that ours were harder to do."

Tinker has settled into offices at the old Laird International Studios, the complex where *Gone with the Wind* was filmed, bought by Gannett for the express purposes of GTG Entertainment. "The quickest way that I can talk about the new company is to say that I would like to re-create the MTM experience. I want us to be able to get our hands on the same level of creative people, as they become available. The good ones are always doing something. You have to be patient and persistent to get them into our new company and do the kinds of programming in comedy and drama that we did at MTM, and that MTM still does. That kind of series television is as much fun as anything. There's something about a series, though it's relentless, that is very satisfying."

Tinker says he doesn't think of himself as a producer. "I sort of produce producers," he said. "I'm a guy who hires producers, hangs out with them, recruits them, and watches them work. I tend to appreciate people who do literate comedy, particu-

Ed Asner initially found it difficult to move the character of newsman Lou Grant from the comedy of The Mary Tyler Moore Show *to the drama of* Lou Grant, *but working with fellow actors like Jack Bannon (left), who played assistant city editor Art Donovan, he found a style that worked both for him and the audience.*

larly. *Mary Tyler Moore* would qualify for me, as *Cheers* would qualify today. It isn't stuff I do myself. It's stuff I like to look at and laugh at."

The "charm" of the business, he says, is "its presence, I think. The fact that I can do it here in my office and go home and watch it at night. It's always with me. I loved that about the NBC job, where I could meddle in anything I wanted to on any given day or night.

"It's not true of the lumber business [Tinker's father was in the lumber business]. I guess you could take a stick of wood home, but it wouldn't be quite the same. I like that about television—that it's only a flick of the dial away at any moment.

"It's a terrific way of making a living. It's not like stealing, perhaps, but it beats working. For me, it's not really working. I frequently find myself thinking, 'This is just like playing!' "

ED ASNER

Wearing a three-piece suit, Ed Asner walks into a conference room at The Egg Factory, a former egg-packing plant that was turned into an office complex by filmmaker George Lucas. He doesn't look comfortable—he should be in his shirt sleeves, tie askew, toiling away in the newsroom at WJM on *The Mary Tyler Moore Show* or the city room of the *Los Angeles Tribune* on *Lou Grant*.

To television viewers he will always be Lou Grant: the tough newsie with a heart—and liver—of gold, the news director who told an employee, "Keep up the fair work."

Asner was raised in Kansas City, attended the University of Chicago, drifted into theater and eventually into New York City, where he discovered the joys and tribulations of live television. But as a struggling actor, he couldn't afford to own a set of his own. "My first work in New York on television was primarily on the Sunday morning shows," Asner said. "*Camera Three, Look Up and Live, Lamp unto My Feet, Frontiers of Faith:* the religious shows, the artsy-craftsy shows. God knows, they were prestigious. I would find myself doing poetry!"

Asner also worked in some of the famous Golden Age prime-time drama series, including *Studio One, Kraft Television Theatre,* and *Armstrong Circle Theater:* "Small roles for the most part," he said. "I wasn't given the opportunity to screw up that much." In 1961, after filming a guest shot on *Naked City* out in Los Angeles, he decided to move to California. A variety of guest roles ensued, and in 1964, he costarred in *Slattery's People,* a short-lived but excellent series that starred Richard Crenna as a state legislator.

In 1969, his role as a police chief in a made-for-TV movie called *Doug Selby, D.A.* caught the attention of Grant Tinker, who was in the process of developing *The Mary Tyler Moore Show.* "Grant passed the word that they should see me," Asner said. "They" were James Brooks and Allan Burns, the cocreators and executive producers of *The Mary Tyler Moore Show.*

I read, and they said, "That's a very intelligent reading. Now we would like you to read it wiggy, wild, crazy, far-out the next time, when you come back."

I said, "I'm not sure what you want. Why don't you have me try it now, and if I don't do it right, don't have me back." They were startled by this laying it on the line. . . .

So I read it crazily. They laughed their asses off, and said, "Just read it like that when we have you back with Mary."

Okay. I came back, and I said, "What the hell did I do?" Couldn't even remember. I forced it, I pushed it, I faked it, and they laughed again. I suppose they were seeing just how malleable I could be, how much of a fool I was willing to make of myself . . .

After I left, I found out a couple of years later, Mary turned to them and said, "Was it that funny?" They said, "That's your Lou."

The show had a memorable cast of characters, including Ted Baxter, the silver-haired and egocentric anchorman played by Ted Knight (reporting a military coup in Albania, he asked, "Albania—that's the capital of New York, isn't it?"), his wife, Georgette (Georgia Engel), put-upon news writer Murray Slaughter (Gavin MacLeod), and Sue Ann Nivens (Betty White), the host of *The Happy Homemaker* (one of her shows was titled, "What's All This Fuss About Famine?").

Asner's own favorite episode of all the seven years, one widely regarded as a classic, is called "Chuckles Bites the Dust." "We had this character on our terrible syndicated channel—Chuckles the Clown," Asner said. "Finally, it was decided to write a script in which he gets killed. He was leading some kind of parade or other, dressed as a peanut, and a rogue elephant crushed him." The resulting one-liners infuriate Mary.

LOU: The guy died wearing a peanut suit—killed by an elephant.
MURRAY: Yeah—born in a trunk, died in a trunk.

LOU: Lucky that elephant didn't go after anybody else.
MURRAY: That's right. After all, you know how hard it is to stop after just one peanut.

"Mary gets very perturbed at the way we're treating this death," Asner said.

All the way through the show, she's busy scolding and nagging, warning us that we better behave when we get to the funeral, because it's going to humiliate her, the station, and everything.

The minister is giving the eulogy. He starts talking about what a man Chuckles was, and all of a sudden, Mary starts to go, breaking into laughter herself.

See, it was brilliant, turning everybody around. We all turned and snarled at this breach of decency. She just totally giggles. Even the minister notices her and says, "That's right, young lady, laugh. That's what Chuckles would want you to do."

Mary starts crying and converting laughter to tears. The minister finally ends with Chuckles's favorite quatrain: "A little song / A little dance, / A little seltzer / Down your pants." Mary just goes wacko, hysterics. I finally get her out of the church. A wonderful show. It was written by David Lloyd, who was, I guess, one of our funniest writers. Our regular director, Jay Sandrich, didn't want to do it. The cast loved it. So Joan Darling was given the assignment, and I believe she won an Emmy for it.

At first, there was uncertainty about the episode.

We came in and began working, and we were very disturbed since it was constantly referring to death and funerals. The older guys in the crew weren't laughing like we had hoped they would. We realized we were up against it, and we worked hard all week. We concentrated; we leaned on each other as much as we could.

Come the Friday afternoon run-through, the dress rehearsal before the Friday night performance, we were four, four and a half minutes short. We all groaned. We. were about to go on hiatus. This meant we would have to come back and ticky-tacky on another scene. The 360-degree perfection of the show would suffer.

We never got laughs in rehearsal. We felt we just had to go out there and play the hell out of it. Got up there, and just in the playing of it, with the audience, we were able to extend the show that four and a half minutes. It came in at perfect timing. Most people think of it as *the* show.

Pulling together was representative of the spirit at the MTM studios, Asner said, "The country club studio of Hollywood."

Below: Reflective of the show's atmosphere of total nonsense and wonderful comic anarchy, the title Monty Python's Flying Circus *had no meaning whatsoever. The six members of this BBC series created a mind-boggling variety of sketches, satires, and animation sequences, many of which had no ending. The series was enormously popular on both sides of the Atlantic.*

Right: A sitcom of the eighties pays tribute to a classic: in a dream sequence in one episode of Kate and Allie *(bottom), Jane Curtin and Susan Saint James played the roles of Lucy Ricardo and Ethel Mertz.*

People just loved coming there. . . . This is not to say it was all Goody Two-Shoes. There were jealousies, and there were ruffled feelings, unbridled tempers at times, but in the main, compared to anywhere else in the world or in show biz, it was the best.

The seven years of *Mary Tyler Moore* were a wonderful blend of working in film and working with an audience. You had the best of both worlds. You were able to perform before an audience, and you were able to capture it on film. Granted, you couldn't come back the next night and improve on that performance, but the wonderful part was that when you were good, you had it for posterity.

It was sweet; it was honest; there was love all around, appreciation, very good ensemble work. Most important, it was beautifully written with an excellent actress in the main role who was willing to be the hub, a source of stability to a bunch of loonies, and was quite gratified with the returns therefrom.

It was seven years of life that went so swiftly, I don't even remember shaving. It was fantastic.

4. DRAMAS

A veteran writer of the Golden Age of live television drama, Rod Serling turned his hand to the creation of The Twilight Zone, *an anthology series of tales of fantasy and terror that specialized in the unexpected twist of plot.*

he Golden Age of live television drama drew to an end in the beginning of the sixties. The advent of filmed television series and videotape ended the spontaneity and intimacy of live drama. As more and more television sets were being sold and the audience was broadening beyond the cities, the marketplace demanded a kind of TV drama different from live TV's social realism. The mass audience wanted action and adventure.

There were some exceptions, and not surprisingly, many of them came from veterans of the Golden Age. Reginald Rose, author of *Twelve Angry Men*, created *The Defenders*, a film series that depicted a father-and-son team of lawyers confronting the social issues of the day, including racism, sexual abuse, and blacklisting; it was produced by Herbert Brodkin. Rod Serling, author of so many fine live TV dramas, delighted audiences with *The Twilight Zone*, a strange and fanciful world of odd creatures and O. Henry plot twists.

But for the most part, the public's appetite demanded escape into a clearly defined world of good and evil. The networks turned to Hollywood, the storytelling capital of the world. Initially, the studios turned their noses down at television. It was a cut-rate invader. But they could not afford to ignore it for long. Television was stealing movie audiences. Ultimately, former NBC executive David Tebet recalled, "Television saved this city. When Warner Brothers was in so much trouble, ABC President Bob Kintner made a deal with them, giving them $10 million a year for three years to make westerns."

By the late fifties, there were more than thirty westerns playing in prime time every week. In the climate of the Cold War and anticommunism, the black-and-white morality of the western reflected the public mood. Warner Brothers was the king of the shoot-'em-ups, producing such series as *Cheyenne*, *Maverick*, *Lawman*, *Sugarfoot*, and *Bronco*. There were many others as well: *Bat Masterson*, *Wyatt Earp*, *The Rifleman*, *Rawhide*, *Wanted: Dead or Alive*, to name but a few, and the two Westerns that left the others back at the ranch—*Gunsmoke* and *Bonanza*. Long after the western genre had bitten the dust, Marshall Dillon and the Cartwright clan continued to whoop it up, until the mid-seventies.

If the public fascination with the Old West faded, the desire for good guy/bad guy shows did not. The locales changed, and heroes and villains shifted from cowpokes and desperadoes to cops and robbers. Going back to the days of *Dragnet*, which premiered on television in 1952 (it began life as a radio series), police procedurals, mystery series, and the adventures of private gumshoes have always been enormously popular on TV. From the violent escapades of *The Untouchables* (a show considered so violent it was held up as an example of the worst of television in the sixties and led in part to the networks cleaning up their acts with such genteel programs as the good *Doctor Kildare* on NBC and his ABC rival *Ben Casey*) through such series as *M Squad*, *Peter Gunn*, *Ironside*, *Hawaii Five-O*, *Police Story*, and *Columbo*, police and detective work have provided an endless source of story material.

The main characters don't have to be uniformed officers or private investigators to fill the good guy/bad guy bill. They can be international spies (*The Man from U.N.C.L.E.*, *I Spy*, or *Mission: Impossible*), lawyers (*Judd for the Defense*, *Perry Mason*) or even keepers of the peace in outer space (*Star Trek*). As Steven Bochco, cocreator of *Hill Street Blues*, *L.A.*

92

Law, and *Hooperman,* said, "Almost everything in television is a cop show. It just is."

The good guy/bad guy syndrome even fits with the phenomenon of the nighttime soaps. Detectives are always knocking at the doors of the mansions of the rich and famous on *Dallas, Dynasty, Falcon Crest,* and *Knots Landing*—and usually with good reason. There's all manner of nastiness going on.

Significantly, all of the drama shows mentioned thus far have been wildly successful all over the world. Filmed episodic drama with plenty of action has been America's most successful television export. In Britain, for example, Christopher Dunkley, the television critic for the *Financial Times,* noted that "British television utilizes and exploits American television much more than the foreign concept of British television might have it. I think people in America probably think that British television consists largely of Dickens and Shakespeare and very worthy stuff of that sort. And it doesn't. It consists of much of American high-popularity products— and that's true in most other foreign countries."

Star Trek has boldly gone to more than a hundred countries. "We were in some deserted village in the wilds on the Caspian Sea," *Star Trek* star William Shatner remembered. "This waiter came up—of course, he didn't speak any English—the man was as remote from civilization as you can get. He said, 'Captain Kirk?' It was bizarre. In the back room of the restaurant where I was eating, on this ancient black-and-white television set, *Star Trek* was playing.

"If *Star Trek* could effect that remote part of civilization, what must *Dallas* and other shows that don't paint a pretty picture of America do to influence people of the world as to what America is like?"

The image of America portrayed in shows like *Dallas* is "appalling," Michael Grade, chief executive officer of Britain's independent Channel 4, said. "But does it matter? I don't think it matters. I don't think people's views of America are shaped by television programs. I think people's views of America are much more complex than that. They are shaped by all kinds of things."

Besides, those international viewers of American dramas are being deluged with such an eclectic mix of images, it would be hard to assemble a representative viewpoint. Along with the pastels and high fashions of a *Miami Vice,* there are the grit and middle-class values of *Cagney and Lacey;* with the gross explosions and car chases of an *A-Team,* there are the thoughtful discussions and moral dilemmas of *St. Elsewhere.*

What's distressing is the lack of the kind of serious drama that typified the early days of television. Cable networks like Arts and Entertainment and public television are the only outlets for them these days, and much of what we see there consists of British imports and little that is written expressly for the television screen. Still, specials and such series as *Great Performances* and *American Playhouse* do allow us the opportunity to see the work of some of the best American playwrights—from Tennessee Williams and Arthur Miller to Lanford Wilson and Sam Shepard—and our finest performers. Commercial television rarely bows to the domestic dramatic tradition of America. There should be more—both adaptations and serious drama written expressly for the TV screen. Only a superstar seems to be able to get such programs on the major networks, and then, only rarely, as was the case with Dustin Hoffman's astonishing performance in *Death of a Salesman* on CBS.

The British television playwright Dennis Potter has said that television drama "ought to be able to

remind you of your own sovereignty as a human being—that is, that the next minute is in your hands, even when it feels as if it isn't." And a Japanese television director, Yoshihiko Okamoto noted, "There should be drama which reveals more of our everyday life, so that the viewer can confront the television screen, not simply lie down with it."

Not all is doom and gloom. The progress made by the creative talents behind such series as *Hill Street*

Blues, St. Elsewhere, Cagney and Lacey, L.A. Law, and *Moonlighting* is encouraging—series that bring a new reality and understanding of human relationships to the standard good guy/bad guy formula. They remind us that popular drama can tell stories that are more than escapist entertainment. David Milch, a *Hill Street Blues* writer who succeeded Steven Bochco as co-executive producer of the series, said, "Appealing to a broad audience and

The deadpan yet congenial countenance of motion picture director Alfred Hitchcock graced each edition of his two television anthology series, Alfred Hitchcock Presents *and* The Alfred Hitchcock Hour. *Every week, tongue firmly in cheek, Hitchcock would introduce tales of suspense and macabre mayhem.*

maintaining quality need not be mutually exclusive ambitions. The fact is, if you tell good stories which identify drama in the rhythms of people's lives as they're lived, an audience will respond."

Part of the reality that these shows are presenting is that life is not all drama or comedy; it's a mixture of both. This has led to these programs being called—only by a few, thank God—dramedies. The ability to move from one to another and still remain credible in the eyes of the viewers is hard to come by. Ed Asner learned this the hard way, when his Lou Grant character had to make the transition from the comedy of *The Mary Tyler Moore Show* to a dramatic series all his own, *Lou Grant*, a series that helped pave the way for the *Hill Street*s and *Cagney and Lacey*s that followed.

ED ASNER

"When we started off, we all knew what we wanted in terms of quality," Asner said,

but not knowing how to get it easily, simply, we went through enormous crew changes and one cast change. I would say that the shakedown cruise finally occurred in the middle of the second, maybe even the end of the second year, and we settled down into smooth sailing.

With *Mary,* the producers were always down on the floor, and there was this yin and yang going on there. With an hour show, generally the producers are either writing scripts up in the office or battling major forces elsewhere. They're not down on the line, because it's a much duller, slower process, and it's a waste of time for them to stay there.

So I really found no guidance. The scripts were wonderful, but how to shape it properly, how much to play for a laugh without an audience? I asked a professional friend, "What do you think of the show?" He said, "Why are you grimacing so much?" I was pushing for the laugh. There were no

laughs, there was no studio audience, so I was trying to create space for the laughs at home.

I'd been under strict direction by Jay Sandrich, who directed most of our shows at MTM, and by the producers, saying, "We're not going to be on the set. You have to keep the flame of Lou Grant alive, da-da-da." So I kept trying to play the Lou Grant of *The Mary Tyler Moore Show.* Finally, there came a time in the middle of the season, when I said, "This is baloney. I've got to play it as I feel it." I was under the gun, and the change in the playing was probably infinitesimal, but it took such a monkey off my back. The relaxation I was able to acquire made all the difference in the world to me. I began to investigate new areas as a different Lou Grant, and the show began to flow more.

Lou Grant's newspaper-city-room motif allowed them to examine a wide variety of topics and issues. "Stories that dominated the press," Asner said. "CIA spying, black disadvantage in the city, Vietnam veterans, white-collar crime, corporate takeovers . . . We did a fantastic show just before we were canceled on the facts and figures of nuclear warfare.

"That one involved two stories: one, following a young girl who had been badly burned in a school bus accident and the hundreds of thousands of dollars in special training and special care that she required. And then showing that, in a nuclear holocaust, there would be hundreds of thousands of people like her, and that the city, which had more than the usual share of burn equipment, was nowhere equipped enough, and the nation certainly was not. It was not going to be just deaths by radiation or blast. It was going to be slow, lingering deaths in the hundreds of thousands—people who could not receive proper medical care."

The episode was called "Unthinkable." Its ratings were dismal, beaten out by the repeat of a special called *TV's Censored Bloopers.* "That *would* beat us out," Asner said. "Bread and circuses—the

Dody Goodman (left) was one of the guest stars who appeared on the courtroom drama series, The Defenders, *starring E. G. Marshall (right) and Robert Reed as a father-and-son team of attorneys. The series, created by Golden Age writer Reginald Rose and producer Herbert Brodkin, was known for its intelligent, adult scripting and its willingness to tackle contemporary issues.*

barbarians may be at the gate, but we got to be entertained."

In spite of that feeling, Asner says, "The miracle is that there *is* good stuff on. It is amazing that with this constant, twenty-four-hour, 365-days-a-year grinding, grinding, grinding out, we end up with as much good stuff as we do. But think of how much more good stuff we would end up with if those in charge did less playing down to the lowest common denominator!"

HERBERT BRODKIN

One of the pioneer producers of television drama was Herbert Brodkin, who continues to produce quality drama to this day. Brodkin worked on *Studio One* and *Playhouse 90* among other live drama shows and believes that much of the success of the Golden Age is attributable to the fact that program executives were just taking their first baby steps, too.

"The networks didn't know enough to prevent it," he said.

We were all beginners. People who had some theatrical background in writing, directing, lighting, scenery—I started as a scene designer—got into television in the early days, and it was all live and then they wanted dramas so we did them! Those were the days when if you had to get a show on at eight o'clock Thursday night, you delivered, and there wasn't time for reediting or hesitation as there is now with film. It was much more a producer's medium than it is now. . . . It was much more fun. It was like being in the theater, with an opening night and the excitement of opening night which pervaded the show and the actors. Sometimes you got the kind of brilliance that you occasionally see in an amateur play production on opening night; of course, *we* used professionals.

In those days, we were almost like England, in the sense that well-known actors would appear on television. We used all the stars, and they got paid very little. But they would be willing to do good scripts and good plays. When we switched from live performance to film, it changed.

The networks had less control over the final product back then; everything happened so fast. There was less sophistication; there was less supervision. Many executives in those days had the same objectives as we producers: They just simply wanted good shows. . . . Everyone was learning. Talent had a chance to show—in writing, especially, and in performance. It was tiring but great fun.

The Golden Age faded because everything went to film. Film could be distributed to television stations all over the world. Distribution reared its ugly head. Once film came in and Hollywood came in, things changed considerably.

The move to film and Hollywood opened television to the great outdoors. Dramas that had taken place in kitchens or jury rooms were out. Character was sacrificed to scenery and action. Brodkin stayed in New York, but he didn't take the demise of live drama lying down. He made the transition to film, but he brought to it the values he had learned in live drama, along with a feeling for dialogue, interior action, motivation, and a willingness to tackle social issues head on. Working with the distinguished writer Reginald Rose, Brodkin produced *The Defenders,* which began airing on CBS in 1961.

"Our intention with *The Defenders* was to do an entertaining series about the reality of life in New York," Brodkin said.

We were, I think, able to tackle some difficult subjects and do them quite well. For the first time in television, the play dealt with the reality of a subject and dealt with it honestly as well as dramatically. . . . We did subjects on television that no one had ever done before: subjects such as prostitution, rape, murder, whatever we saw in the daily papers. It was exciting and it was fun.

The series got on the air, I think, only on a kind of fluke, because our pilot was rejected. But it was [CBS chairman] William Paley who pulled it off the shelf and said, "Let's try to make this." . . .

When we had completed the first half-dozen episodes in the spring before it went on the air the following fall, the then president of CBS thought that what we were doing was just awful. So we stopped for an evaluation, which went on for six weeks, and we just rested. When they had evaluated what we had done, we went back and did more of the same thing. When it went on the air it very quickly achieved a high rating. *The Defenders* was a show that was talked about the next morning by everybody and almost changed the face of television. Then something called *The Beverly Hillbillies* came along, and some others like it, and changed it right back.

Our motivations [on *The Defenders*] were honest, and we dealt with subjects honestly to the best of our ability. Today, the networks are exploitive; they use the subjects of crime and violence not for the inherent honesty in the subjects but for the excitement of getting a rating, of seeing who can get the biggest audience tuning into the nastiest subject. I think that's basically what the difference is.

I think the networks have underestimated their audience right from the beginning. I think the audience was there and was receptive. I say *was,* because the networks have now had twenty-five or thirty years of training people not to like good entertainment, good drama, so that they have

Norman Walker, renamed "Clint," was the laconic star of Cheyenne, *the first hit western from the Warner Brothers stable.*

trained their own audience, and they will, I hope, one day be hoist by that. I think it will take a long time to bring the audience back to the way it was in the time of the early to late fifties and early sixties. They have been trained in the wrong way.

WILLIAM ORR

When the production of drama series shifted from live to film and from the East to West Coast, Hollywood was not prepared for the television invasion. Bob Hope joked that movie moguls regarded television as "that furniture that stares back at you." But eventually, the studios gave in. They finally recognized the potential gold mine in television production. One by one, they succumbed, all of them realizing that economic necessity demanded it.

After some initial hesitation—and outright hostility—Warner Brothers became one of the first to get involved in television production. The year was 1955, and the head of television production for the studio was William Orr.

"ABC went to several of the major studios including Warner Brothers and asked them to produce for television," he said.

First off, Jack Warner had not appreciated television, since it was cutting into attendance at the theatrical motion picture tremendously. As a matter of fact, he wouldn't even allow a television set to be part of the dressed set for a picture. Nobody watched television in Warner Brothers movies at that point—nobody. . . . But our theatrical business had been going down . . . and it was a matter actually of "if you can't beat 'em, join 'em." So we did; we went into business with ABC. . . .

I had been an executive on the features side for ten years, and I had no idea that there was the possibility that I would be placed in television. So I was placed in charge one Friday afternoon, much to my surprise, because at that time if you went into television from the feature end, it was like getting scarlet fever. However, seeing as it seemed to be necessary, I went over and got into it, and once I got into it, it was a lot of fun.

As did the producers in the days of live TV, the Hollywood producers of filmed TV had a lot to learn.

It was very quick, you had to make decisions rapidly, you didn't have time to consult and do this and that, and I enjoyed it. The first year was horrendous because we had not prepared early enough and we didn't know enough about all the problems of getting on the air at the right time.

I got into television probably three months too late. We had very few scripts, we didn't have too many stories, and we were fumbling around trying to figure out how you made television. . . . Our big problem was being behind the time to get on the air. Not being old pros at this, we were all

One day, on *Cheyenne,* I picked up the report I used to get from the set. The sixth day [of shooting] was the last day, and we didn't have enough film shot to make the minutes. I figured we were about eleven minutes too short. So I got hold of the producer and I told him. He was a new producer. He'd been a good writer and I'd made him a producer, but he wasn't terribly well versed in these things, so I invited him over to my house. He came over about ten o'clock, having been to a cocktail party he said he couldn't get out of. We stayed there and he wrote scenes and I wrote scenes, and then we'd compare our scenes, discuss what our scenes would be about. We got enough scenes, we thought, to do more than eleven minutes—so we'd have something to trim—and at five o'clock I said, "You've got to get to the studio first thing in the morning and get hold of the casting office. In fact, you should call them from home the minute you get up and get hold of a girl we need to play a part, get the sets organized, get hold of the unit manager and whomever else and get this thing going—we'll shoot these extra scenes sometime during the day"

I didn't sleep very well thinking about this, so at a quarter to six, I woke back up, did the things I told him to do, got up, and went to the studio about eight-thirty. He sailed in. I said, "Hello. How's everything?" He said, "Well, fine, I'm gonna call up the girl and get her." I said, "There she is." He said, "Well, we gotta get the sets." I said, "We're in one." It was just a matter of inexperience. He didn't realize that in order to do it, you'd better get there early in the morning and get it done, so we shot that extra bunch of scenes that day and it worked out fine. It wasn't a happy time at the moment, though.

There were advantages to shooting television shows at a major motion picture studio. "Warners and every other studio in town had made myriads of westerns, so when we did *Cheyenne,* we had big scope," he said.

We would cleverly integrate stock film from our own company, and we would write stories to the stock, knowing that when Cheyenne went out onto the western street on the lot, he would get on a horse and we would ride him out to some prairie that was probably in Arkansas or somewhere, and

fumbling around. It meant that we would spend untold hours—I'd be up until three or four o'clock in the morning—trying to get these scripts ready to shoot.... That whole year I was looking for an assistant and didn't have time to look!

Although Warner Brothers produced a number of other kinds of TV shows in the fifties and early sixties (including such contemporary action shows as *77 Sunset Strip, Hawaiian Eye,* and *Surfside Six*), it was for its westerns that the studio became best known. The first of them was *Cheyenne,* starring Norman "Clint" Walker. As in the first baby-step days of live television, Orr and his colleagues at Warner Brothers were learning as they went along. That meant that everyone was nervous, and that everyone pitched in, no matter how esteemed their position.

James Garner (below left) and Jack Kelly played the brothers Maverick, Bret *and* Bart, *western dandies who brought an unusual wit and sophistication to the TV shoot 'em up.*

Davy Crockett, king of the Wild Frontier, made a major TV star of Fess Parker when he appeared as Crockett in a series of adventures on Walt Disney's Disneyland. *No raccoon was safe as the demand for copies of Crockett's coonskin cap swamped the stores.*

then we'd use the stock to intercut. We'd get a couple of cattle and have Cheyenne ride on the back lot, shoot up over a cattle horn, go right back to the stock, he looked like he had ten thousand head. . . . That gave great scope to the series. . . .

Some of the stories were based on old Warners pictures, but I found we had very few stories, so I went down to the local bookstore in Beverly Hills and bought three or four books, anthologies of cowboy stories, took the essential ideas out of them, and they became *Cheyenne* and ultimately *Maverick* and *Sugarfoot, Lawman,* all of them. We paid five hundred to seven hundred and fifty dollars for the rights to use those stories. The authors thought this was quite nice because nobody had ever bought these short stories for films before.

Today those writers would have agents, lawyers, and business managers; possibly they would be

wangling for the chance to direct. It was a simpler time then, but only briefly.

It didn't take long for Hollywood to make television a big-time part of the show business.

MICHAEL MANN

Someone is pursuing Michael Mann with a very important question: "Should we portray them as contemporary bikers or Sergio Leone types?"

"Nah," Mann replies, "make 'em contemporary."

Mann's office, at Universal Studios, is definitely contemporary: black, stark, high tech, stylish—appropriate for a man who's the executive producer of a show that set its own distinctive style—*Miami Vice.*

According to legend, *Miami Vice* began with a memo from Brandon Tartikoff, president of NBC Entertainment. The note said, simply, MTV COPS. Mann cannot confirm the story, but it would appeal to his love of the blunt. A plaque in his office is engraved with a quote: DON'T USE THE WORD "BUTT." THAT'S CRYPTO-FAGGOT "HILL STREET BLUES" TALK. The source of this aphorism, not readily found in Bartlett's, is Michael Mann.

"I was only interested in making motion pictures," he said. "I had gone to graduate school and lived in Europe for six years, studying films and making films—short films, documentaries, some art films. Worked for Twentieth Century–Fox in a production executive capacity in London for about a year and a half. . . . I came to L.A. in '71, and I thought that films suffered from a tyranny of words. I had no interest in television at all. So I wound up getting my first legitimate gig as a writer in televi-

sion, which is exactly how things usually work here," he said, laughing.

That first job was working as a writer for Aaron Spelling and Leonard Goldberg on *Starsky and Hutch*. From there, he went to work on *Police Story*. "A lot of really good writers came out of *Police Story*. It was an anthology show, there weren't continuing stars, so each story was different. Joseph Wambaugh was still heavily involved when I was there. He was a real champion of quality."

Then, he said, his career "started happening very quickly. I wrote one pilot, which became a television series, *Vegas*. After that, because I was fairly successful as a writer for television, I told ABC that I really didn't want to write anything else unless I could direct it. We found a script called *The Jericho Mile*. I did a rewrite on that, shared the writing credit with the original writer, directed it, and it did very well."

The Jericho Mile, a television movie starring Peter Strauss, did very well indeed. The story of a prisoner who becomes a marathon runner, it received four Emmy awards. It got Mann his first feature—*Thief*. He expected to keep working in movies, but he came back to television. "There are certain things you can do in television that you can't do in features," Mann said. "I have always had a tremendous appreciation for the immediacy of television and for the topicality of television. . . . Because we do so many hours on *Miami Vice*, I can make one about Nicaragua, I can make one about a motorcycle gang from twenty years ago who now are major drug manufacturers in Miami, which is factually based. . . . I have an idea today, we have a script about three weeks from now, we shoot it two weeks after that, and it's on the air four weeks later. It's fast, and I like the speed of it."

Still, given the Hollywood system, Mann didn't

Cowpoke Tom Brewster (Will Hutchins) was popular with the womenfolk, but the other cowboys said he was one step lower than a tenderfoot. Hence the name of his series—Sugarfoot—a popular ABC western produced by Warner Brothers.

Killing was wrong on the fifties western, but a man had to do what a man had to do. Premiering in 1955, Gunsmoke was the longest running western on television. It starred James Arness (center) as Marshall Matt Dillon, and Dennis Weaver as his limping, slightly dim deputy and sidekick, Chester B. Goode.

102

expect to find himself back in TV once he had started to direct movies.

My agent said, "You should read this script we have." It was a ninety-minute version of a pilot called *Gold Coast.* "Universal wants to know if you want to take the thing over and work with Tony Yerkovich, who wrote it." I got to page ten of this first draft, and the writing was actually brilliant. Anybody on the street could read this and say, "Hey, this pilot is great! This thing's going to work. It'll work as a feature film; it'll work as a miniseries; it'll work as a television series; it'll work as anything." The characterizations were great and Miami is hot. I knew Miami, I knew South Beach already, and I could see these guys walking around in that sunbaked Deco landscape. So I got involved and that was it. We made *Miami Vice.*

What really was new about it when it appeared on the scene is that the people who were making it did not make it like you make television. . . . If there's one isolatable quality that caused *Miami Vice* to be different when it hit, it was that a lot of the people who worked very hard on the show were very committed people who care a lot about what they do. And what they do is make movies. We looked at it as if we're making a little movie every week, and we're going to make it as good as we know how to make it.

It's for that reason that *Miami Vice* reportedly costs as much as $1.5 million an episode. Mann also attributes part of the show's success to his knowledge of how organized crime really operates.

I could tell if something in a script felt phony, like a rerun of *Ironside.* That is not how people are operating now. There is a known set of rules, observable laws that govern the political economy of organized crime. Crime is a business. It's run by professionals . . . and successful professional criminals rarely go to jail. There are as many dynamics to that economy as there are dynamics to Wall Street.

A lot of people working on the show are street people or urban people, have an urban sensibility, so they're not going to have some TV idea of what an organized crime boss is. It's not going to be some guy walking in with an ascot. . . .

Lorne Greene (below, second from left) was the TV western's ultimate father figure, playing Pa Cartwright on Bonanza. *His sons were played by Pernell Roberts (Adam, left), Dan Blocker (Hoss, right), and Michael Landon (Little Joe).*

So it was both the street sensibility toward content and an approach to making movies—that's what made the first season, at any rate, different than the other stuff on the air.

But what about the "look" of *Miami Vice,* the style that seemed to capture so many imaginations? "It starts with how I work as a film director," Mann said.

On a film, after I've written it and have figured out what the content is, I then go through a very calculated process of saying, "What film form tells the story best? A neorealistic verisimilitude where it's seamless and people walk into a darkened room called a theater but it's just like they're really there out on the street? . . . Or through a kind of diffusion filter, where the film is very much on the screen, removed from them—it's very beautiful, it's obviously a fantasy that they're looking at? What is the form that best tells the story?"

Sometimes you hit and sometimes you miss. I think with *Miami Vice,* in the first season, anyway, we certainly hit. I decided what I really wanted to sell, in effect, was heat—you know, as in temperature. The place is hot. It's sunbaked. There was an Impressionist way of working with vibrating pastels, where if you really want to create white heat, you don't paint a canvas white. You put a lot of yellows, then greens and light blues next to each other, and put a little piece of white in the middle of it and it starts to really feel hot.

Lawman, starring John Russell as Laramie Marshall Dan Troop, was one of the many western series that salvaged the financial condition of the Warner Brothers studios in the fifties and sixties.

Even though he worked as a bounty hunter, Josh Randall, played by Steve McQueen, was a good guy on the western, Wanted: Dead or Alive.

I also decided—I make up these arbitrary rules—that in the show's world, all low-rent people live in Art Deco, and all high-rent people live in postmodernist, and nothing in between. I don't want any fifties architecture, I don't want French provincial for rich people in Palm Beach. It's just the two extremes and nothing else—except for funk, like a Cuban coffee shop or something. We were exploiting the industrial landscape in Miami, which is really rich, too.

Mann makes it clear that a great many people are responsible for making the look possible—the production and costume designers, among others—nor does he think of himself as the "auteur" of *Miami Vice.* As a result, he claims to be relatively immune to criticism that *Vice* is more style than substance.

This is very much a producing activity for me. There's a big difference between being a director and being a producer. When I hear criticism about *Miami Vice,* I'm not as sensitized to it as I would be if somebody talked about [my feature film] *Manhunter.* I usually shoot my mouth off in defense of *Miami Vice.* I feel that I'm defending all these other people I work with, and that's about two hundred and fifty of them on each show.

Miami Vice is variable. It's like a high-risk venture for an investor. I'm not talking about the money or the budgets on *Vice.* It's creatively and artistically high-risk. It's easy, mechanically, to go into a studio and shoot on an existing set for six or seven days. Maybe five days in the studio and two days out—like on an average *Hill Street.* That's not to knock *Hill Street . . .* but it's extremely difficult and risky to approach each hour of an episode like a forty-nine-minute motion picture and try to jam all the shooting—three locations in a single day, all the stuff that we do—into an hour of television. Which means that when we do well, it's going to be an extraordinary product, and when we do poorly, it's going to be abysmal.

The style of the show you get for free, because when you invent it, it replicates itself, it's there every week. Everybody knows what to do. The guys know what color to use, what shapes to stick in front of the camera, what to dress the people in. You buy the clothes once, you got them for the whole season. Content, you got to make it up brand-new

Wagon Train *was a long-running NBC western whose cast of characters changed as the seasons went by. Ward Bond starred as the original wagonmaster, Seth Adams, until his death in 1960. He was succeeded by John McIntire (second from left). Other cast regulars included Terry Wilson (left) and Frank McGrath (driving the chuckwagon), who played cook and comic relief Charley Wooster.*

every week. We will always fall down on content sometimes.

Ultimately, though, Mann rejects the style-over-substance criticism. "We do stuff that nobody else does. I don't know shows that have dealt with Third World problems, with poverty, with hunger, with Nicaragua, with rape the way we have." But what about the violence on the show? "It's very easy to confuse violent subjects and violent attitudes and very passionate, strong-felt emotions with physical violence. Censors confuse them all the time. We

have had arguments with Broadcast Standards, who say, 'Well, you can't do that.'

"I say, 'What's wrong? What did you see?'

"'Well, he did this, he did that. . . .' We run the film back, and what he imagined he saw, there was none of. It was just the strength of the moment. They still try to cut it out, and then we have big fights."

Mann doesn't believe that he would do much differently if Broadcast Standards didn't exist. "Maybe we would have some scenes where you'd actually see a gun pointed at somebody's head on

"Just the facts, ma'am." Jack Webb starred as the taciturn Sergeant Joe Friday on Dragnet, *America's first hit police series, in 1951.*

Bill Cosby was the first black actor to share equal billing with a white costar on the sixties action series, I Spy. *Robert Culp and Cosby played Kelly Robinson and Alexander Scott, international espionage agents who traveled the world posing as a tennis star and his coach-trainer.*

camera," he said. "We can show the gun, we can show the head, but we can't have the gun and a head in the same frame, which to me is absurd, because I can create the impression that the gun is to the head as strongly as, if not stronger than, if I actually had a gun pointed to somebody's head.

"That's the kind of meaningless rules and restrictions—there is no internal, consistent logic that they apply to anything. . . . But I don't think we'd do anything differently. You don't want to alienate the audience. This stuff is going into people's homes at nine o'clock and at ten o'clock."

But is there excessive violence on TV? "I think that *A-Team* violence is much more dangerous, and it does much more to desensitize people because it makes violence cartoonlike. You don't really get hurt by shooting lots of bullets at people, it says. It's okay—people die neat—it's cool to be shot and die. You'll hold your arm and you'll be able to go on and come back next week.

"You get hit by a projectile going about twenty-three hundred feet a second, you do not just hold your arm and show up next week."

Michael Mann is a classic example of someone

Robert Stack (right) starred as Prohibition enforcer Eliot Ness on ABC's The Untouchables, *an action series that was criticized as being the most violent show on the air. Among the series' guest stars was Keenan Wynn (left).*

who comes from the but-what-I-really-want-to-do-is-direct school, and he's getting his wish, but he loves television too. "I think there's more right with television than wrong with it. In the last three years, I've seen television become more adventuresome in terms of content and chance taking than the motion picture industry. If anything, the motion picture industry is starting to become as adventurous as television became a couple of years ago."

Occasionally, Mann sees himself as an artist, he says, but for all the talk of aesthetics, motivation, and message, the bottom line is simple: "I don't put *Miami Vice* on the air to be a journalist or to be a priest or to be a detective. This isn't the Justice Department; it's the Michael Mann Company, and we tell stories we like to tell."

STEVEN BOCHCO

Steven Bochco, the man *The New York Times* called "perhaps Hollywood's brightest and most innovative producer of television drama" has helped give viewers two of the most creative, intelligent and entertaining series on modern TV—*Hill Street Blues* and *L.A. Law.* Each of them took a standard television genre—the cop show in *Hill Street,* the lawyer show in *Law*—and turned it on its ear, producing programs with many characters and overlapping plot lines, shows that reflect the reality of life in a world where there are no easy answers, where the good guys don't always win. In fact, you may not always be sure in these shows who the good guys are.

Bochco was raised on New York's Upper West Side. His father was a concert violinist. After graduating from Carnegie Tech in Pittsburgh, Bochco headed west.

I had an MCA writing fellowship when I was in college, and I used that to sort of con my way into a summer job at Universal Studios between my junior and senior years. They put me in the story department as an assistant to its head, and at the end of that summer, they invited me to come back permanently when I graduated.

When I returned to Universal the following summer, which was in June of 1966, I went to work in the feature story department. I guess at that time, my ambition ran toward being a motion picture writer.

But inevitably I got caught up in the television mill, because, perhaps even more so then than now, Universal was a primary supplier of television to the three networks. It was really a remarkable operation, and for somebody who was very young and just starting out, it was a great opportunity to work on all kinds of things. They had me doing stuff like adding five minutes of story to eight different episodes of a new series called *Ironside* with Raymond Burr. In their first eight, by the time they edited out all the terrible stuff, each episode was somewhere in the neighborhood of five minutes short. So I had to write new additional material. They would go in one day and shoot them all and cut them in to get these episodes up to length.

From little writing jobs like that I moved on to somewhat more extensive things. I really got directly involved in prime-time television program production in 1969 or '70, when I went to work on a show called *The Name of the Game,* which ostensibly was a show about magazines, but really was a cop show, a mystery show—almost everything in television is a cop show. It just is. Sometimes they disguise themselves as lawyer shows or whatever, but it's all cop shows.

Bochco was a writer on *Columbo* and *Macmillan and Wife* and a couple of other less well-known cop shows—*Delvecchio,* which starred Judd Hirsch and featured two future *Hill Street* stars, Charles Haid and Michael Conrad, and a charming private eye show, created with Stephen Cannell, called *Richie Brockelman, Private Eye.* Then he went to work at MTM Enterprises, where in 1978, he produced a short-lived police series, *Paris,* starring James Earl Jones.

Hill Street Blues was a milestone in episodic television drama, a police series that conveyed the harsh reality of life in an inner-city police precinct. Its stories were taken from the newspapers and the streets. Multiple story lines would intersect, resolve, or have no ending, just like life. Pictured here are undercover detective Mick Belker (Bruce Weitz) and Officer Andy Renko (Charles Haid).

Like his Hill Street Blues, *Steven Bochco's* L.A. Law *(created with Terry Louise Fisher) features a large ensemble cast and multiple, sometimes overlapping story lines that come closer to an approximation of real life than the episodic series of the past did.*

What's the appeal of cop shows?

Good guys, bad guys, good and evil, you know, shoot outs, car chases—they're adrenaline addictive. They also tend to provide, in entertainment terms, closure: You set up a problem. You have a crime. There's a bad guy out there. Your guys come roaring in. They ask some questions. They chase the guy down, and they catch him. They shoot him. They kill him or arrest him, they put him in jail. There's something very satisfying about all that . . . particularly in a day and age in which the world is increasingly gray, and there are problems we cannot address. We are impotent in the face of terrorism and crime in the streets. The kind of television entertainment that gives you that easy answer to something is pretty satisfying.

I think a lot of them have been fundamentally the same over the years—even up to and including *Miami Vice*. The triumph of a *Miami Vice* is not so much in its content but in its form. It has substantially repackaged the genre in very stark and interesting ways.

On the other hand, *Hill Street Blues* looked at the process more than the result, and in dramatic terms, it really created a very different way of telling the story.

Especially after his experience producing *Paris*, Bochco was not eager to undertake another police show. But he and fellow writer-producer Michael Kozoll were intrigued with an idea then—NBC President Fred Silverman had for a realistic, no-holds-barred cop series. "All of the shows we had done up to that point gave us a guideline in terms of what we *didn't* want to do," Bochco said. "We had pretty much covered the territory, and neither of us had much to offer that was fresh to that kind of storytelling. The thought of just doing another cop show and reworking that same old formula wasn't very appealing.

"So when it became clear that NBC really did want a police melodrama, we set about trying to create a show that was going to break all the rules."

Bochco and Kozoll wanted it made clear that they wouldn't be bridled with network interference. Before they even wrote the script for the series' pilot, a "summit meeting" was held with several representatives of MTM—including Bochco, Kozoll, and Grant Tinker, who was then president of MTM—and Jerry Stanley, the head of the Broadcast Standards department at NBC. "I had asked for this meeting about a script that didn't exist," Bochco remembered.

Our motivation in asking for the meeting was to let them know, going in, that we were going to be doing something

David Janssen (left) was The Fugitive, *a doctor wrongly accused of murdering his wife. He crisscrossed the country in search of a mysterious one-armed man, the real culprit, stopping along the way to become involved in the lives of such guest stars as Harry Townes (right).*

that was going to give them grief, and that if they were going to apply the same standards to what we were going to be doing that they applied to all their other programs, there was simply no point in going forward. Because we were, by design, going to do something that did not present balanced points of views, that did not present a kind of racially balanced mix of ethnic types in this ghetto. That we were going to step on all kinds of toes, that we were going to use language that, at least to some degree, approximated the reality of an inner-city police precinct. And if they were not prepared for that, then we just might as well not waste each other's time.

They kept saying, "Well, I don't know how we can judge something that doesn't exist." And we kept saying, "Well, you're going to have to. You're going to have to give us certain assurances." And we went back and forth. Nothing was resolved. Except that we certainly had gotten their attention, so that when we wrote the script, they kind of had been prepared for what they got.

NBC, I think, genuinely felt that what we were doing was special and different and fresh. I don't think there was any argument about that. Whatever anxiety they had was not a function of us doing bad work. I think their real anxiety came from the fact that there was nothing like this on the air. They were afraid, and understandably, that people wouldn't quite know what we were doing.

Nothing like it had ever been done before. "There was no template for an audience," Bochco said. "We had to train an entire audience how to look at us. It took time, because we were confusing. We were putting so much information on a frame of film, overlapping dialogue, multiple story lines, just tons of characters moving through the frame, thirteen regulars, fragmented story lines, stories that didn't end, a jumble of sounds . . . I think, stylistically, from a writing point of view, our willingness to slap very harsh melodrama hard up against outrageous, almost slapstick, nonsense comedy, was unique—we hadn't seen that in television before. The kind of unrelenting darkness of the piece

was pretty different. Even the music was different. . . ."

Bochco gives credit for the overall "look" of *Hill Street* to the director of the pilot, Bob Butler. "Mike and I had written a script that looked different," Bochco said. "We were writing dialogue down both sides of the page and we were scripting all the background stuff, and, of course, people said, 'You can't do that.' Butler said, 'Yeah, we can. We'll do it. We'll use a hand-held camera, and we'll just pick it all up. It'll overlap, and you won't hear anything. It's okay.' He was absolutely willing to do that.

"His visual sense of what this thing should be was very unorthodox, and it worked. It was remarkably aided and abetted by Greg Hoblit [originally the series' line producer, later its co–executive producer], who inherited the responsibility of maintaining and expanding the look and feel and taste of the show in terms of its production values. Between Bob and Greg you had two men who saw this thing as a challenge. No, 'Gee, we can't do this,' but 'Gee, how *do* we do this?' "

A public-television documentary, *The Police Tapes*, produced by Alan and Susan Raymond, also had a profound effect on *Hill Street*. "It was a documentary about cops in the South Bronx. They just took video cameras, and they followed these guys around in their squad cars and into domestic beefs, tenements, and murders, and showed them dragging perpetrators into the station house. They'd have interviews with top command officers and then guys in the squad cars.

"Like any good documentary, that camera became absolutely invisible to the subject. It caught a level of reality that was really remarkable.

"I'm proud to say we robbed them blind."

Casting was a key element in creating the feeling of an ensemble among the cast.

I got to hire all my friends. Charlie Haid [Andy Renko], Bruce Waitz [Mick Belker], and my wife, Barbara Bosson [Fay Furillo] and I went to college at Carnegie Tech in Pittsburgh. Jim Sikking [Howard Hunter] was an old friend of mine; our kids went to school together. I had worked with Michael Warren [Bobby Hill] on another series. I had worked with Michael Conrad [Phil Esterhaus] on *Delvecchio* some years before. We had remained good friends ever since.

Because of the ensemble nature of the piece, we were not burdened with the necessity of hiring stars, famous actors. It would have totally skewed what we were doing. So it was an opportunity to put together a wonderful ensemble of gifted, highly experienced actors who had never really made it.

We got real lucky with our chemistry. Daniel Travanti [Frank Furillo] was a gift, really. I had never met him before. He was the first actor who came in to read for the part, and he got the role. Two hundred actors later, he was still the guy. Veronica Hamel [Joyce Davenport] was the very last actress we saw for her role.

We had an enormous amount of good fortune in putting that group together at that time. You simply cannot discount luck as a factor in the success of a show.

The success of *Hill Street* was far from immediate. "I had an awful lot of people whose opinions I respect enormously, friends of mine, who would all acknowledge that this was a remarkable piece of business," Bochco said.

But they would also reluctantly say that they didn't really think it was going to catch on. They didn't think that people would want to look at something that was so busy and dark and intense and fast and furious. So it took some time.

There were several incarnations of Charlie's Angels, *female crime fighters who were employed by Charles Townsend, head of a private investigation agency. We never saw Charlie; we only heard his voice (John Forsythe). These were the original Angels: (from left) Jaclyn Smith, Farrah Fawcett-Majors, and Kate Jackson.*

114

Peter Falk made the title role of Columbo *so much his own, it's hard to believe that the series' creators, Richard Levinson and William Link, originally offered the part to Bing Crosby. This episode featured Jeanette Nolan and Martin Landau.*

In the first year, it was, in fact, a barely watched show. In its first season, it was the lowest rated show ever picked up for a second season. We basically have the media to thank for that, because they really got behind us. But those ratings were so low that the anxiety level at the network was pretty high.

I'm not privy to all of whatever went on behind the scenes at NBC. Though we had our debates and our arguments, when it finally came down to execution, they left us alone. They honored the commitment that we had exacted from them at the very beginning, which was to make this show the way we wanted to make it.

That was very gratifying, because then, with all the Emmy recognition we got and the attendant publicity, people figured they'd better take a look at what we were doing. And once they did, we had them.

But network support and popular and critical acclaim didn't end Bochco's feuds with NBC's Standards and Practices. "They have a job to do," he said, with a touch of resignation in his voice. "They impose what is ostensibly a standard. But what you realize as you move along in the process is that the standard is whatever somebody says it is until you're willing to spend ten more minutes arguing it than they want to spend arguing it. Then they say okay. Suddenly it's not a standard anymore. It's an amorphous thing."

The relationship between Bochco and Standards and Practices remained stormy.

Hill Street was a show that pushed at their bindings. We were at war all the time about stuff. It was simply in the nature of the show. It was a volatile show, and our stories were volatile.

We had cops blown into domestic situations: incest, half-naked people, stuff that maybe you don't normally see on the tube. We were rude and occasionally dirty, because that's not an antiseptic environment, you know. We just tried to be as gritty and realistic and as funny with all that stuff as we could be. We were constantly getting into hot water

with Broadcast Standards and arguing over what was and wasn't acceptable.

We won the vast majority of those arguments, and I think to Broadcast Standards' credit, they would tell you that we all won. As we began to push at the boundaries of what was considered acceptable they began, little by little, to perhaps relax some of those standards. We just got better and better at what we were doing. And then shows like *St. Elsewhere* benefited from that. I think in general, because of that warfare, we were able to expand what you could do in an hour of television. Quite honestly, I think the industry benefited from it.

The time that I was there . . . went by like a split second. It was so tumultuous. *Hill Street* was this collection of madness and energy and lunatics and shooting stars and probably the most exciting five or six years I've ever spent in my life.

Hill Street took its toll in a way, too. "In a given season of twenty-two episodes, you would chew up the kind of story material that would fuel five years on a more conventional show. So in the course of

Raymond Burr played ace defense attorney Perry Mason in the long-running series of the same name. He won every case but one, ably assisted by the smooth detective work of private investigator Paul Drake, played by William Hopper, the son of Hollywood gossip columnist Hedda Hopper.

five years, the amount of original storytelling you had to do was just staggering."

During those *Hill Street* years, Bochco also had an enormous flop with which to contend. He produced a series about a baseball team called *Bay City Blues.* "I don't think it was about something that a substantial portion of the viewing public gave a hoot about. It was about young people deeply involved in an essentially frivolous situation with no life-and-death situation on the line week after week." The series was canceled by NBC after four episodes.

When Bochco moved from MTM to Twentieth Century–Fox in 1985, the *Bay City* lesson stayed with him. He decided to develop a series about the legal profession, *L.A. Law,* because, he said,

it's about something. If it succeeds, you're going to be going to your typewriter every day for three, four, or five years. And if you're going to go to that typewriter, it better be about something you can write about.

The law is always about something that's exciting, complex and dimensional. It incorporates everything you want to write about thematically. You've got these driven people who are excellent at what they do and have egos and love lives. It then becomes a very rich canvas that you can then legitimately get involved with for a long time.

I think you have to be able to locate, hour to hour, something that taps a deep emotional vein in the viewer—something in some way that's primal, and that's life, death, rage. One of the things we've managed to do in *L.A. Law* that surprises and delights me is that in a show that is overwhelmingly verbal, we've still been able to really tap into stuff that is wrenchingly identifiable to a great many people.

L.A. Law does so with lively dialogue that rings true. Life in a high-powered law firm is very much the way Bochco and his partner, Terry Louise Fisher, a former attorney, have portrayed it—maybe not as sexy, though.

How would he compare *Hill Street* and *L.A. Law?* "*Hill Street* was really a show about people holding despair at arm's length, with a minimum of power to change the environment or to derive a whole lot of personal satisfaction from simply winning day to day. A win on *Hill Street* was staving off disaster for another day.

"*L.A. Law* is populated by people who are infinitely more successful. They make more money, they drive nicer cars, they have prettier girlfriends, they're possibly smarter, and they win more. I don't think that the characters in *L.A. Law,* as a rule, feel

Raymond Burr followed his success as Perry Mason with the role of wheelchair-bound detective Ironside. *Among the series' writers was Steven Bochco, later to become one of the creators of* Hill Street Blues *and* L.A. Law.

powerless or overwhelmed in their environment. While it may have a kind of cynicism to it, it fundamentally is probably a more positive show in the sense that it does hold out the possibility of its characters winning."

His love for television is unrestrained. "Television is exciting, because it's immediate. You don't have to spend a year and a half of your life working on one little thing and then see it go into theaters for maybe ten days, and it's gone. That doesn't appeal to me. I like the diversity of the activities that I'm involved in with television. I like the con-

stant production. I like the fact that in a season of television you make twenty-two, twenty-three, twenty-four hours, and you don't have to hit a home run every episode. You try to, but you're in for the long haul. You're working on a body of work. You're writing and you're producing and you're having meetings and you're running around. And suddenly, every week, another one is on the air. And then you're off to the next one.

"It forces you to move along. It allows you not to get obsessive about the work. That appeals to me a great deal."

BARBARA CORDAY

Barbara Corday is a rara avis in at least two ways: As the president of Columbia Pictures Television from 1984 until late 1987, she was the first woman to head a major studio's television production division. What's more, unlike many studio executives who came from legal, talent agent, or financial backgrounds, she is a product of the creative side—a gifted writer and producer.

Corday and her writing partner of many years, Barbara Avedon, created the series *Cagney and Lacey*, a barrier breaker in its depiction of two women in a close personal and professional relationship. She grew up in New York City, a member of a show business family. "We got a television when I was nine years old," she said. "There was a very eclectic group of shows in those days, and I think my family watched just about everything that was on.

"There weren't very many role models for young girls on television in those days. I always identified with any children who were on television. I loved a show called *I Remember Mama* that had wonderful

Cagney and Lacey, starring Tyne Daly (right) as Mary Beth Lacey and Sharon Gless as Chris Cagney (left) is a drama series notable not only for the fact that it is a police series with two female leads, but for the way in which it goes beyond the typical cop show to examine the family lives of its two main characters and the personal relationship between them.

kids in it. Because I was raised in Brooklyn in an apartment, anything that was on a farm or in a house I just immediately gravitated toward. Even if it was reality, it was fantasy for me!"

She entered show business professionally as a publicist, first in New York and then in Los Angeles, but she really wanted to be a writer. "I met Barbara Avedon, who was already a television writer. We became very good friends through the peace movement during the Vietnam War. She was the head of an organization called Another Mother for Peace, and I was one of its many volunteers. Barbara and I became very good friends and started coming up with ideas to work together. Slowly, we evolved into a writing team and had a nine-year partnership.

"We worked on a great mix of shows, a lot of episodic television. We wrote things as diverse as episodes of *Maude* and *Medical Center*, some pilots, a couple of television movies. . . .''

Corday explained the difference between writing comedy and writing drama. "Writing a dramatic show, at least for Barbara and me, was two people sitting in a room being very intense, working a certain number of hours a day, being almost in a cocoon. Writing a comedy, generally, there are more people involved, it's more a communal undertaking. It can be very hysterical, an entirely different set of problems and set of circumstances."

While continuing her work with Avedon, in 1979 Corday went to ABC as director of comedy development. She was made a vice president a year later. "We did about ten pilots every fall season and six pilots every midseason. That's somewhere around fifteen to eighteen pilots a year, and I was there for three years. That's a lot of shows."

She explained how a network gets involved in the creation of a series.

You meet I don't know how many hundreds of writers and producers every year. You listen to pitches. People come in and they pitch you a show, and you discuss it. You may put a script into development, or if it's somebody very well known, somebody who has a lot of credits as a producer and writer, you might actually give them a pilot commitment. There might be a star who's very well known—*they* might get a pilot commitment.

You work on that script with the producer and the writer all along the way. You discuss the idea; you discuss the story. They turn in a first draft. You discuss. They go off and do a second draft—usually over a period of several months.

If it's good, you actually make the pilot, on film or tape. You begin the casting process. The producer, the writer, the network executive, the director, all those people are brought in and you start looking at actors.

You shoot the pilot, and then there's a period of time in our business called the selling season—like there is in probably a million other businesses—where all these pilots get turned in to the network. There's about thirty people who sit in a room at the network, watch the pilots and decide what shows they want to pick up for the following season.

Everyone in America has an idea for a television show. I have almost never gotten in a taxi in my life that the cab driver has not had an idea for a television show. People don't realize that it's the execution. So when somebody pitches me an idea, the ideas that attract me are the ideas of a passionate writer and producer. If a writer I respect and admire feels very strongly about an idea, that attracts me even when sometimes I don't agree with the idea. I'm attracted to his or her feelings.

During her time at ABC, Corday was working on projects of her own, including a noble but failed experiment, a series called *American Dream*. It was about a struggling young family, moving from the suburbs to an urban, changing neighborhood. "It was one of those terrible experiences, where it never had a chance," Corday said. "It was never in the same time period more than twice in the entire six episodes that were on."

And then there's *Cagney and Lacey*, a Corday-

Ryan O'Neal and Barbara Parkins were two of the many stars of Peyton Place, *an ABC series in the sixties that was a prime-time-soap predecessor to* Dallas *and* Dynasty. Peyton Place *was also unusual for its time because it was broadcast as often as three times a week.*

Avedon project that was many years in the making. "The idea for *Cagney and Lacey* came in a conversation with my husband, long before we were married, thirteen years ago." Corday's husband, Barney Rosenzweig, is executive producer of *Cagney and Lacey.*

I had given him a number of books to read about women and the feminist movement. In one particular book, *From Reverence to Rape,* a history of women in the movies by Molly Haskell, she traces women's roles in films through the decades. One of the points that she made was that there had never really been a female buddy picture, a movie similar to the Paul Newman–Robert Redford movies. Barney said to me that we really should try to do that.

So I went to my partner, and we came up with cops—the Cagney and Lacey characters. We wrote it originally as a feature film, and we could not get it made. Had we made concessions, it might have gotten made. There was one studio head who said that if we would get Ann-Margret and Raquel Welch to play the parts, he would make the movie. We chose not to do that.

Then we tried to sell it as a television series, and nobody wanted to make it. We tried to sell it as a television movie, and two networks turned us down. The third [CBS], our last possible hope, said yes. It went on, and within two days of it being on the air, they called and said, "Could we make a television series out of it?"

The made-for-TV movie had starred Loretta Swit and Tyne Daly, but Swit was tied up with *M*A*S*H*, playing Hot Lips Houlihan, and could not appear in the series. The first six episodes starred Daly and Meg Foster. "Although Meg is a wonderful actress, with whom I would be happy to work any time," Corday said, "we felt that Meg and Tyne were too similar on screen. We had a serious problem. Both the network and the viewers were saying, 'We can't tell these two women apart.' CBS offered to pick up the show again if we would replace Meg. We made the concession. We all agreed

that it was the right thing to do." Foster was replaced with Sharon Gless, and the show became a success.

Part of its success is tied to the fact that the series came along at the right time. Corday thinks a series like *Cagney and Lacey* probably would not have worked fifteen years ago. "It took a lot of consciousness raising for *Cagney and Lacey* to work," she said. "There is a very strong eighteen- to forty-nine-year-old audience out there that has been raised with the consciousness of the women's movement. If you're eighteen years old in this country today, you don't remember what life was like before the women's movement."

It's evidence of a maturity in much of today's prime-time programming, Corday believes. "What you're seeing now has changed quite a bit. If you go back and look at some of the old cop shows, there were certainly some very good ones, but you didn't get as much of their home lives, their personal lives, you didn't get as deeply into the characters as people do now. People want more from their shows. *St. Elsewhere,* for instance, is not just a better hospital show than some of the old ones, because some of the old ones were terrific. It's different; it goes deeper; it digs into people's characters more; it explores the relationships more."

Shows such as *Cagney and Lacey* provide positive role models for women, a concern of Corday's, although she is quick to say, "I think it is not absolutely necessary to have a *Cagney and Lacey* on every other hour. I think that a young woman growing up can get positive feelings from a woman in a small role, if it is a positive role. I don't think that a woman has to play the chairman of the board of Exxon to be a positive role model. I think you can be a positive role model and be a mother or a housewife or a teacher or a school principal."

Corday expressed concern about the impression of women's roles younger women are still getting from the reruns of classic shows from the fifties and sixties. *I Love Lucy*, for example: "This is not a slur at Lucille Ball, who is a giant in our industry, but that show does not speak to today's young women, and yet five- and six- and seven- and eight-year-olds all over the country are still watching it twice a day, as they are many other shows. I am more concerned about them believing that you have to connive to get five dollars out of your husband, or that you have to trick him into letting you drive the car, than I am concerned about the children's programming that they're watching. Although in their day they were wonderful shows, I don't think that little girls and

little boys are going to get good role models of what husbands and wives should be to each other from those shows."

As for coming from the creative rather than the corporate end of the business: "I think the advantages far outweigh the disadvantages, the advantages being that when a producer comes in to talk to me about a show, I know what he's talking about. I'm not somebody who came from a law firm or an agency or someplace like that. If a producer comes in and sits down and says to me, 'See, in Scene Three, the reason I need to do it this way is because . . . ,' I know what he's talking about. I'm very sympathetic to the casting process and to actors and to all that sort of thing. I understand how difficult it is to make a show every week. It's an extremely hard job to make a television series. I know what every person on that show is doing. I know what their jobs are. So I think the producers and writers trust me and are willing to confide in me and talk to me about what their problems are."

Having once been a network executive, Corday realizes how difficult it is to sell the network something new. "The network programming people always want something different, but they don't want it too different. They want you to be able to describe it in terms of something that's already been on, but a little different. It's very dicey.

"It's kind of like being in the dress business. If I came in and tried to sell you a sack dress, you'd say to me, 'Wait a minute, it doesn't have a waistline, why would I want to wear that?' But if a few key people started wearing it, all of a sudden, that thing without a waistline doesn't look so bad. The television business is very similar to that. Somebody with passion and with credits has to sell them something different. Then the next person has an easier time selling something different."

Few suspected that the simple, homespun charms of a series like The Waltons *would lead to a ratings success, but the CBS series lasted for nine seasons. Poor but never down-and-out, the Waltons were a family struggling to make ends meet in rural Virginia during the Depression and World War II. The cast included Ralph Waite and Michael Learned (standing, left) as the parents, Richard Thomas as their eldest son John Boy (standing, right), and Will Geer and Ellen Corby as grandparents Zeb and Esther Walton.*

As for what the next "something different" might be, Corday said, "I have two ideas on what the next shows are that could be successful. You may remember a show called *Family* some years ago. I believe there needs to be on television the other side of *The Cosby Show*—whatever that is. A serious, dramatic show that has to do with the eighties-going-into-the-nineties family. We have not had a major dramatic family show on television for a long time.

"The other thing that is clearly missing and pains me is that there are really no minorities in the forefront of dramatic programming. We've never seen an hour show about a Hispanic family. That has to come soon."

She finds much of television repetitive. "It's not chancy enough. It's not bold enough. It allows small groups of people to dictate too much to it. It's very parochial, much too narrow for the world that we live in today.

"What's right with it is that two hundred million people can be entertained every day and every night at any hour that they wish by a number of programs that boggles the mind. That's quite extraordinary."

GLENN GORDON CARON

The Twentieth Century–Fox movie lot is one of the few left in Los Angeles that really conjures up the glory days of Hollywood moviemaking. Maybe that's because when you get past the security guard you're automatically on a movie set. Gene Kelly turned the exteriors of many of Fox's offices into a replica of turn-of-the-century New York for *Hello Dolly!* in 1967, and Fox made the decision to leave it that way—a movie lover's dream.

Fox is also the home of Glenn Gordon Caron, the young creator and executive producer of the successful and stylish series *Moonlighting*.

Moonlighting, the detective series starring Cybill Shepherd and Bruce Willis, is about the Blue Moon Detective Agency, the only asset model Maddie Hayes (Shepherd) had left when her business manager absconded with her career earnings. She runs the agency with wisecracking, good time private eye David Addison (Willis), and their loyal, if perpetually bewildered, office manager, Ms. Dipesto, played by Allyce Beasley.

Moonlighting takes episodic-television traditions and throws them out the window. The show's scripts are filled with humor, sexual innuendo, and innovation: a show done totally in black-and-white, for example; a big-budget parody of *The Taming of the Shrew*; a dream ballet sequence, choreographed by Stanley Donen; all punctuated by knowing asides to the camera. Sometimes these experiments fall flat, but *Moonlighting* takes the chance.

It's appropriate that Caron should have his offices at Fox, for he is, above all, a movie junkie. While he is a fan of television, it's the movies he keeps going back to for inspiration. As a student at the State University of New York at Geneseo, he booked movies for the college film series. "We would steal the sixteen-millimeter print afterward, take it, and run it on a—it wasn't even a moviola, it was just a single scope with two rewinds. We'd look at how the scenes were cut and then scream about them to each other—why this worked, why that didn't work. We would have knock-down, dragout fights about the way *Straw Dogs* was cut. It's very hard to work up that kind of head of steam about television."

Graduating from college, Caron knocked around for a while in New York and Chicago, studying improv in Chicago with Del Close and Second City. Eventually, he moved to Los Angeles, never intending to go into television. "I started writing because I couldn't afford to make a film," Caron said.

Somebody said to me, "Why don't you write a film? Costs about three bucks, and if you get a good job and they have a Xerox machine, it costs you even less."

I started to do that, and at one point, my work started to get a little bit of attention, and an agent—he's my agent now—Elliot Webb, signed me. He was with ICM at the time, which is one of the big talent agencies in town.

I don't know if that is standard; I know it was certainly the case with me. I think the way they sign you is they kind of look at you and go, "Movies, movies, movies . . ."

You go, "Great!" and you sign.

Once they've got you, they go, "Television . . ."

You go, "Huh?"

They go, "Television, it's a wonderful place to start your career, blah-blah-blah . . ."

I kind of scratched my head and said, "But I don't want to work in television. I don't *watch* television."

They said, "Why don't you go home and watch some television?" So I went home, and I turned on the TV, and

Combining high elegance with outlandish humor and double entendres, Moonlighting *is a comedy romance that masquerades as a detective drama. The series brought TV stardom to Bruce Willis and revived the career of seventies movie star Cybill Shepherd.* Moonlighting's *popularity has allowed it to experiment with a variety of wild format ideas—from a parody of Shakespeare's* Taming of the Shrew *to a sequence in which Shepherd and Willis appeared as clay animation figures.*

there was a show premiering called *Taxi,* which I just thought was terrific. I picked up the phone the next day, and I called Elliott up, and I said, "I'd like to do *Taxi."*

That's really how I started in it. Very strange.

Taxi, which ran on ABC for four seasons and on NBC for a fifth, was one of those shows—such as *The Mary Tyler Moore Show* and *Cheers*—that found real comedy in human relationships, without eschewing the one-liners and sight gags of more traditional sitcoms. Caron compared it to the experience of writing *Moonlighting:* "We don't sit down and say, 'Let's write some comedy.' This is going to sound kind of artsy-fartsy and pretentious, but what we try to do is sit down and say, 'What's the truth?'

"I bristle a bit at 'This is a comedy, this is a drama.' What we try to do is get to the truth, whatever that is, and if the people involved are inherently interesting and inherently funny, then certainly some humor will emerge. But we don't sit down in a conscious way and say, 'We're comedy, we're drama.' "

Caron has worked in both, piling up an impressive list of credits for a guy who's only in his early thirties. He was the story editor of *Good Time Harry,* a short-lived series about a sportswriter that had a cult following among critics and the few viewers who could find it buried in the NBC schedule; a writer and producer on the series *Breaking Away* (based on the movie of the same name); a writer and producer of *Remington Steele;* and the creator of two pilots produced by his own company, Picturemaker Productions. Both pilots, made for ABC, failed to become series, but the network was impressed by Caron's work.

Lew Erlicht, who was running the network at that time, took me out to lunch. He said, "Look, what you do is weird. I'm okay with that, and I want to put you on television, but you've got to help me. You've got to write in a conventional genre. Something that I could schedule."

I said, "Like what?"

He said, "Let's do a detective show," and I just, I mean, my eyes rolled to the top of my head. I think I said something to the effect of, "That's what America needs, another detective show."

He said, "Well, just think about it, and think about a star." He rattled off a bunch of star names—you know, some of the women who had appeared in *Charlie's Angels* and some other things. I kind of left the lunch depressed—because I've been very lucky. I've almost never done anything my heart wasn't in.

But I thought about it for a while, and I went back to him. I said, "Let's get together. Let's have a meeting. I have an idea of what I want to do." So we all got together, and it was a twenty-second meeting. I said, "I'll do your damn detective show"—I mean, I think that was my tone—"but what I want to do is a romance."

Lew said, "Fine. Go ahead and do it." He may have said, "What's the premise?" And I think I might have told him about a model who's lost her fortune and she's left with all these things and one of them's a detective agency and there's this guy and hooda-hooda-hooda. But I mean, maybe forty-five seconds tops . . .

So I went off. In fact, I remember leaving his office, walking down the hall, and suddenly the door opened, he said, "What's it called?"

And I went, "Ahhhh—*Moonlighting!"* I don't know where that came from.

The result was a totally unexpected delight. "A lot of what *Moonlighting* is, is a function of my boredom with the form," Caron said. "Me trying to stay awake. One thing that makes it different is that there's this sense that these people [David and Maddie, the leads] know they're on television. They watch television. They're bored with the form, too.

"The audience is also obviously TV savvy," Caron maintains. He believes that a show like *Moonlighting* might not have been able to pull off

its tongue-in-cheek attitude about TV ten or fifteen years ago. "I'm not sure that the history of the relationship between the viewer and the television set was deep enough at that point to get away with that. But the idea certainly isn't new. You ever watched the old Hope and Crosby pictures? Invariably, once a picture, they turn to the camera and say something like, 'Can you believe we're doing this?' It's certainly not a new idea. I think even Shakespeare fooled around with it—I did a series with him, by the way. He's very overrated. . . ."

He *does* find it hard to pin down all the various popular-culture influences on the series.

There are phonograph records that influenced *Moonlighting*, music I was listening to at the time. There are movies that I've seen that seem to have nothing to do with *Moonlighting*, and yet, they are important to me, and so they'll creep in at some point. . . .

One thing we did do deliberately—Bob Butler, who was the director of the pilot [and also director of the pilot for *Hill Street Blues*], suggested that we sit down and watch *His Girl Friday* [Howard Hawks's reworking of the newspaper comedy classic *The Front Page* with Rosalind Russell and Cary Grant], because I kept talking about how the dialogue has to go a hundred miles an hour. Bob Butler said, "Why can't they talk at the same time?" So we watched *His Girl Friday;* in fact, we showed it to Cybill and Bruce to get a sense of what the limits are, because Hawks did it better than anybody. That's a direct influence.

But there are other things knocking around in there. I'm a huge Frank Capra fan. And, by extension, a huge Joe Walker fan; he was the cinematographer on the Capra pictures. Gerry Finnerman who's our cinematographer, lights with hard light, which tends not to be the rule today in television. Takes a little longer, but I'm a big fan of turning off the lights and playing a scene in the dark. I'm a big believer that people say things at night that they wouldn't say during the day. They say things when it rains that they wouldn't say when it's sunny. A lot of that comes from watching the Capra pictures.

Body Heat sort of got me reinterested in the whole James M. Cain sort of geometry on a mystery—*Double Indemnity* and all that. Particularly during the first five episodes that we did, early into the first season, we played with that geometry quite a bit.

Caron enjoys working in television for many reasons:

You get an idea on Monday, you write it down on Tuesday, you shoot it on a Wednesday, and it's on television the following week. Bruce Willis always kids—he calls it Film College. I get a texture in my head, or a color, or someone else will—an idea—and we have the means with which to try it, to reach for something. And some of these things are nuts.

They defy any kind of rational . . . you know, I had this idea in my head, storytelling with dance, which hadn't been done in a long time. I said, "Wouldn't it be wonderful to just do a seven-, eight-minute thing?" So you call Stanley Donen, thinking he'll hang up on you, because he's the master, and he says yes! How often does that happen?

I remember two years ago, when we had the idea of doing the black-and-white show. I was certain that I'd go to ABC, say I want to do this show in black-and-white, and the roof would fall in. They weren't concerned.

That's why I work in television, because the palette is certainly as broad as film, and the freedom is there for me, and (knock wood) the audience, for the moment, is there.

That's the other thing—it's the biggest house in the world. You're playing the biggest theater there is, and when you do it well, they sure tell you. When you don't, they tell you, too. The feedback's pretty immediate. It isn't like a motion picture, where you make it, and for six months everybody sort of sits and ruminates about it, and then you put it in theaters. It's a different experience. That's why I work in television.

The movie addict in Caron is obsessed with the look of *Moonlighting,* one of the series' most distinguishing features. "I had always seen the show as a romance," he reminded. "Sort of harkening back to what my notion of romance in film was—going back to those Capra pictures, in which Barbara

Stanwyck would come in and sort of tell the truth to Gary Cooper. Those scenes always seemed to play in the dark, so we were determined, if and when we were allowed to do the series, to get someone who was comfortable with that." They hired Gerald Finnerman, who was trained in the old school of Hollywood camerawork.

All of this, of course, is expensive, and *Moonlighting* has a reputation for being one of the most expensive hour-long shows on TV. Caron doesn't bristle at the suggestion—but he says immediately and unequivocally, "Want me to do my speech?"

The thinking in television, which makes no damn sense to me, is that a half hour of television costs X, and an hour of

television costs Y, no matter what that television is. It strikes me as an insane hypothesis. The parallel is, you're hungry, whether you go to McDonald's or whether you go to "21," it should cost the same; they both fill your stomach. It's nonsense.

I once sat down and figured it out. I believe we are the cheapest show per ratings point, certainly on ABC, and when you really get down to it, that's what ABC is selling. There are other shows that are in the same ballpark as us. ABC is getting their money's worth. If they're not, they have the wherewithal to do something about it. I don't apologize for what the show costs at all.

If you want quality, I think you have to expect to pay for it, and I think the viewers have said in a very clear way that they want quality. Not an unreasonable thing to ask, because you have to remember that when the viewer sits down and turns the channel selector, he doesn't differentiate between ABC, NBC, CBS, and HBO. Which means that my show that costs a million something, or Michael Mann's or Steven Bochco's, is more than likely competing against a movie made by George Lucas that cost thirty-something million. It's still free to the consumer. Sure, he writes a check at the end of the month to HBO, but when he sits down and makes the choice, nobody's asking him for his money. . . .

So from where I sit, a show like *Moonlighting* is cost effective. Everybody's making a profit. The question is how big a profit. The thinking that needs to change isn't here. I'm not sure it's in Hollywood. I think it's in New York, on Wall Street.

Another facet of *Moonlighting* that has made the show somewhat controversial is its out-and-out, blatant sexiness. Yet, Caron claims not to have had the problems with network censors mentioned by other producers and writers. "We have a terrific relationship," he claimed.

Beginning with the pilot, we've had an agreement with them that if there's something they're uneasy with or uncomfortable with, I film it and show it to them on film, with the understanding that if they continue to have a problem with it, we can offer them some remedy. They very rarely ask us to do that.

128

In the premiere episode of the lavish dramatic series Dynasty, *oil magnate Blake Carrington (John Forsythe) took a new wife, Krystle Jennings (Linda Evans), beginning a maelstrom of plot twists and turns typical to the prime-time soaps. When English actress Joan Collins joined the cast as Blake Carrington's conniving ex-wife, Alexis, the series got just the shot of comic-book, arched-eyebrows evil it needed. Ratings soared.*

My argument to them has always been, see it in context. On a page, you can't take into account all those other elements that are what a film is. They've always been kind of great about that.

I think the one thing that upsets them a little bit is that, unfortunately, they get to see it incredibly late, because we've fallen into a pattern of delivering our shows very late.

It's their air, you know? It's their movie theater. Ultimately, I'm not responsible. I mean, I'm responsible for the quality and the content of *Moonlighting*. I'm responsible to the viewers. But they [the network] are responsible at some point to the government and all that kind of thing, so it's very hard to begrudge them that voice.

Why are writers like Caron willing to take on so many responsibilities as a producer? "Producing in television is a natural outgrowth of wanting to control the work," he said, "since the ideas tend to begin in the writer's mind and also because the writing is probably the most elusive commodity in the whole chain of events that yields a television show. So from a business point of view, there's a natural inclination to say, 'Let's make the woman or man who's doing the writing in charge of the whole darn thing.'"

Television has won over the film student:

It strikes up this kinship, you know? I see it on our show: the relationship that the audience has with the show. It becomes personal in a way that no other medium can because of its immediacy—that's what television does best.

I don't think in history any part of the entertainment business has taken on the challenge that TV does, which is to create sixty-six new hours of entertainment a week. Hollywood in its heyday didn't do that. Measured against that yardstick, we're doing okay.

What's wrong with TV? We're asked to make it too fast. We're asked to make it too inexpensively. There's a tremendous temptation to homogenize everything—an overabundance of concern about offending. I think part of the dramatic experience has to do with unsettling you a little. I mean, even as children—*Lassie Come Home*—if you were alive and the picture worked for you, you cried at the end. That was what it was about.

Steve Bochco says—I'm going to misquote him, but the thrust of what he said was that all art begins with a point of view. And the temptation in television is to deny point of view. We want to be fair to everybody. No good drama, no good art comes out of that.

5. DOCUDRAMAS AND MINISERIES

he docudrama and the miniseries are subsets of television drama. Some of them are based on the latest trashy novel, sensational murder, or sex scandal; others trade in what Larry Gelbart called "the disease of the week," the triumph of an individual over illness, poverty, illiteracy, war, separation, divorce, prejudice, drug abuse, child abuse, wife abuse, husband abuse, or the simple inability to get a date.

But they have also provided American audiences with some of the finest in quality drama. A miniseries such as *Roots* or *Holocaust,* while made to appeal as popular melodrama, also serves to awaken viewers to history and the legacy of pain and suffering that has been experienced by many of those around us. Sometimes they can do so far more powerfully than a straightforward documentary. Such was the case when *Holocaust* finally was broadcast in Germany. "Thousands and thousands of people phoned to make personal confessions: 'It's true. I have seen it,'" German television producer Peter Marthesheimer said. "I had seen a lot of programs on German TV which had been made with more accuracy, with more brains, with more delicacy. I had been moved in my head, in my brain. But this was the first time I had been moved in my stomach. The impact was because it was a Hollywood drama." It was effective because it placed the events of the Holocaust against the fictional lives of two German families, one Jewish, one Nazi, and told it as an emotional story about people.

Defining a miniseries is simple: It's a TV series of a limited run—that is, it will only last a finite number of episodes—eight in the case of *Roots,* for example, or only four in the case of *Holocaust.*

Docudrama is somewhat harder to define. It is usually based on an actual event: i.e., *The Execution of Private Slovik,* which told the story of the only American soldier executed for desertion during World War II; *Blood Feud,* an account of the fighting between then–Attorney General Robert Kennedy and Teamsters boss Jimmy Hoffa; or *Tail Gunner Joe,* the story of Senator Joseph McCarthy. Docudrama can place fictional characters against the backdrop of real events: for example, the aforementioned *Roots* and *Holocaust,* or *The Winds of War* and *War and Remembrance,* both based on Herman Wouk's World War II novels. Some would also define as docudramas those made-for-television movies that take on an issue and examine it through fictional characters: for example, *Something About Amelia,* which treated the delicate subject of incest; *An Early Frost* showed a family coming to terms with the son's AIDS; *The Day After* posited what life would be like in a small Kansas town following a nuclear war. Finally, the rarest form is the docudrama that uses documentary techniques to tell a fictional story: for example, *Special Bulletin,* which used the format of a network newscast to tell the story of an incident of nuclear blackmail, as did a made-for-cable movie, *Countdown to Looking-Glass,* which led the audience through the events leading to the possible outbreak of World War III.

The central issue that raged and burned around the early docudrama was the simple notion of what constitutes truth: Is it right and fair to ascribe words and actions to a real character who may or may not have said and done what the scriptwriter has placed in his or her screenplay? Is this not deceitful to the viewer, leading to a misunderstanding of truth?

This dispute, however has become rather a tempest in a teapot. "Most of the research now being done on how television audiences perceive television would suggest that people are not stupid about this," television critic Christopher Dunkley said.

"It's the old suspension of disbelief that you have in the theater. Do I really think this was happening to the real Richard III? Not really; I don't. I think that's probably all that's happening with television audiences." People know the difference between a drama and the news. The days when Orson Welles could terrify hundreds of thousands with his *War of the Worlds* radio broadcast would seem to be firmly behind us.

Miniseries and docudramas can trace their ancestry back to the Golden Age of television drama in the United States and the traditions of dramatic

television in Great Britain. Live dramas based on actual events were a common occurrence during the early days of TV drama in this country. Director George Roy Hill oversaw a live production re-creating the sinking of the *Titanic*, and Jack Lemmon once played John Wilkes Booth. Many of the Golden Age alumni are still working in television today, creating docudramas and miniseries and addressing the same ideas they confronted during the days of live TV.

And long before docudramas and miniseries were popular in this country, they were standard operating procedure in Great Britain. Historical dramas were frequent, and most series in Britain produce far fewer episodes per year than series in

the United States, so the idea of a limited series is not unusual. (This applies to comedy as well as drama. For example, only forty-five episodes of *Monty Python's Flying Circus* exist. They were produced a handful at a time over the course of several years. Some of the ones you're seeing today were created twenty years ago.) This allows the producers and writers to achieve greatly enhanced creativity and quality: You're not wed to a production mill grinding out show after show week after week; you have time to think. This has led to such wonders as *Brideshead Revisited*, *The Jewel in the Crown*, and the extraordinary work of Dennis Potter, probably Britain's finest television playwright. His two miniseries, *Pennies from Heaven*

Derek Jacobi starred as the emperor Claudius in a masterful television
adaptation of Robert Graves's I, Claudius, *a fascinating story of intrigue in
ancient Rome. The British series was first seen in America on public television's*
Masterpiece Theatre.

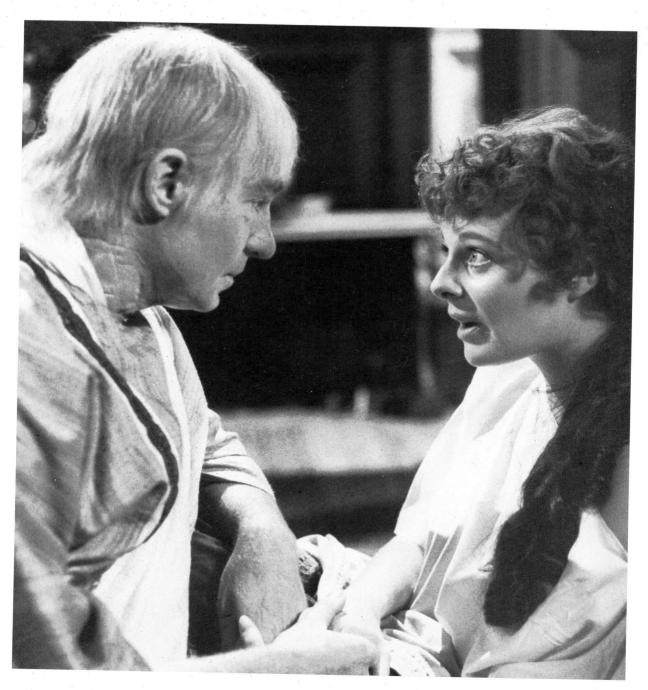

Another downstairs crisis: Jean Marsh (center) played Rose, a senior member of the household staff on Upstairs, Downstairs. *She was also one of the creators of the series, which costarred Gordon Jackson (left) as head butler Mr. Hudson and Angela Baddeley as the cook, Mrs. Bridges.*

Bob Hoskins and Cheryl Kennedy starred in Pennies from Heaven, *a fascinating miniseries from Great Britain that had its characters mime to musical recordings of the twenties and thirties to express their innermost yearnings. The series was made into a motion picture in America, starring Steve Martin and Bernadette Peters.*

136

(1978), which told the story of a man's extraordinary sexual torment, and *The Singing Detective* (1986), about a mystery writer crippled by disease and tortured by hallucinations, use popular songs of years past to express the characters' innermost thoughts in truly astounding and troubling ways.

It is believed that it was not until such British miniseries as *The Forsyte Saga*, *The First Churchills*, *Elizabeth R*, and *Upstairs, Downstairs* were successful on public television that producers and network executives decided that they were a viable form for commercial television. The ratings success of *The Blue Knight* and *QB VII* led to *Rich Man, Poor Man* and a slew of others—*Washington: Behind Closed Doors*, *The Thorn Birds*, *Eleanor and Franklin*,

Kennedy, *King*, *Chiefs*, *Centennial*, *The Atlanta Child Murders*, and on and on.

The enormous costs of some of the more elaborate miniseries, especially costly flops such as ABC's *Amerika* in 1987, have threatened the genre's survival. But both the miniseries and the docudrama are types of programs that the audience has demonstrated it enjoys. Their budgets may be cut back, but they will, in all probability, survive.

J. P. MILLER

After the Golden Age ended, writer J. P. Miller, author of *The Days of Wine and Roses*, continued to

Dame Peggy Ashcroft and Tim Pigott-Smith, whose character, the bigoted Lieutenant Merrick, played a pivotal role in the miniseries, The Jewel in the Crown. *Based on Paul Scott's four novels,* The Raj Quartet, *the series was a popular success on British and American television.*

work in television. His efforts have included the Emmy award–winning *The People Next Door* and two made-for-TV miniseries that would fall into the genre known as docudrama—*The Lindbergh Kidnapping Case* and *Helter-Skelter,* the story of Charles Manson and the Tate-LaBianca murders.

Miller hates the word *docudrama.* "May I be permitted to make a short speech?" he asked, laughing. "There is no such thing as a docudrama. It's like a humpless camel or a unicorn—they don't exist. It's either a documentary and it's true, or it's a drama and it's not true. When you say a docudrama, you're saying that it's a documentary that's been dramatized. That's just drama! What they call a docudrama is just part of television's sickness.

. . . I don't care how true the scene is, the minute you have an actor saying those lines that Charlie Manson said, it's no longer documentary, it's drama, because it's a different person, different inflection. I wrote the words. Charlie Manson didn't really say them. I wrote what he said, I said he said that, and this actor is doing it. So the whole thing is a wipe out.

"What you have to do [in docudrama] is give the impression that it's real, but you have to do that with all dramas, don't you?"

Miller continues to develop projects for TV and the movies and has written three novels, but he's good-humoredly skeptical about the future of network television.

Charles Dance surveys human horror and desolation in the wake of Indian independence at the end of the British series, The Jewel in the Crown, *a drama that depicted the final years of colonial rule in India.*

Steve Railsback was the maniacal Charles Manson in the CBS miniseries Helter-Skelter, *the story of the Tate-LaBianca murders in 1969. The two-part docudrama was written by J. P. Miller and based on the book of the same name by Vincent Bugliosi, who was the prosecuting attorney in the trial of Manson and his cult followers.*

Alex Haley's Roots *hit television with a dramatic intensity that made it the highest rated series in TV history. Twelve hours of storytelling seen on eight consecutive nights,* Roots *traced the history of a black family from slavery through emancipation. LeVar Burton starred as the young Kunta Kinte.*

I'm not too optimistic about it. I think they're all competing with each other to put out as many penny-dreadful programs as they can. It's whatever brings in the viewers, and it's all numbers. I swear I think if they could get the Chicago slaughterhouse on TV and people watched, they'd do it. There's really no morality involved in it.

I think it *has* to get better. It's absolute rock bottom. It's just cheap shots. It's current events dramatized, and usually badly. . . . I don't watch television drama. I can't stand it.

The hope, maybe, of television drama, strangely enough may be in the miniseries. That's the thing movies can't do—you're not going to go see a six-hour movie. They make people come back if they're well done, three, four nights in a row. You have time to develop characters, you have time to do various things that you can't do in a two-hour TV movie. You can do a whole miniseries without a car chase. Maybe we're edging back toward quality drama.

DAVID WOLPER

Many of the people who were early participants in the production of television are more successful than ever. One of them is David Wolper. Wolper came into television entertainment from a different direction. He was an independent producer of documentaries, but, he said, "I found it very difficult to get my documentaries onto the three networks. Every time I got one on, I had to fight to get it on, because the network news departments make their own documentaries. It's much easier to sell drama to the networks, so my decision to change was based on questions of money and energy both. I could make more money with drama, and I didn't have to expend so much energy getting it on the air."

Wolper produced the television adaptation of Alex Haley's best seller, *Roots,* in 1977. Since then, there have been other miniseries for Wolper such as *Roots: The Next Generations, The Thorn Birds,* and *North and South,* a massive Civil War potboiler.

Wolper found himself in yet another career in recent years. On top of his other activities, he has produced such extravaganzas as the opening and closing ceremonies of the 1984 Summer Olympics in Los Angeles and New York's 1986 Liberty Weekend, celebrating the centennial of the Statue of Liberty.

"I have my own theory on what kinds of projects would make good miniseries," he said.

A good miniseries must fulfill categories: One, the book it's based on has to be a big best seller—not just a best seller that's sleazy but a distinguished best seller—the subject matter can be kind of edgy, but the book itself has to be considered a distinguished book. Two, the story has to be about a great sociological event—the Holocaust, slavery.

And three, it has to be about a great historical event or have a historical figure as the center point of the film. I always say a good story does not a miniseries make, the story's not enough. . . . You have to hold people for three or four or five or six consecutive nights. They've got to make up their minds before they come and then say, "Okay, we're gonna spend this week at home. It's subject matter I want to see, and I want to give that much time of my life to watching it." There has to be a reason to watch it.

Roots filled all the criteria. It concerned a great sociological event—slavery in the United States—it was based on a gigantic, best-selling book, and it told part of American history. . . . That's why I felt that it had a good opportunity to be successful. . . . I believed in what it was talking about, but I make films for a living, so I felt the subject matter would make me money, and I made it for that reason. . . .

I like to reach big audiences because I feel American television is designed for that. I don't just want to entertain, and I don't just want to inform, I want to do both together, and doing both together is one way to get a very large audience. . . . When *Roots* came out one of the critics called it "middlebrow *Mandingo*." I wasn't happy with that, but he was right for the wrong reasons. It *is* middlebrow; it isn't highbrow and it isn't lowbrow. American television is middlebrow, and I wanted to produce something that was important in a middlebrow way so a large audience could appreciate it, understand it, and get something out of it. People actually turned off basketball games in bars around the United States and put on *Roots,* because they wanted to learn, and they wanted to learn on their own terms. They wanted a terrific drama, excitement, stars, and, under those conditions, they were more than happy to learn.

Roots represented twelve hours of television, broadcast over eight nights. "Eight successive nights was a great idea," he said.

It was one of the things that made *Roots* the big success that it was, because people would get up in the morning, go to work, and talk about what they saw last night, and if you didn't watch *Roots* you were out of the conversation.

I have a feeling however that that was not the reason it was played on eight consecutive nights. There's big competition among the three networks for ratings, and they rate on a week-by-week basis. . . . I thought ABC was a little nervous about it, so they put on all the shows in one week. If it was a disaster, they'd get rid of it all in one week, and they'd lose that week—"Okay, we got rid of that. Now let's get on to the next week." If they had put it on every week and it was a disaster, once a week, it would have hurt them. Some people there [at ABC] were a little nervous about *Roots.*

It was a daring concept for American television. I mean, you're living in a country of ten percent blacks and ninety percent whites, and you're doing a whole story where the whites are the villains and the blacks are the heroes. . . .

We knew *Roots* was going to be a challenge to the American people. They were going to have to take a lot of blows watching it—they're going to be guilty, they're going to see that the white man is a man who enslaved the black, and it was going to be a very tough experience for the American audience. I tried to use black actors who were familiar to the American television audience, blacks who were stars of other television shows, so that it would be somebody they would be familiar with. So when a black actor came on, oh, they had seen him in another television show—they knew who he was, that he was an actor—they didn't feel the total threat that you could possibly get from it. . . .

More people saw *Roots* in that one week than have seen Shakespeare in all the performances on stage since he wrote all the plays. . . . There was a little town in New Hampshire that kept a record. The man in charge of the water supply always knows when there's a good show on because, at a certain time, when a commercial comes in a television show, the water pressure goes up and everybody is using the john. He said, "I knew *Roots* was a hit when it came to the second commercial. It was the biggest surge of water in the history of the town."

Las Vegas has all these shows that go on at eight o'clock at night. They had to cancel, move the shows earlier or later so people could go back and watch. . . . Congress was meeting, and they had to get out early so everyone could get home to see *Roots.* Movie theaters knew that something was going on because nobody was in the movie theaters. . . . It just caught on and spread. . . . I think what people were moved by was that it was a story about peo-

ple, a family story about people. . . . They happen to be black, but you went right along with them because you related to all the family. . . . That's what got everybody, and once they got caught in those characters they wouldn't let go. Night after night, they wanted to know what happened to the characters. They couldn't step away from it and say, "Okay, I saw enough." Each night we left them with the idea that they wanted to see what happened to those characters. . . .

ABC News took a poll immediately after *Roots,* and it showed that people were more sympathetic to the plight of blacks because they had seen the roots of where all the problems came from.

Wolper has always maintained that the public knows they are not dealing with the absolute, point-by-point truth when watching a docudrama. "Docudrama has been criticized a lot for not giving an accurate picture of a major historical event," Wolper said.

I think the people who have been criticizing have been taking the wrong tack and seeing docudrama as something it isn't. . . . When I do a docudrama, I always say that there's nothing that's recorded—except in a courtroom or in Richard Nixon's office. . . . Outside of that, when famous people talk they don't have a tape machine on, so we're going to have to create dialogue in all docudrama or not do docudrama at all. . . .

What we do is we create dialogue to give you a sense of what went on at that time. . . . When I do a docudrama, you will probably see it once in your lifetime, maybe twice, so it is not a reference book. . . . If you want to find about Truman and MacArthur, there are fifty books about the firing—you'd go there for the information. I do not know what Harry Truman said to MacArthur when he got off the plane and they shook hands. We have to write that.

Don't go to a docudrama looking for a research paper. Go to a docudrama to enjoy the experience of having been there, seeing the people act out the event, and get an overall feeling of the ambience of the event, not the detail of every little item in the event.

Because they have more airtime in which to develop a story, miniseries can offer viewers more detailed plots and examine characters and events in greater depth. In nine and a half hours, broadcast over four evenings, NBC's Holocaust *told the story of a Jewish family struggling to survive the horrors of Nazi Germany. Below, Rosemary Harris, Fritz Weaver, James Woods, and Meryl Streep, and at right, Fritz Weaver, Rosemary Harris, Kate Jaenicke, and George Rose.*

144

HERBERT BRODKIN

Overcoming his disdain for much of what he sees on commercial television, Herbert Brodkin remains active in the TV business, creating quality programs despite what he regards as near-impossible odds.

One of his accomplishments was the NBC mini-series *Holocaust,* the nine-and-one-half-hour fictional account of the Nazi terror that went on to win eight Emmy awards. Brodkin tossed aside criticism of the work as a trivialization of the darkest episode of the twentieth century. "The subject was so powerful and so real that *Holocaust* achieved a place of its own, created an atmosphere of its own,

*Playing an American naval officer in the years leading up to World War II,
Robert Mitchum starred in the massive television adaptation of Herman Wouk's
novel* The Winds of War. *Among the huge supporting cast were David Dukes
(left), who played an American foreign service officer.*

so that it wasn't treated the way an average television film would be treated. On the other hand, I had a high-placed executive at ABC say to me, before we went on the air, "Thank God we don't have *Holocaust*." But *Holocaust* had the highest rating of a dramatic show that NBC had ever had."

Brodkin has become a seasoned practitioner of the docudrama. In addition to *Holocaust*, he has been responsible for *The Missiles of October*, a dramatization of the events surrounding the 1962 Cuban missile crisis; *Skokie*, based on the story of what happened when members of the American Nazi party announced plans to march in Skokie, Illinois, a city with a large Jewish population of Holocaust survivors; and dramatizations for Home Box Office of the lives of people who would not be considered appropriate—or profitable—subject matter for the commercial networks: a Soviet dissident *(Sakharov)*, a distinguished television correspondent *(Murrow)*, and a black crusader fighting South African apartheid *(Mandela)*.

He recognizes the difficulties in dramatizing something that actually happened. "There are lots of problems—is it authentic, is it honest, have you changed it? . . . What we try to do is make a play, a dramatic play, which is true to the essential center of the event. Within scenes, of course, dialogue has to be made up, has to be created. A comparison is what Shakespeare did—he took real events, real kings and created works of art. I don't say that we are as good as Shakespeare, but we're in there pitching all the time."

Brodkin has been pleased with his experience working for a pay cable company such as HBO.

It may be that the networks are busily creating their own demise. I don't know. If that is so, it will be long after I'm gone, but if the public is beginning to turn away, they are turning away to shows that are done on HBO and Showtime

Martin Sheen has appeared in more made-for-television movies and docudramas *than any other actor—from* The Execution of Private Slovik *to his role as* John F. Kennedy *in the miniseries* Kennedy. *Blair Brown co-starred as Jacqueline Kennedy.*

Daniel J. Travanti of Hill Street Blues *played legendary broadcast journalist Edward R. Murrow in a television movie produced by Herbert Brodkin for Home Box Office.*

and that kind of thing, which are now possible and being done at higher budgets. The networks are losing audience, no question about it. Whether or not they will lose enough to affect their supremacy remains to be seen. It is also possible that companies like HBO may succumb to the same frailties that the networks have succumbed to. I hope not, but there are signs of it. . . . Even HBO has to deliver a rating.

I have always felt that television drama has really two important facets: One was to entertain and the other was to teach. And if you combine them into a drama, that to me is the true function of television. It seldom happens now. They're mostly looking for entertainment, and entertainment on any terms—no matter how reprehensible, how coarse, how immoral, how dishonest. Television in this country has missed its chance to correct a great many things that are wrong with this world. The true function of television is to communicate—to teach as well as to entertain.

6. TALK SHOWS AND GAME SHOWS

The Goodson-Todman production company produced game show success after success. Among them was Beat the Clock, hosted by Bud Collyer (right), on which contestants had to perform wacky stunts within a set period of time. For a brief time, one of the show's employees, hired to try out the stunts before they were attempted on the air, was James Dean.

rime time. That's the period between
the hours of eight and eleven at night,
six nights a week, the peak TV viewing
time in the country.* The commercial
networks' air is filled with situation
comedy and episodic drama. But in the
hours before and after, what programmers call the "fringe" time periods, much of the
programming is different. Sure, there's a glut of
syndicated network reruns, but there are also news
shows, soap operas, and two program genres that
remain particularly hardy, as they have since the
beginning of television—talk shows and game
shows.

With the exception of running the test pattern at
all hours of the day and night, talk shows are just
about the cheapest kind of programming on television. All you need is an affable or thought-provok-
ing host, some guests, chairs and/or a couch (desk
optional).

There are still many local talk shows on stations
all over the country where guests make the tour
plugging their new book, diet, record, or political
philosophy. Early on, the networks realized that
talk shows could be an effective and inexpensive
tool to lure an insomniac audience away from the
old movies of *The Late Show.* But at first, even the
hosts of these shows were a little dubious. When
Steve Allen debuted as the host of NBC's *Tonight
Show* on September 27, 1954, he told his audience,
"We especially selected this theater because it
sleeps, I think, about eight hundred people . . . This
is kind of a mild little show. It's not a spectacular—
monotony is more the idea." He made a prophecy,

*On Sundays, prime time starts an hour earlier, at seven
o'clock, but that first hour can only be used for news programs
(à la *60 Minutes*) or family shows (*Punky Brewster, Our House,
The Disney Sunday Movie,* etc.).

Big band leader Kay Kyser (left) brought his Kollege of Musical Knowledge to NBC in 1949. Contestants were asked to name songs played by the band or sung by the group The Honeydreamers (right).

too: "I want to give you the bad news first," Allen said. "This program is going to go on forever."

Allen had no idea how right he would be. After he left *Tonight* in 1957, to devote more of his energies to his prime-time variety show, he was succeeded by the voluble and unpredictable Jack Paar, who stayed with the show (despite some famous feuds and emotional outbursts that once included walking off the set while the show was on the air) until 1962. Then came Johnny Carson, and the *Tonight* show is still going strong.

When Carson leaves *Tonight*, he will in all probability be replaced by the host of another talk show that is also produced by Carson's production company: David Letterman. "He's changing what people have been accustomed to seeing," Carson

Emcee Hal March ordered contestants into the "isolation booth" so that they could not hear answers from the audience—but also for added dramatic effect—on the popular game show, The $64,000 Question.

Productions' executive vice president David Tebet said of Letterman. "He's come up with a brand new kind of humor." Who else is hosting a show that includes a regular "Stupid Pet Tricks" segment, elevator races in the RCA building, and a program during which the picture rotated a full 360 degrees? To succeed Carson, "He's going to have to broaden his audience a little bit," Tebet said.

Only Merv Griffin has come close to approaching Carson's longevity as a talk show host, with chat programs that aired on NBC, CBS, and in syndication, but over the years there have been others whose talk shows have enjoyed several years of success—Mike Douglas, Joey Bishop, Irv Kupcinet, David Frost and Dick Cavett, whose reputation for both wit and erudition found him a place on PBS after his talk show was canceled by ABC.

There have been notable disasters as well. Witness such syndicated late night shows as *Thicke of the Night* or *The Late Show Starring Joan Rivers,* gone in a smoky haze of poor ratings and old press releases announcing how they would knock Johnny Carson from number one.

With the exception of Carson, the only national talk shows that have had any great recent success are those that eschew the old couch-and-desk format for an arena setting in which the host wanders from guests to studio audience, getting everyone involved in the topic under discussion, whether it be nuclear arms control or—more likely—whether women should be allowed to expose their breasts in public. Phil Donahue and Oprah Winfrey can seize on the most arcane of issues and churn them into boiling controversy. "What they have to resort to in subject matter is sometimes a pain in the neck," Merv Griffin said. "You know, the sex lives of Lithuanian doctors and dentists is not all that interesting."

What really concerns a talk show pro like Griffin

is what he perceives as a constant lowering of the American audience's attention span. "In the beginning of talk shows, you could go twelve, fourteen minutes with an interview. Now, if you don't get it done in four minutes, with all those little remote controls the audience has now, they can just shut you up."

One type of show that still manages to rivet a home audience's attention is the game show. They are as popular now during the daytime and early evening television hours as they once were in prime time. "Game shows go back to the early days of radio," game show host and producer Wink Martindale noted. "There were game shows like *Stop the Music* and *Break the Bank.* Game shows were a staple in radio. So when television came along, it just automatically happened that this genre was easily moved over to television. It just had to happen." Another key consideration is that game shows

Suitably attired in cap and gown, Joe Kelly (seated right) asked the questions on one of TV's first game shows, Quiz Kids. *Produced at NBC station WNBQ (now WMAQ) in Chicago, the program featured child prodigies who were experts on all manner of subjects. Viewers who succeeded in stumping them were awarded cash prizes.*

"are produced a lot more simply than situation comedies or movies for television these days," Martindale added. "They are more cheaply produced and people enjoy them."

Game shows captured the audience's imagination with increasingly large cash prizes and contestants with fascinating stories or phenomenal memories for esoteric information. In the fifties and early sixties, game shows were consistently on each season's list of top 20 programs: Goodson-Todman's *I've Got a Secret,* on which people would try to stump the celebrity panel with such true confes-

sions as "I saw President Lincoln assassinated"; *The Price Is Right,* on which contestants try to guess the correct retail price of power boats and living room sets (many American game shows have been successfully duplicated in other countries, but *The Price Is Right* was a disaster in Brazil; with inflation hovering around two hundred percent, Brazilian contestants could never guess the correct price): *The $64,000 Question,* on which Dr. Joyce Brothers appeared as an expert on boxing, and actress Barbara Feldon, years before *Get Smart,* was an authority on Shakespeare.

Kids turned the tables on the adults and asked the questions on Youth Wants to Know, *broadcast from Washington from 1951 until mid-1958. World leaders and decision makers, such as Yugoslavian Ambassador to the United States Vladimir Popovic, seen here, provided the answers.*

The American fascination with game shows is still with us. They combine surprise, a spirit of competition—both at home and in the studio—prize money and a somewhat unhealthy desire to see other people make spectacles of themselves. The screaming, ecstatic winners of *Wheel of Fortune*, the becostumed players on *Let's Make a Deal*, the dismal alleged talent that was paraded on *The Gong Show*, the contestant on *Family Feud* who, asked to name one of the evilest men in history, consulted with his fellow team members and confidently replied, "Rudolph Hitler."

Concentration, Password, Jeopardy, What's My Line?, Truth or Consequences, People Are Funny, Beat the Clock, To Tell the Truth—game shows will always be a part of the television schedule. But the entire genre almost vanished from the screen in the late fifties and early sixties. The question of their honesty created a scandal and very nearly destroyed them.

JACK BARRY

One of the key figures in the quiz show business was Jack Barry. He was a game show host and a producer, the star of such early shows as *Tic Tac Dough, Juvenile Jury*, and the children's show *Winky Dink* (the program that allowed you to draw on your TV with a "magic" screen). He was interviewed for the *Television* project shortly before his death in 1984. At the time, he was still hosting and producing the game show *The Joker's Wild*.

"It seems to me that Americans are by and large game players," he said. "We are nuts about football and baseball. Not everyone can play, but you can get some kind of minimal feeling by participating in a game show, even if it's from your own home.

Americans are gregarious, Americans are competitive, and they like to play games. I never shared the feeling that it is the prize money that makes a difference. It's the competition—people at home pitting their abilities against the people on stage."

Barry was involved in the production of *Twenty-One*, a game show that almost destroyed all the others. A disgruntled contestant accused the producers of rigging the game in favor of the man who defeated him—Charles Van Doren, who was so successful on *Twenty-One* he became a national celebrity. Doren confessed that he was given information

To Tell the Truth was one of television's most popular game shows. Airing in prime time on CBS for over ten years, the program was hosted by Bud Collyer, but when the series went into syndication in 1969, it was taken over by Garry Moore (pictured here). Three people would claim to be a certain individual; only one would be telling the truth. A panel of celebrities such as (left to right) Bill Cullen, Peggy Cass, Orson Bean, and Kitty Carlisle had to figure out which contestant was the genuine article.

on the questions and answers. As coproducer, co-owner, and host, Jack Barry found himself in big trouble. "I think that we would all have to share a joint responsibility, but I don't shirk my own responsibility," he admitted.

I was reared in the tradition of early radio as an announcer and master of ceremonies on various programs. I just knew that on any informational program, the participants were given help in one form or another. It was done purely to make the shows more appetizing. You couldn't have a successful program if nobody answered any questions; that goes without saying. Consequently, the tradition grew. I certainly didn't invent it, but I knew about it for many, many years before there was a *Twenty-One.*

I became the master of ceremonies on a program that was popular in the 1950s called *The Big Surprise.* It was a successor to *The $64,000 Question.* And on that program, I had firsthand knowledge that the participants weren't being given questions and answers. So when my partner and I devised the show called *Twenty-One,* in the first few weeks, we didn't resort to the practice. But after the third or fourth week, we had a couple of contestants who missed almost every question. It was painful. The sponsor and the advertising agency called and said, "Don't ever let that happen again."

Well, with my background and knowing what had gone on in almost every other program, I said, "Don't worry. It won't ever happen again." And it didn't. We gave help to the contestants we wanted to win. It was a standard common practice in the United States.

I can't say definitively, but they [the networks] would have to have had rocks in their heads if they didn't know. It was the talk of the industry, had been for many years, particularly on the large programs. With the gigantic sums of money being given away, the people in the accounting department who did the bookkeeping had to know, and in my opinion, did know.

Then-president of CBS Frank Stanton says otherwise. "When the news of the rigged network quiz

shows came out, we were concerned," he said. "We came out of that in good condition because we weren't nailed on it in any respect. There were some shows that I thought had the potential for rigging, and I removed them from the air. With one fell swoop, I took off, I think, ten hours a week of game-show programming. I never could be sure somebody wasn't slipping out to a pay phone and calling someone to tell them something about the answers. To remove the possibility, I simply wiped the slate clean. I took them off on a Friday and

Airing on CBS from 1950 until 1967, and for several more years in syndication, the game of What's My Line? *was basic: Guess a contestant's occupation. What made this show so popular was the witty repartee and glamour of its celebrity panelists, epitomizing New York sophistication for millions of viewers across the country. Pictured here, perennial panelist and prominent publisher Bennett Cerf greets the Supremes.*

started with a whole new ten hours of programming the next week." One of the programs canceled was *The $64,000 Question,* although no actual evidence of cheating was ever found against it.

The brouhaha that erupted after Van Doren's confession, which included Congressional hearings and the publicly expressed outrage of President Eisenhower, almost led to the extinction of the game show.

"I had become the most publicized master of ceremonies in this industry," Barry said.

Somebody had to take the fall for everybody else, and I was exiled from the industry for about ten or twelve years. . . . I couldn't get any employment with any of the United States networks. I did work for a few years in Canadian television.

Then, due to some sober-thinking human beings in our television industry, namely Bud Grant, now the president of CBS Entertainment, Fred Silverman, who was then head of programming at CBS, and several others, they helped reinstate me. . . .

It took me a long time to admit even to myself that the practice was not good judgment, to say the least, and was even unfair. When it is seen all the time, you become accus-

Former radio announcer Bill Cullen emceed a number of quiz shows and was a regular panelist on I've Got a Secret, *but the game with which he will be forever associated was* The Price Is Right. *Contestants attempted to win prizes by coming closest to estimating their retail value without going over the actual price.*

Bob Barker remains one of television's most ubiquitous quiz-show hosts. For eighteen seasons, he emceed Truth or Consequences, *a game in which contestants had to answer a question correctly and promptly or pay the "consequence"—performing some kind of absurd and mildly embarrassing stunt.*

tomed to it, and you don't think anything of it. But I have had a lot of years to think about it. The practice is wrong. It isn't being done anymore, certainly not by us, and I doubt by anybody else. . . . It was okay for the winner but not so good for the loser. I surely would never participate in anything like that again.

The effects of the quiz scandal are still felt today. "There are so many safeguards now, there's practically an FBI agent watching over game shows during every taping session," fellow host and producer Wink Martindale said. "The way shows are produced today, I think it would be almost, if not utterly, impossible to fix a game show in today's marketplace. If somebody did get by with fixing a game show again, there would be a very real chance that the game show would be destroyed forever."

MERV GRIFFIN

Merv Griffin has been a key figure in the television business almost from the very beginning, the ubiquitous host of both game shows and talk shows for three decades. He is also a shrewd television businessman. Two game shows he created—*Wheel of Fortune* and *Jeopardy*—have been the number one and number two rated syndicated TV shows in the United States. In 1986, Griffin sold his company, Merv Griffin Enterprises, to the Coca-Cola Company for a reported $250 million.

He has his own memories of the early days of television game shows. "There were disasters all the time. I was the emcee on a game show for Goodson and Todman called *Play Your Hunch.* Everything you could possibly imagine happened on that show from a stagehand dying in the middle of the show to me doing a demonstration with an orange and cutting right through my hand, blood run-

ning into the orange juice. They were the most amazing days in the world."

Another of Griffin's early emcee chores was an on-location talk show called *Going Places* in 1957.

Going Places came to me through a gentleman named Martin Stone, who was responsible for the *Howdy Doody* show. He had this show that would tour around all the great tourist spots of Florida. I used to fly to Florida every weekend and emcee this show.

"It was live, and it was on late Sunday afternoons, all over the United States, and there were guest stars. The first show was from the Jordan Marsh department store's new dock in Miami. People could come in their yachts and go shopping. We had the Cypress Gardens Water Skiers, so my opening announcement said, "Let's open this fabulous dock here with the Cypress Gardens Water Skiers, starring Dick Pope, Junior."

162

I said, "Dick, are you ready?" And he said, "Ready, Murth." I thought, *"Murth?* I hope my friends didn't hear that."

After he finished, I said, "Now, here's the mayor of this great city of Miami to officially open this dock, Mayor Randall Christmas." And he said, "Thank you, Herb."

I was dying inside. The producer was falling against the remote truck, screaming, laughing. And then the orchestra leader called me Mark.

Later, I saw *The Miami Herald,* and it said, "Be sure and watch *Going Places* today with Merv Griffin opening the Jordan Marsh dock and its emcee, Mary Griffin."

You're humbled, always, from the beginning.

Going Places featured a lot of animal demonstrations. "We were doing a demonstration of these exotic snakes of the Okefenokee Swamp. On the air, they had little children with snakes wrapped around their necks. It really repulsed me—it was a difficult show to emcee.

"This man had hold of a cobra, and while he was talking to me, it struck the side of the camera, and the cameraman thought it was after him. Everyone threw their earphones off and ran out, leaving me and the cobra and the trainer, who couldn't get control of him."

On another occasion, *Going Places*'s cameras traveled to the Viscaya estate. "I decided that day that I would sing a song," Griffin said. "They put me in a little boat. The waters were rough in that little channel. I took the guitar player with me. He had worked very late in a jazz place and probably had too much to drink. We got out there, and I was singing, and the guitar player, live, threw up all over me.

"So in the early days, we all learned our lessons well. People say, 'Why are you so calm?' Well, I'm so calm because I have seen everything happen. I never had the experience Dick Cavett had where a man died right in the middle of his interview. But

A former big band vocalist, Merv Griffin has made his mark in both the game and talk-show fields. The creator of two of the most popular game shows in television history, Wheel of Fortune *and* Jeopardy, *his popular talk show ran in syndication until 1986. Talk shows became the new vaudeville circuit for unknown performers and such show business legends as Jimmy Durante.*

he was probably asking boring questions." Griffin quickly added, "I told Dick that, so he'll understand."

Griffin's career as a talk show host began in 1962, as a Monday night replacement for Jack Paar on *The Tonight Show,* which shared a studio with Griffin's daytime game show, *Play Your Hunch.* Not realizing that, Paar one day walked into the middle of a *Play Your Hunch* telecast by accident. Griffin handled the impromptu situation well, and Paar was impressed. "Let him take over on a Monday night," Paar suggested. "See what he does. He's funny."

On Griffin's first night, he said, "I knew the audience didn't know who I was, so I went out and said, 'I know you don't know who I am. Your wife knows who I am because I spend a lot of time with her during the day. I can't stand here and tell you who I am, so I brought my agent, Marty Cumber, with me.'

"I hired Al Kelly, who was the world's greatest double-talker. I said to him, 'Marty, it would be more humble of me to allow you, as my agent, who has all this faith in me, to tell the audience who I am.' Of course, he started out, 'This fine boy is one of the great frataznats of all time.'

"You actually saw people in the audience sit forward—'What did he say?' He did about three minutes, and as it built, the audience realized it was being put on, and they just screamed."

But at the time, Griffin thought he had bombed. Producer Bob Shanks had to keep him from heading home. "They shoved me back on, and that was it. The ratings for that night went through the ceiling. The next day, the press all said, 'Where'd he come from?' I guess the press doesn't watch daytime television." Griffin's success on *The Tonight Show* resulted in his own daytime talk show, the first of many forays into the talk show genre.

Steve Allen's intelligence, quick wit, and willingness to do just about anything for a laugh made him the ideal host when NBC premiered The Tonight Show *in 1954.*

During his tenure as host of The Tonight Show, *Jack Paar's unpredictability created several public incidents, including a feud with Ed Sullivan over the amounts of money each paid their guests. Paar took a turn on the guest's chair to tell his side of the story as his second banana Hugh Downs looked on.*

Johnny Carson has hosted The Tonight Show *since 1962, successfully fending off every rival talk show the other networks have attempted to throw against him. Sidekick Ed McMahon (left) has been with Carson from the beginning, when the program was telecast from NBC's New York City studios and featured such guests as Richard Kiley and Selma Diamond.*

Following a run on ABC, Dick Cavett brought his talk show to public television, where every program usually featured a single guest. Richard Burton was one of Cavett's most fascinating catches, regaling the audience with stories of his acting career and turbulent personal life.

"I had a few backstage rules," Griffin said. "I never wanted anybody to write any questions for me. I wanted them to write areas of research, which I would take upstairs for two or three hours prior to the show. I like improvisation.

"I never saw a guest star before the show and made a rule, most of the time, never to see them after the show. It's too hard to interview your friends, and there was that spontaneity of the audience actually seeing us meeting for the first time. That always triggers something interesting.

"When Jack Paar quit in 1962, I asked him, 'Why are you leaving, Jack?' And he said, 'There's nobody left to talk to.'

"I thought, 'Oh, that's depressing,' because I was just starting my talk show. But we did find twenty-three years of people to talk to—many newcomers who are now major stars."

Why are talk shows such a television staple? "In the beginning there were just a few of us," Griffin said. "Then, because of the financial gains to be made from such a low-budget show, every local

Phil Donahue makes the audience an integral part of his daytime talk show, soliciting their opinions and encouraging everyone to ask questions of his guests.

want to know the technique of psychiatric interviews, you watch Merv.' "

I said, "Why?" And he said. "Well, I'm not going to explain it all to you, if you don't know what you're doing, but you go through many doors to find the answer you want."

In a sense, that's true. The greatest example of that was when we booked Spiro Agnew after he was forced out of the vice presidency. Every day, one of his associates would call and say, "Now don't ask this, don't ask that, don't ask this." I had ninety minutes with him, and by the time we got to the day we were going to tape him, I had nothing to say to him beyond hello.

The staff said it's too much of a chance, let's duck out of it. I said, "No, it might be the best school in the world for me, to see what I can get past him."

The press was a little rough on me; they said that I was too gentle with him. But they didn't stay with it. Once you have a subject in front of you, and you schmooze and relax and get them so that they're comfortable with you—I asked him every single question I was told not to. And only one did he refuse to answer, because he had some litigation going on in Maryland.

station put on their own local talk show. The number of talk shows that have come and gone is immense.

"Isn't it television at its best?" he asked.

For years, we lived with images of the stars that were created by the Hollywood columnists and the great studio press departments. Suddenly, on talk shows, you saw these larger-than-life figures sitting on a show and telling the true stories of their lives. That's probably what killed off the great and famous columnists of Hollywood, the Parsons and the Hoppers; people saw the stars coming on and talking about their lives, and they were far different stories than the pap that the press had been putting out.

"Sometimes, you can talk a guest too far back into their past, and it almost becomes a psychiatric interview. I met Doctor Martin Grotjahn, who was probably the dean of American psychiatrists, a great gentleman who had written a book called *Beyond Laughter.* He said to me, "Interesting to meet you. I always tell my new young psychiatrists, 'If you

There is a connection, for Griffin, between the talk show and the game show. "Game shows, once again, are improvisational. Paar came out of game shows; Carson came out of game shows; I came out of games. It was the great learning platform for people who had a clock in their head, a sense of timing."

He has successfully devoted much of his career to determining the secret of a hit game show: "the audience at home," he said. "There's nothing more thrilling to somebody at home than getting the answer before the contestant does or before anybody else in the room does. I think that's why, for example, in Chicago, they have these bars that show *Wheel of Fortune* every night on big screens. Everybody comes in and bets on different people who can get the answers before the contestants.

"It's not enough to watch people on a screen

David Letterman takes his talk show, Late Night with David Letterman *out into the field for "investigative" reports on everything from the eating habits of celebrities at Chinese restaurants to the inside story on life at Manhattan's Yummy Donut Shop.*

168

playing games or acting silly when there's no participation."

Wheel of Fortune, Griffin said, was based on

games my sister and I used to play in the back of the car on summer vacations. Mom and Dad would say, "We're taking you to Carlsbad Caverns to watch the bats fly out." We'd ride in the back of the car for days, and we'd sit there and play a rather violent game called hangman. Every kid in America played it. You'd put in blank spaces, and you'd guess a letter, and if it wasn't in the puzzle, you'd start hanging a man. I think everything I've drawn on in my career goes back to my youth. . . .

And so, one day, just fooling around in the office here, with the creative staff, I threw out this idea, and we started to work on it. We worked for a year on it. We then made a pilot. I first showed it in my house to Mike Eisner, who is now head of Disney, and Brandon Stoddard, who is head of ABC. They both saw it, and they said, "Well, it's not a show." I thought, "Whoops . . ."

Without changing it at all, I showed it to Lin Bolen at NBC, and she bought it. But she said, "I want to do a show in a boutique." So they put us in the middle of this—it looked like a store. That didn't work. It looked frumpy.

The set was redesigned to resemble what it is today. "We then brought in [Edd] 'Kookie' Byrnes [from *77 Sunset Strip*]. He did a pilot."

Byrnes was replaced with Chuck Woolery, who had hosted the original pilot, and a woman named Susan Stafford. "Then I found Pat Sajak, who was a local weatherman on NBC here, and then came the famous Vanna White, who now is one of the larger-than-life cult figures in America. The cover of *Newsweek, People, Esquire,* every major paper. It just doesn't stop."

According to Griffin, *Wheel* is now seen in forty countries, including six behind the Iron Curtain. Its influence is everywhere: "Sam Donaldson says to the president in a press conference, 'Mr. President,

how did you think the first televising of Congress went today?' And he said, 'I thought they did very well. If they do any better, they can get on *Wheel of Fortune.*' Not a bad plug, from the president."

As for *Jeopardy:*

I invented the game sixteen years ago. It's probably the toughest game that's ever been on television. I went in a year ago and took the test for contestants and failed—and I'm the executive producer.

Jeopardy came from my wife turning to me during the quiz scandals and saying, "Why don't you do a game?" I had said to her, "I wish I could do a quiz show. I love questions and answers."

She said, "Why don't you do a show where you give the answers?"

I said, "Well, they just did that, and everybody's in jail."

She said, "No. Five thousand two hundred and eighty."

"How many feet in a mile?"

"Good. Seventy-nine Wistful Vista."

"What's Fibber McGee's address?" I thought, "Whoa." Landed in New York, called the staff together at eight o'clock that night, and said, "Listen to this." And we started working.

But again, it was a year and a half of structuring. It's not enough to have an idea, because really the idea of *Jeopardy* is just answer-question. That's the only thing different. But structuring the game, categories, amounts of money, things that can happen, things that won't happen, was very difficult.

When I first showed it to NBC, I rented a theater in New York. Instead of having Jeopardy, Double Jeopardy, Final Jeopardy, I had Jeopardy and Double Jeopardy together, and the board was so big it came off the stage and went out into the audience. There were fifty categories! NBC said, "Could you make that a little smaller?"

The *Jeopardy* experience left Griffin with a real distaste for network research.

When I first put *Jeopardy* on the air, two weeks after it was on, the head of NBC research department, Paul Klein, came to me with these huge charts, and he said, "Merv, look what happens on your show. . . . The questions are way too tough. You've got to bring them down to a sophomore-in-high-school kind of questions and answers."

I said, "Well, that's not the game."

He said, "You have to do it or you won't last thirteen weeks. The testing groups don't know what those answers and questions are. You've got to change it. That's an order from the network."

I said, "Okay," and he left, and I never told anybody that he was ever there. We went right on with the show, and it ran eleven years [on NBC].

Not too long ago, I did a game show pilot, and in the middle of the pilot, as we would complete each segment, the head of daytime said, "Hold it now," and he ran into a roomful of people he had hired saying, "Was that good?"

That's never been entertainment. . . . If you make *Gone with the Wind* you don't ask anybody on the street, "Is that good?" You put it out there and you take your chances. You will either have done your job well, or you're a disaster.

He'd run out and say, "They didn't understand." Finally you just get to the breaking point of saying, "Listen, I've got a track record. I got you the number one show on your network for twenty-three years. Leave me alone, and let me do it. If it fails, it fails."

That's not ego speaking, but the confidence of a successful game show entrepreneur. Griffin knows what works and what doesn't. "The game is the thing," he said. "Same as Broadway where the play's the thing. You can have shows where people can win millions—there's a million-dollar game on right now, but nobody cares, because the play's the thing, the game's the thing. You can never get around that."

Ever since the fifties, nighttime talk shows have been an addiction for millions of American insomniacs.

7. VARIETY

Bandleader Lawrence Welk hosted a musical-variety show filled with schmaltz and what he called "champagne music," a kind of video Muzak that appealed to middle America. Among the regulars on the show were dancers Barbara Boylan and Bobby Burgess, a former Mouseketeer on The Mickey Mouse Club.

There was a time in America when the variety show was as much a staple of the prime-time schedule as situation comedies and dramas. Now they barely exist.

Variety programs reflected some of the earliest show biz traditions—especially vaudeville and the circus. Acts that came from those circuits were tried and true, featuring material that had survived years of traveling on the road from town to town. You could put them in front of the camera and let them do their thing. As a result, the airwaves were filled with singers, dancers, jugglers, magicians, and animal acts.

Many of these programs were hosted by comedians (for example, George Gobel, Tennessee Ernie Ford, Milton Berle on *Texaco Star Theater,* Sid Caesar on *Your Show of Shows*). But you didn't necessarily have to have performing talent yourself to emcee a variety show. Witness Ed Sullivan, host of the granddaddy of all the variety shows, *The Ed Sullivan Show,* originally called *The Toast of the Town.* Sullivan was a Broadway newspaper columnist who never really mastered a feeling of comfort in front of the cameras. His hunched shoulders, halting delivery, and unmistakable voice made him a required imitation for every professional mimic in the country. But Ed Sullivan had an eye for talent—all kinds of it—and for twenty-three years, he was able to provide Sunday night audiences with something for everyone—an eclectic mix of pop songs, opera, stars from Broadway and Hollywood, comics, and circus acts from around the world. Others would try to duplicate his success with programs such as *The Hollywood Palace* on ABC, but Ed Sullivan was unique. Where else would you be able to see the Beatles, the Moiseyev Dancers, Elvis Presley, and Albert Schweitzer?

Music was central to variety shows. Many of them deliberately set out to create a feeling of intimacy, making you a part of their musical "family." Fred Waring and Lawrence Welk successfully did this by featuring members of their bands and choruses in medleys and specialty numbers. Garry Moore and Arthur Godfrey did the same thing, letting audiences in on the comings and goings of various cast members. Godfrey—whose programs on CBS radio and television accounted for some twelve percent of the network's revenues—gained nationwide notoriety when he excommunicated a member of the family on the air—the personable boy singer Julius LaRosa, whom Godfrey had decided was getting too big for his britches.

One early musical variety series anticipated the advent of music videos by thirty years. *Your Hit Parade,* a transplant from radio, presented a countdown of the top songs in the country. Each was presented with a big production number. When a song was on the charts for weeks at a time, imaginative producers and choreographers had to strain their creativity to come up with different ways to present it. There are only so many ways you can do "Shrimp Boats (Are A-Comin')."

The most successful singers in the country were given their own variety shows: Perry Como, Dinah Shore, Rosemary Clooney, Kate Smith, Andy Williams—all enjoyed popular success. Nat King Cole was a rarity—a black performer with his own show. But despite his prodigious musical talents, NBC was unable to attract a national sponsor—companies were wary of affecting business in the South—and Cole was off the air after little more than a year.

In addition to the regular weekly series, musical stars were spotlighted in grand television specials—for a period of time always trumpeted as "spectaculars"—sixty- or ninety-minute extravaganzas that

Four of the regular cast members on Your Hit Parade: *(left to right) Russell Arms, Gisele MacKenzie, Dorothy Collins and Snooky Lanson. A precursor of the music video, each week the show presented production numbers around the week's Top Ten songs. When a song lingered on the charts week after week, the producers had to come up with a new gimmick for every show.*

In the fifties, many local stations presented their own versions of American Bandstand, *teen shows like* Hi-Jinx! *in Los Angeles, where kids could dance to the latest hit records.*

*Singer Janette Davis (left) was one of the "kids"
featured on* Arthur Godfrey and Friends *and* Arthur
Godfrey's Talent Scouts. *Godfrey's on-camera persona
was warm and friendly, but his popularity faded when
stories of his temper and firing of members of his TV
"family" became more and more public. In one famous
incident, he fired singer Julius LaRosa on the air.*

were showcases for great performances. Most variety shows were enjoyable, disposable entertainment, but sometimes the spectaculars veered toward art. Noël Coward, Tallulah Bankhead, Ethel Merman, Mary Martin, Lena Horne, Fred Astaire, Gene Kelly, and Judy Garland (who, briefly, also had her own variety series) were just a few of the superstars who starred in TV spectaculars.

Occasionally, stars appearing on network television can still electrify an audience: the *Baryshnikov on Broadway* special, produced by Dwight Hemion and Gary Smith, or Michael Jackson's performance of "Billie Jean" on the special *Motown 25: Yesterday, Today, Forever.* But the variety *series* has all but vanished. *Saturday Night Live,* with its music acts and stand-up comics, retains elements of the variety show, as does the syndicated series *Hee Haw,* featuring country-western music and cornpone jokes. The interest in variety shows seems to have waned, although occasionally a Donny and Marie Osmond or a Dolly Parton have another go at it.

Larry Gelbart thinks the last successful variety series was *The Carol Burnett Show.* Grant Tinker remembers *The Julie Andrews Hour* (1972–73) fondly, but notes that the series was not a popular success. What happened? Gelbart posited that the comedian was what held the variety show together and that's no longer the case. Former NBC executive David Tebet believes that *Rowan and Martin's Laugh-In* was the cause—the show's hectic pace *was* its variety, and television would never be the same. Others look to MTV and the music video as the culprit or to the unrestrained access that cable services like Home Box Office and Showtime can give to a star like Liza Minnelli or Bette Midler. Finally, many of the elements of variety—especially music acts and comedians—now appear on talk shows like

Tonight and *Late Night with David Letterman* instead. Musical performers and movie and TV stars find an appearance on a chat show as valuable to their careers as variety shows once were, and it is much less taxing and time consuming.

So the variety show is dead—until the next one comes along. Merv Griffin recently shot a pilot for a variety series called *The Coconut Ballroom,* a show with a big-band-and-dance format. So far, no takers, but who knows, given the strange and wondrous cyclical nature of television, variety can come back. Just imagine Mick Jagger with his own variety show, introducing Kiri Te Kanawa, Keith Richards, juggling bears, and the Bolshoi Ballet . . .

One of the regular features on Dick Clark's American Bandstand *music show over the years has been "Rate the Record." Two teenagers hear one of the week's new record releases and decide whether it will be a "hit" or a "miss."*

GEORGE SCHLATTER

George Schlatter, in many respects, fits the classic image of a Hollywood television producer. He's a wheeler and a dealer, a husky, bearded mass of energy, always looking for a project, always eager to find an angle. Perhaps the best description of Schlatter and his work was provided by Tony Schwartz, writing in *The New York Times* in 1982 after Schlatter's NBC series *The Shape of Things*

had been canceled. "Like every Schlatter effort, *The Shape of Things* was a novel idea executed with supercharged energy on a medium generally characterized by neither," Schwartz wrote. "Unfortunately, it was also vulgar, gratuitous and not very funny. Mr. Schlatter is a bit like the girl with curl. When he's good, he's very good, and when he's bad, he's terrible."

George Schlatter is one of the people who gave us *Rowan and Martin's Laugh-In* and *Real People.*

Variety shows offered everything from jugglers and sword swallowers to acrobatic troupes like the one that performed with guest star Kirk Douglas on CBS's The Ken Murray Show.

Red Skelton specialized in broad, "big yucks" comedy, developing a repertory of stock characters such as Clem Kadiddlehopper, San Fernando Red, and Freddie the Freeloader. Over the years, his Red Skelton Show *featured a remarkable variety of musical guest stars, from the Rolling Stones to opera diva Helen Traubel (right).*

When Milton Berle's Texaco Star Theater *aired on Tuesday nights in the late forties and early fifties, all other activity ground to a halt. Theater attendance dwindled. Everyone was watching Uncle Miltie, television's first superstar. Berle donned a zoot suit to greet guest star Duke Ellington.*

182

Comedy is hard work. Rehearsing for his Texaco Star Theater, *Milton Berle had a reputation as a tireless perfectionist and a relentless taskmaster, both on himself and other cast members.*

Whether or not you liked *Real People*—and many critics didn't—it was a huge popular success.

Schlatter also perpetrated a show called *Speak Up, America*—it lasted ten weeks—and among his other accomplishments, he lists the first program on television in which no one, including the commercial announcer, was over the age of fourteen.

He went to work in commercial TV in 1956 at NBC, when Hal Kemp, a network production executive, hired him to book guests for variety shows. He has worked with many of the biggest names in show business, including Dinah Shore, Frank Sinatra, Judy Garland, and Diana Ross.

Born in St. Louis, he sang with the St. Louis

Sid Caesar's nutty professor character on Your Show of Shows *appeared as everyone from Professor Sigmund von Fraidy Katz, expert on mountain climbing, to Dr. Heinrich von Heartburn, expert on marriage. He was often aided and abetted by cast members Carl Reiner (left) and Howard Morris. Caesar and Imogene Coca were the comic mainstays of* Your Show of Shows *and* Ceasar's Hour. *The shows' writers included Mel Brooks, Larry Gelbart, Neil Simon, and Woody Allen.*

184

186

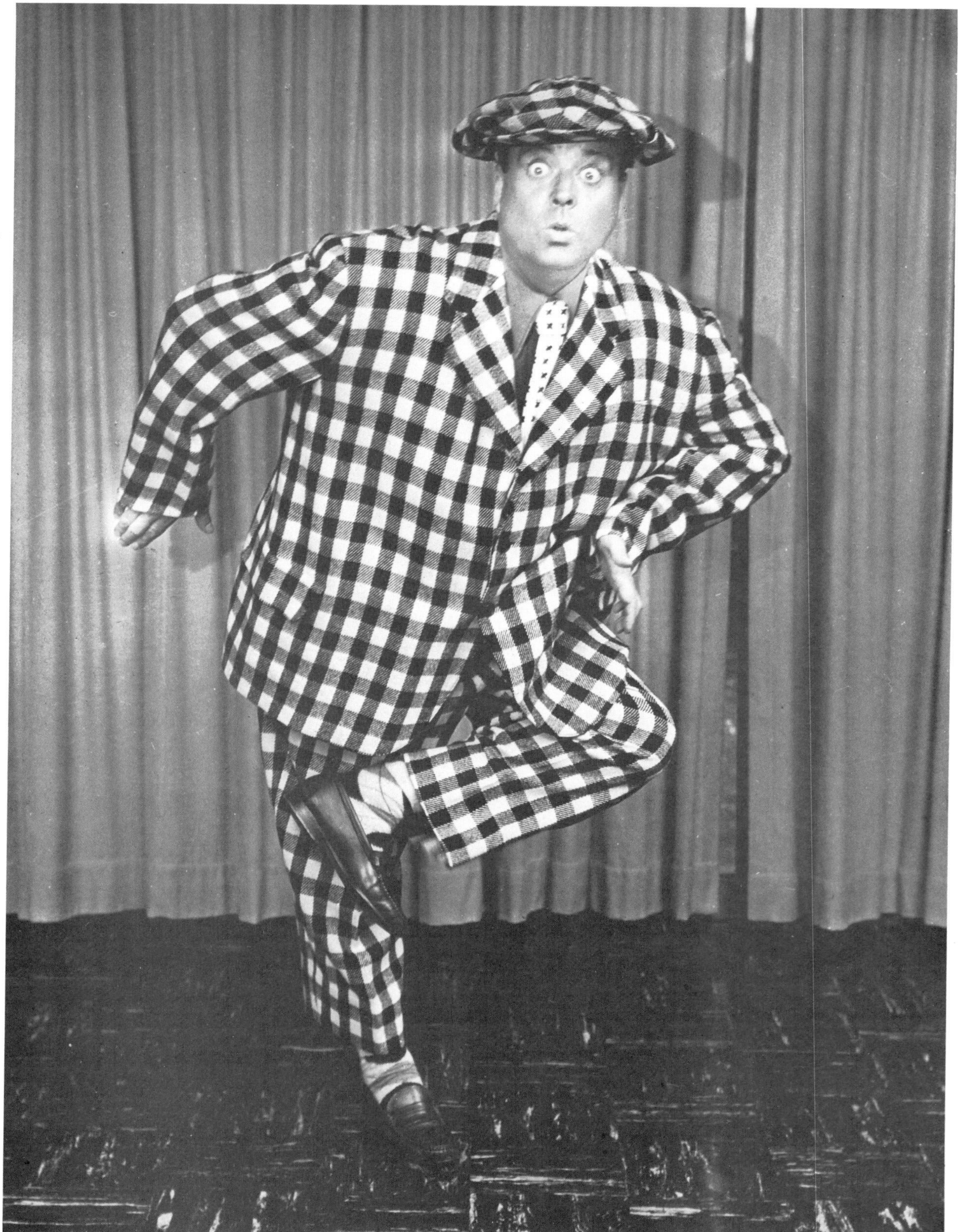

Jackie Gleason got his first television break on the Du Mont Network's variety show Cavalcade of Stars. *He would become TV's "Great One," one of the most gifted television comedians in the history of the medium.*

Dean Martin and Jerry Lewis were among the hosts of the fifties' Colgate Comedy Hour, *the variety show NBC pitted against* The Ed Sullivan Show *on Sunday nights. Martin and Lewis alternated the hosting duties with such stars as Jimmy Durante, Donald O'Connor, Eddie Cantor, and Bob Hope.*

Municipal Opera as a youth and began producing shows when he was a student at Pepperdine University. He got a job as an agent with MCA at the age of nineteen.

I booked nightclubs and acts—singers and dancers. Then I got a job at Ciro's, which was a nightclub on the Sunset Strip. I did a TV show called *Party at Ciro's,* which was on ABC locally. All the stars in Hollywood came on that show.

Then I wanted to get married, and my wife said she would marry me only if I got out of saloons. So I went to NBC to book *The Dinah Shore Show,* which was the first color series, many years ago. It was during the Golden Age of variety shows. As I got into it more and more, I started to come up with shows and ideas, and eventually, they let me produce my own. I was with NBC for a long time. Then I left NBC, and I went to CBS to do *The Judy Garland Show,* a job for which you got stunt pay.

I loved her. I had a good time with her. It was like living in an avalanche, but I did love her and had a wonderful time. God, she was an exciting woman. . . .

Garry Moore (right) didn't sing or dance very well, but his pleasant personality and relaxed style made him the popular host of a successful weekly variety show on CBS that featured such regulars as Durwood Kirby and Carol Burnett and guest performers like magician Milbourne Christopher (left).

188

Mary Martin's appearance in the title role of a lavish TV musical version of James M. Barrie's Peter Pan *in 1955 helped create one of television's most memorable spectaculars. Wendy Darling was played by Kathleen Nolan (left), who went on to star in such comedy series as* The Real McCoys *and* Broadside.

Ed Sullivan's stoop-shouldered posture and halting delivery were imitated by every professional mimic in the country, but his Ed Sullivan Show was the longest-running variety show on television, a Sunday night spectacular that glittered with Broadway performers, circus acts, opera singers, Hollywood stars, and musical greats. Below, film director John Huston, and far right, choreographer Katherine Dunham.

Schlatter was replaced as executive producer of *The Judy Garland Show* after five episodes had been taped. The series would not last a full season. But within four years, Schlatter would be present at the creation of an enormous hit, a hit that many believed changed television in general and TV comedy in particular for good: *Rowan and Martin's Laugh-In.*

At that point, in 1967, television had really kind of settled into a rut. There had been no change. And here came this show that combined radio and theater and burlesque, motion pictures, nightclubs, and revues. It came into a relatively tranquil period, when you had *Gomer Pyle, U.S.M.C.* and *Mayberry, R.F.D.* and *Leave It to Beaver* and *My Three Sons* and cowboy shows. It was all rather quiet and nobody talked about any kinds of problems at all, particularly not humorously. . . .

Then we came, and we started talking about the Pill and the Vietnam War and racial tension. We made it acceptable to make humorous observations about serious issues. After that, it was acceptable to air *All in the Family* and *Maude* and *The Jeffersons.*

Laugh-In combined all known forms. The biggest single influence on *Laugh-In* was Ernie Kovacs. [Jolene Brand], my wife, was the girl on *The Ernie Kovacs Show,* so Ernie and I

had a very close relationship. We used to argue a lot about the necessity of punch lines. Because, if you remember, Ernie was just weird. He did some great things, but you never really knew when they were over. He had a certain disdain for the audience. It gave him individuality, it gave him charm, and it gave him a unique appeal.

On *Laugh-In,* I took what Ernie did with the medium—the use of the medium as more than a means of transmittal—and we applied the technical advances that had been made in television to humor. So we stepped up the pace, the energy. We took out all of the fat and cut away everything that was unnecessary.

We taped, and then we started editing, editing, and editing. It was a major moment. We had a brilliant group of

The signing of Judy Garland for a weekly variety show in 1963 was hailed as a major coup for CBS. But in spite of some extraordinary musical moments with Garland, the series lasted but one season, battered by the ratings power of Bonanza *on NBC and a series of upheavals in the production staff. George Schlatter was* The Judy Garland Show's *first producer. He was replaced after the first five tapings.*

writers, all of whom later became producers and directors. And we had a brilliant cast. I don't know if you could ever assemble a cast like that today, and if you assembled it, I don't think you could hold on to them, because the whole agent procedure is different. I think you'd lose Goldie Hawn the third or fourth week, but she stayed with us as long as her deal. So did Lily Tomlin and everybody.

No one was really sure that the audience was ready for a show of just funny things without ballads and things to change the pace, or whether or not the audience was ready to accept a show that dealt with serious issues.

Everybody was a little bit shocked and thought it was too fast, and said, "Well, it's okay once, but will it survive with that kind of speed?" I thought, really, we could.

So did the viewing public. Once it became a series, *Laugh-In* was an almost-instant hit. "We didn't really know at the time what impact we were having, because we were locked up in editing rooms and writing rooms," Schlatter said. "I was working seven days a week, so I never got out. And finally, at the end of the first fourteen shows, when we got out of the building and saw what we had done, we were thrilled and delighted.

"It was a warm, wonderful, exciting, happy time of my life, because we could say anything; we could do anything. We were a big enough hit that we could get away with anything. You know, President Nixon came on and said, 'Sock it to me?' Which we found out later might not have been that bad an idea."

Laugh-In managed to offend just about everyone at least once. "Truman Capote got us sued once. He came on and said, 'I would like to apologize for having said that Jacqueline Susann looked like a truck driver in drag.' We said, 'Well it's nice of you to apologize to her.' He said, 'I'm not apologizing to her. I'm apologizing to the truck drivers.' Two days later, we got hit with a lawsuit.

"We did a joke once, on one of the early *Laugh-*

*In*s, we did a thing on 'News of the Past, Present, and Future.' We said, 'News of the Future, 1988'—this was 1968, twenty years ago—'News of the Future 1988: With marriage in the church now an accepted practice, the Archbishop and his lovely wife, the former Sister Mary Katherine, both announced, "This time it's for keeps, if only for the sake of the children." ' The switchboard almost exploded."

Obviously *Laugh-In*'s humor created problems with the censors. "It was pretty much hand-to-hand combat," Schlatter said.

Occasionally bayonets. You must understand what was going on in 1967. Nobody could say the word *pregnant* on the air, and here I had Joanne Worley standing at a piano singing, "The things I did last summer," and she was obviously about ten months gone. She was pregnant one week, and sang, "I *should* have danced all night."

The censors would come downstairs and say, "What are you doing?" I said, "Come on, people have babies. How do you think we got here—by bus? People have been pregnant for centuries and it didn't destroy society." We would get a pregnant joke on the air, but they were very nervous. And they were very nervous about political jokes.

The way we used to get a lot of jokes on was very interesting. They wanted these jokes, but they also wanted to be safe. They wanted those ratings and that impact and that energy and success, but they also wanted it quiet.

The way we would beat the censors most of the time was with the band. We would do a joke and tell the band, "Don't laugh." As long as they didn't hear the band laugh, it was okay. If the band laughed, though, they would say, "You can't do that." So we would have the band laugh at straight lines, and they'd say, "No, no, no—cut that!" We'd say, "Oh, you caught me." Then we'd have the band sit there and bite their lips when we did some other outrageous things.

I don't know if a man my age should be proud of having gotten *Laugh-In* on the air, but it was cat and mouse then, you see. If you can imagine me twenty years younger, like a kid in a toy store, perhaps you can forgive some of the adolescent overtones of what we did.

Schlatter currently is involved in the production of specials for cable and a syndicated series called *George Schlatter's Comedy Club.* Having been involved with so many series and specials—including variety shows—Schlatter has some theories about why variety has virtually disappeared as a genre on American television:

I think MTV and the music business in general is not conducive to variety shows. Carol Burnett did a show with Robin Williams and Whoopi Goldberg and Carl Reiner. It's marvelous, but it was difficult to generate the kind of excitement that there used to be for performers. The movie stars today don't really want to do guest shots, and the musical performers don't want to. It's difficult to capture the performance of a Bruce Springsteen or a Mick Jagger in a variety show. That form doesn't seem to work as well as it used to. It was lovely, though; it was great. One year, there were twenty-five different variety shows and a lot of specials, and it was fun. It may come back, but in a different form.

MTV changed it by putting so much money into three minutes. And the artists themselves changed a lot. Outrageous music is difficult for everyone to relate to, and to have a successful variety show, you need a very broad audience. It's very expensive: sets, costumes, rehearsals, and so on.

Also, musical performers today really don't want to rehearse that much. They just want to do what they do. Part of the fun of variety was changing what they do.

But Schlatter sees a positive side to the move away from variety shows as well, a change that's taking place on cable. "HBO and Showtime have come out with these personality specials, where you see Liza Minnelli on stage, her whole act," Schlatter said.

Robin Williams did a show from the Metropolitan Opera stage. He came out and did two hours of the most brilliant comedy I have ever seen in my life. It was very intimidating,

194

because you sat there and said, "Is it possible for anyone to ever top what he did?"

That would not be possible on network television because he could not have the build of energy and performance and the accumulated effect that he had with an uninterrupted performance.

Cable is giving people new things to strive for. I think it's also a positive change in the business, because we're introducing more innovation, which we must do. Television must continue to change, if it's going to survive as an intelligent medium.

It eats its young. Television is a cannibalistic kind of show business. No matter how big a hit you are on television, it's temporary. You know that a show will come along that will one day beat you.

DICK MARTIN

In the 1960s, Dick Martin and his partner, Dan Rowan, were working nightclubs and making frequent appearances on other people's television variety shows. Virtually overnight, television zoomed them into millions of living rooms and conjured up instant fame.

It happened with *Rowan and Martin's Laugh-In.* They weren't the only ones who became sudden celebrities because of the show. Such stars as Goldie Hawn and Lily Tomlin first achieved fame on *Laugh-In.* An indication of the show's popularity is the number of catch phrases that arose from it: "Sock it to me," "You bet your bippy," and "Look that up in your Funk and Wagnall's." Twenty years ago they were the height of hip.

"NBC pitched a show to us because we had become very hot from the Dean Martin summer show," Dick Martin recalled.

We were Dean's first summer replacement in 1966, and we did rather well. It was a very high rated show, so they said,

"Would you do a show of your own, *The Rowan and Martin Show?*" We said, "Yes, but we don't want to do a variety show, we would like to do something a little different. . . ."

A lot of the ideas came from the nightclubs where Dan and I were appearing and the TV shows we were doing then, like *The Perry Como Show* and *The Jerry Lewis Show* and *The Ed Sullivan Show.* All the sketches we did were four to twelve minutes long. . . . We decided that brevity was the answer to a lot of people's prayers on television, and it turned out to be that way.

[NBC] was mildly receptive, so we pitched this idea and they said, "Go find a producer." We found a producer [George Schlatter], did a special, and it was warmly received by the television audience and highly received by the critics, so NBC said, "We'll give them thirteen shows." They threw us opposite [*Here's*] *Lucy* and *Gunsmoke,* the number one and three rated shows! So we were in the position of being the giant killer. . . . In nine weeks we became the number one television show in the country.

Up until then, there had been televised radio and televised vaudeville, of which Milton Berle was obviously the king. He took his great vaudeville and stage show knowledge and photographed it. It was hilarious, of course; it always will be, but it was never an electronic use of the material. . . .

I was a big fan and a very good friend of Ernie Kovacs. . . . He would do things in his shows electronically that were brilliant, and so we borrowed whatever we could of the

Tom (left) and Dick Smothers had a very successful musical-variety series on CBS in the late sixties, The Smothers Brothers Comedy Hour. *It was canceled by the network after a number of public fights with the brothers over censorship of the show's irreverent topical humor and their choice of guest stars like folksinger-activist Pete Seeger.*

electronic part but tried to go more and more for brevity. . . . In order to do it electronically, we had to do it in many, many, many, many cuts. It was really the videotape editor's delight.

We had thirteen marvelous writers, and the fact is that it was the first show I can ever remember where there were no rules—no beginning, no middle, no end. . . . You don't have to write a sketch for so and so, just write whatever you want and see what happens. We were able to fit most of them in. . . .

The unusual nature of *Laugh-In* made having an audience—usually so essential to Rowan and Martin's kind of comedy—a problem. "We did the first three shows and decided that having an audience was using people, making them sit there through hours watching things that had no cohesion, nothing that they could construe as a show. So we decided not to have an audience. We had open house—that was another innovation—we just opened the doors and we would have one hundred, two hundred, three hundred people there at a time, but they had no obligation to stay, and we had no obligation to entertain them as such."

Those who did stay saw some remarkable occurrences. "They would see the most startling things," Martin said.

All of a sudden John Wayne would walk on the stage and do six or eight lines and walk off. . . . John was the first big star who broke the barrier, because when John Wayne first appeared, the show hadn't been on the air yet. We asked him to say, "Well, I don't think that's funny." He had no idea where it was going in the script, but we did. He had great faith in a man named Paul Keyes, who was our head writer and the producer after George Schlatter. Wayne just did it, and all of a sudden it opened up for Jack Lemmon and Kirk Douglas and all the other big stars. . . .

The show is in syndication now, and I am constantly amazed and surprised and delighted to see myself working there on the screen with Zero Mostel, Marcel Mar-

ceau—people who didn't do television in those days—Truman Capote, Gore Vidal. After Lily Tomlin had done so many Ernestine rip-offs of Vidal, he came on, good-naturedly. With William F. Buckley, we had a thing where we sent him a telegram: WOULD YOU BE ON THE SHOW? He sent a telegram back saying, NOT ONLY WILL I NOT BE ON THE SHOW, I AM INSULTED AT BEING ASKED. So we sent him back a telegram saying, WOULD YOU BE ON THE SHOW IF WE FLEW YOU ON A PLANE WITH TWO RIGHT WINGS? He said, "Yes, I can't resist that!"

Although the humor on *Laugh-In* was always light, Martin insisted that the show was politically oriented. "We tried desperately to keep it balanced, and we had writers who were at opposite ends of the pole. Richard Nixon was running for president and agreed to come on and say, 'Sock it to me?' He did this, and we offered the same opportunity to Hubert Humphrey. His advisers turned it down. If you recall, Mr. Nixon only won by one million votes. A lot of people have accused us!"

The Sonny and Cher Comedy Hour, on CBS from 1971 until 1974, was one of the last successful musical-variety shows on American television. The series ended when the couple divorced. A subsequent attempt to reunite them in a new series failed.

Laugh-In stayed on the air until the end of the 1973 television season. Two and a half years later, a comedy and variety series was created that took *Laugh-In*'s combination of satire and broad comedy and gave it an even brighter, sharper, relevant edge—*NBC's Saturday Night Live.*

LORNE MICHAELS

Lorne Michaels is sitting in an office at NBC with a window that looks out onto the floor of Studio 8-H, where Toscanini once conducted the NBC Symphony, now best known as the home base of *NBC's Saturday Night Live.* Willie Nelson's band is down there, tuning up for rehearsal.

Michaels is back as executive producer of *Saturday Night Live,* the series he created in 1975. When it went on the air, it took a while to catch on, but once it did, the series became an important part of the baby-boom generation's weekend viewing. It was the only comedy show that seemed to address their concerns and interests: sex, drugs, politics, television—not necessarily in that order. Well, maybe in that order.

Many of the movies' young comedy stars first gained public notoriety on *SNL:* Chevy Chase, John Belushi, Dan Aykroyd, Bill Murray, Eddie Murphy. Its live, improvisational nature bred a lot of wonderful talent and a lot of burnout. Michaels himself left the series after its first five seasons to work on other projects, including an abortive NBC prime-time variety series, *The New Show.* He returned to *SNL* in 1985.

Michaels says he simply wanted to create a show for the generation that had grown up never knowing a world in which television was *not* an essential part of life. "I grew up in Canada," he said. "As I was growing up, we had a mixture of Canadian television, American television, and English television— the best of English television was shown on Canadian television. I watched everything. I remember television sort of being a miracle. . . ."

But a television career wasn't a conscious deci-

Carol Burnett's Cleaning Lady, like Red Skelton's Freddie the Freeloader and Jackie Gleason's Poor Soul, became a trademark character. An animated version appeared in the opening titles of The Carol Burnett Show, *which had an eleven-season run at a time when most other variety shows were in decline.*

sion on Michaels's part. "I was very conventional. I did shows in high school and at the University of Toronto—revues, and I acted in plays and directed shows, but I think I was headed more toward theater or to film. I was from the what-I-really-want-to-do-is-direct generation." Instead, he became a

writer. "The first sort of serious jobs I got were with a partner [Hart Pomerantz]. We began writing for comedians. I just got led into it. My partner was older and a little more sophisticated, and I tagged along. Through a series of happy accidents, we got to write for some good comedians, and that material got shown to other people. We were sent out to California to do a television series, and that led to another television series."

That second series was *Rowan and Martin's Laugh-In,* not the happiest of experiences. Michaels and Pomerantz were junior writers. "Our work would be rewritten, and we would have no connection to the rewrite. Also, the writers were not encouraged to come to the studio on taping days because those were supposed to be writing days. . . . My fantasies all had to do with sort of Kaufman and Hart out of town in Boston, rewriting the second act at four o'clock in the morning, drinking a lot of coffee, but we were very separate and divorced from the show." That unpleasant time encouraged a curiosity "about producing or production in order to protect your scripts."

The two writers returned to Canada and the CBC, where, Michaels said,

I was given a lot of control and was allowed to produce and write and actually perform in the shows as well. Hart and I did four specials a year for three years. I did a couple of other pilots and series up there as well.

I learned how to do television mostly because the CBC was this tremendous training ground. If you were prepared to work from midnight to eight, you could edit all you wanted. I began to feel very comfortable in a television studio. . . . I was able to learn an enormous amount in a very short time.

When I came back to California in 1971—because I'd been asked to come back as a writer on some shows—I found that I knew more than most people who were at a

The Coneheads: Prymaat (played by Jane Curtin, left), Beldar (Dan Aykroyd), and their daughter Connie (Laraine Newman) were three of the most popular characters in the history of Saturday Night Live. *A family of extraterrestrials posing as visitors from "France," the Coneheads were inspired, in part, by a visit Ackroyd made to the famous carved stone heads of Easter Island.*

Lorne Michaels, executive producer of Saturday Night Live, *made frequent appearances on the show during its first season, including the night he offered to pay three thousand dollars for a reunion appearance of the Beatles—$750 apiece.*

similar stage of development, because I'd been given more opportunities.

I then worked with Lily Tomlin on a series of specials with her and Jane Wagner [Tomlin's partner, the author of *The Search for Signs of Intelligent Life in the Universe*]. Lily was the first person to go to a network and say, "I think this kid can produce." That's where my formal start as a producer in America came.

The idea for a show like *Saturday Night Live* had been percolating in Michaels's brain since 1969, during his CBC days. "We began getting *Monty Python* in Canada," he said. "At least to me, the Pythons were to comedy what the Beatles had been to rock and roll. What you got from the Beatles was the sense that these people, who probably could have done other things and were smart and bright, had chosen to express themselves that way. I'd seen *Beyond the Fringe* in a theater, and I obviously had listened to Nichols and May and the [Carl Reiner– Mel Brooks] "Two Thousand Year Old Man." I was not unaware of American comedy and American television comedy, but this seemed so different, and so much more writerly."

In 1972, Michaels made a presentation at NBC's headquarters in Burbank to Herb Schlosser, who was then head of programming on the West Coast, and Larry White, Schlosser's chief aide. The show he had in mind then was not to be done live. *Monty Python* had not shown up yet on American public television, so Michaels showed their movie, *And Now for Something Completely Different* to give the executives some idea of what he had in mind. "There was no response whatsoever," he recalled. "There was a sort of stock answer then, which was that English comedy didn't work in America. I wasn't actually trying to do the Python show over here. I was just saying that this style is very interesting to watch, and notice the ability to not finish

the scene—to just go on, to take the heart of a scene, and not have to do that predictable thing of beginning, middle, and end, where the audience knows what's going to happen way ahead of you." The reaction: thumbs down.

NBC's feelings about Michaels's idea changed when Herb Schlosser, now the president of NBC, decided something new had to be designed for late Saturday nights. "Up to that point, Saturday night had been *Tonight Show* reruns. In 1975, Herb Schlosser declared there would be a new show in this time period, that it would come from New York, and that it would use Studio 8-H. . . ."

The original idea was to test a variety of pilots in the time slot, but eventually, Michaels's show was the idea on which NBC decided to take a chance. "It was pretty much the show that I'd been talking about to anyone who would listen for about three years," Michaels said.

Everybody had been describing shows for twenty years as new and experimental. It had become a cliché. I was too young to know it was a cliché, so I was very passionate and very intense about it. . . .

It didn't vary much. . . . There'd be a cast of seven and there would be rock-and-roll elements. I realized that the more I talked about it, I was really building around all my compulsions, all the things I was interested in. . . . I wanted short films, because there was a lot of interesting work being done by filmmakers. I wanted the host to be different every week, and I wanted stand-up comedians. . . . I used to say that I knew all the ingredients, I just didn't know the recipe. . . .

I just did a show that I would watch if I were the audience. Everyone else I assembled in the first year really had just sprung from the audience. With one or two exceptions, they weren't people with very long résumés . . .

I think they [NBC] thought it would be a more traditional variety show. Somebody once said that they were expecting Rich Little and the Marine marching band on the first show. Because it was live, nobody saw it until it went on. The censor saw it, of course, and the programming executives, but nobody really knew what you could do and what you couldn't do.

On the first show, there was this enormous argument which sort of distracted everybody—whether George Carlin could wear a T-shirt or whether he had to wear a suit. The compromise, which was reached by [former NBC executive] Dave Tebet, was that he could wear a T-shirt, but he would have to wear a jacket on top of it. Those were the sort of fights we were having in 1975.

Michaels started becoming aware of the impact the show was having when he began hearing people in restaurants talking about it over Sunday brunch.

"I started getting ticket requests from NBC executives, but it was not them who'd be showing up—it was their kids. You began to realize there was now an audience of kids, up to twenty-five or thirty, who were tuned into the show. . . . You'd see a football or baseball game, and in the stands there would be people wearing cone heads.* Chevy Chase and I went down to Washington twice during the first season for Gerald Ford things. We went to some sort of Senate affair, and Eugene McCarthy said to me that the first thing that was discussed on the Senate floor on Monday mornings was 'Weekend Update' [a weekly segment of the show that satirizes the news]."

The live nature of the show has always been a part of its excitement and appeal. "That's still the power of the show," Michaels said. "There is something different about it being done in real time, very different in the performances. There's no controlling it. I nudge it to completion, you know, and try to steer it along a bit, but you never know. For example, last week, we were a minute long going into the final twenty minutes of the show. Where's it going to come from? You can't cut bars in a musical number without advance warning. Sometimes, people can pick up the pace, sometimes you're dropping introductions, sometimes you're cutting whole chunks out of a sketch, sometimes you're going with a shorter sketch that you had cut at dress rehearsal. . . . We're almost never under because I always want too much."

Originally, the show was scheduled to run fifty-two weeks a year, but reason took hold. New shows were produced only until the end of May, and the

cast went on hiatus, although a few new programs were produced in July and August.

We did twenty-six the first year, twenty-four the second year. . . . They [NBC] didn't think that it could be rerun because it was live, that people wouldn't sit still for reruns because they never had before. But when the reruns started rating better than the originals, eventually we honed it down to twenty shows a year. . . . We just didn't know, because we were making up what we could and couldn't do.

I had been around successful shows on the periphery, but I had never been at the center of one. I think that somehow, everyone being the same age, we were sort of an all-for-one, one-for-all kind of group. We lived in a sate of grace for the first three or four years.

I don't know how long groups can stay together in a kind of innocence. I think there's a point at which the age of experience takes over, and people view each other and themselves differently. They become conscious of "Is this the best sketch for me to be doing?" The *work* ceases to be the guiding thing and this other word—*career*—begins to take over.

Saturday Night Live has always been a show in which the team's personal lives have provided source material for SNL sketches "for lack of anything else," Michaels said. "You couldn't possibly do ninety minutes a week without a lot of it overlapping. If somebody's just broken up with their boyfriend or girlfriend, you would get a sketch about that, sometimes not consciously. You would also get a lot of restaurant sketches, because writers tend to spend a lot of time in restaurants going, 'What do you want to do?' 'I don't know.' . . . Oddly enough, in this new format, we haven't had a lot of suburban-living-room sketches, which we used to have a lot in the old show. Part of the reason is that we're so conscious of our history that everybody's trying not to do what we've done before, so if an idea even

*One of the most popular running gags of *SNL*'s first few seasons was a series of sketches featuring an extraterrestrial family, the Coneheads, trying to get by on Earth posing as immigrants "from France."

Pat Boone first became a hit on Arthur Godfrey's Talent Scouts. *His wholesome, all-American looks and vanilla voice made him a big star. His family huddled around the living room TV set when Boone's own TV series,* The Pat Boone–Chevy Showroom *premiered on ABC in 1957.*

comes close to something we've done before, it gets knocked out. There's a tyranny to that. . . ."

The basic production schedule for *Saturday Night Live* has not changed much since Michaels first drew it up in 1975. At first, it was a six-day schedule, but by the middle of the first season, he said,

We realized we could probably do it in five, and then began to see how long you could leave things, because

the nature of the writer's personality is to leave it to the very last moment. . . .

We have a writers' meeting on Monday, which the host, if they're in town and can make it, is welcome to come to. People present ideas, but generally they've had very little time to think of ideas because they didn't get home until very late on Sunday [after the Saturday night broadcast], and they've only had one day to do their laundry and shop.

Each week, no matter how good or bad the week before was, there's a host sitting there going, "I hope this isn't one

of the weeks when it's not good." People write right through to Wednesday at three o'clock in the afternoon, which is when a read-through begins.

During that writing time, Michaels says,

I tend to move around and find out what most people are working on to see if there's a certain balance in terms of the cast and to see if I can help with the ideas. . . . Four to one is about the ratio of pieces written to what we actually use. . . .

After the read-through, I meet with the host and with some of the writers, the director, the designers, and the music department to see what's going into the show and can fit into the studio. It starts being designed that night, and they start working on the sets at the shop in Queens the next morning.

We start rehearsing the music first on Thursday, from one to three, then we do some promos, and then we start blocking sketches as the sets arrive.

On Friday, we go from one P.M. to eleven, and block all the pieces we haven't blocked. Then, at eleven, we have a short production meeting, at which point we determine the running order. . . .

On Saturday, we do a run-through and a dress rehearsal. We do the run-through from one-thirty to five-thirty. We have dinner, then we block "Weekend Update" [done last because it's tied to breaking news].

We do a warm-up for the dress rehearsal audience, which starts about seven or seven-thirty. Dress rehearsal at eight until about nine-thirty or ten, at which point we will have three meetings: a writing meeting, a technical meeting, and notes to the cast . . . Sometimes, if we have no time, we fuse the three meetings. . . .

At the script meeting, you try to decide which pieces to cut and what internal cuts we're going to make within pieces. You try to assess whether something got hurt by where it is in the show, whether the performance was off, or whether it just isn't working. A writer cannot solve every one of his problems—the piece can have a beginning, middle, and end with no fat on it and it's seven minutes long, but that particular subject matter or idea isn't worth seven minutes. Before the dress rehearsal, you would have had a

battle to the death about where the cuts would be, but after dress rehearsal, it's, "Well, what about these three minutes here?" "Okay." Comedy is very much about the ear.

What's always been great about this show is that no matter how taken with ourselves we've been, every week three hundred civilians from the boroughs come in and say, "Why did you think *that* was funny?" When something doesn't work, you have to scramble.

I asked Michaels about the changes that took place in the show after he left as executive producer in 1980. "When the original cast left, I think it changed," he said.

Everybody was compared to the original cast, and then they went through so many casts so quickly. . . . Then, when Eddie Murphy came along, it became "The Eddie Murphy Show," and he was paid differently, so it lost that feeling that it was a group, an ensemble that had to, if nothing else, like each other and work with each other. I think his brilliance so outshone everything else that was happening that it became a different show.

It's a little better organized, better run now, because I'm older, but you still can't find certain writers when read-through starts, and certain actors are not around when they're supposed to be, and I still, at every dress rehearsal, can't believe the show could be that bad—"This one has really hit a new low. I'm being punished"—and then the miracle happens. You can't *guarantee* the miracle is going to happen. You just sort of hope that it will happen and things will get better. Sometimes they don't.

The show still has the power to outrage, although there are limits. "Suffice it to say, anything to do with small children or sex or the divinity of Christ is still basically taboo. My feeling is that if it's funny and it's about ideas, it's all right if it's on television. After twelve years, people should know not to watch this show if that's what they're worried about.

"It gets better each week. Hopefully, it will be perfect—someday."

8. THE NEWS

F or three and a half days in November 1963, virtually everyone in the nation did the same thing: sat in front of a television set and watched incredible events unfold—the body of President Kennedy being brought back to Washington from Dallas; Lyndon Johnson moving into the White House; the lying-in-state in the Capitol rotunda; the shooting of Lee Harvey Oswald by Jack Ruby; the service at St. Matthew's Cathedral in Washington; young John Kennedy, Jr., saluting his father's casket; and the lighting of the eternal flame at Arlington National Cemetery.

It was during those days that all of us suddenly realized the importance and power of network news. It kept us in instant touch with what was going on and allowed us to share in a period of national sorrow and healing.

Television news is one of the primary reasons for the very existence of the commercial networks. With their enormous resources and technical capabilities, they can get us to just about any part of the world in seconds. If you had tuned in the *NBC Nightly News with Tom Brokaw* on the night of April 14, 1986, you would have heard correspondent Steve Delaney telling Brokaw, live, "Tom, Tripoli is under attack," as U.S. bombers were bombing Libya. When the space shuttle *Challenger* exploded, the three networks were on the air within minutes and stayed on the air, live, until early evening, when President Reagan addressed the nation. (Ted Turner's twenty-four hour news service, the Cable News Network, was the only network that had carried the launch live.)

Television shapes the way we perceive events, and in so doing it often affects those events themselves. Anything that happens without the presence of the TV camera has become the visual equivalent of the tree falling in the forest. Did it make a sound? Did the event take place? Because of TV news, we have seen inaugurations and political conventions, congressional hearings and presidential press conferences. TV brought the Vietnam war right into our homes, and in so doing, helped fuel antiwar sentiment in America. We watched the presidency of Richard Nixon crumble and the candidacies of Gary Hart and Joseph Biden evaporate into thin air.

Such thoroughness of coverage was not always the case. In the beginning, when the networks began broadcasting news in the late forties, it was little more than televised radio. There were few visuals, no pictures or graphics to illustrate the stories. It was simple rip-and-read from the wire services and the newspapers.

The first TV news show to feature newsreel footage was on NBC, *The Camel News Caravan*, sponsored by Camel cigarettes. John Cameron Swayze was the first star of TV news. He introduced the various newsreel pieces on the *Caravan*, and when there was no film available, he too read from wire service accounts, "hopscotching the world for headlines." (Having a sponsor like Camel Cigarettes did present a few problems. No one was to be seen on the program smoking a cigar. The tobacco company bowed to world opinion for one exception: Winston Churchill.)

Some extraordinary television journalists emerged in the fifties: the great Edward R. Murrow, John Charles Daly, Walter Cronkite, Chet Huntley, David Brinkley, Howard K. Smith, Edward P. Morgan. But in looking at their early programs, right up through the mid-sixties, it is interesting to note how studio-bound they remained. On-the-scene reporting was scarce in the days when jet travel and satellite technology were still in their infancy.

Another reason for the paucity of on-location re-

Among Dave Garroway's many NBC duties was hosting the Sunday series Wide Wide World, *a show that examined a single subject with a variety of reports, many of them live, from around the nation and the world.*

porting was the camera equipment. The big thirty-five-millimeter sound cameras were too bulky to allow any kind of mobility. It was not until the late fifties and early sixties that lightweight sixteen-millimeter film and sound equipment were developed that could be carried from place to place and maneuvered into all kinds of tight situations.

It happened just in time. The television news business reached maturity in the sixties, a time when there was more happening in the world than at any time since World War II. The Kennedy administration, the civil rights struggle, the emergence of the Third World, Vietnam—events came fast and furious. With the development in the seventies of ENG (electronic news gathering) reporters, producers, and camera crews could hit the street with lightweight videotape cameras. The videotape eliminated the need for processing and could be used over and over again.

Today, each of the three commercial networks spend between $250 million and $350 million a year on news. Each fields approximately eight domestic and fifteen overseas news bureaus, staffed by one hundred correspondents, each of whom earns an average of more than $150,000, according to *Broadcasting* magazine. The technology continues to grow as well. With the new "flyaway uplinks," a complete satellite earth station can be packed into fifteen cases, loaded onto an airplane, and rushed anywhere the news is breaking for live reports.

With CNN, the morning news shows, ABC's *Nightline,* local news, and weekend newscasts, we have access to what's going on any time of the day or night. In spite of cutbacks in the network news budgets, we still are offered an astounding variety of TV news sources. But too often, television news is an all-seeing eye but not a brain. Some critics maintain that with all the coverage available, in an

effort to get as many stories on the air as possible, actual reporting is limited to "Here they come, there they go" journalism: the diplomats are entering the meeting room and now they're leaving.

It's not enough to stop and look. We have to be able to stop and think, to understand what we're seeing. TV pictures can be so vivid and immediate that sometimes little thought is given to the background of a story or its future implications. Most network analysis is reserved for those rare moments when there are no pictures to show.

The networks still produce documentaries, but not as many as in the days of Murrow. A few subjects are given the full, in-depth treatment. In fact,

sometimes an entire evening of prime time is devoted to a single issue, although not on a night that's too crucial to the ratings. Other topics are given the quick once-over on such magazine shows as *60 Minutes, 20/20,* and *West 57th.* Some subjects get just the amount of attention they deserve; others require more.

For more information, one resource is public television. PBS may not have the wherewithal of the commercial networks or CNN, but it does provide thoughtful analysis with *The MacNeil/Lehrer Newshour,* the work of Bill Moyers, such documentary series as *Frontline* and *Eyes on the Prize,* and such shows as *Wall Street Week* and *Washington Week in Review.* They may not be able to send a special report from Rabat in three seconds, but they offer useful, often expert reportage and commentary.

The commercial networks may be heading toward just this kind of in-depth reporting, more background and analysis on fewer stories. That's partly because of the budget cutbacks: Such coverage can be cheaper to produce. But it's also a function of competition between the networks and the news shows being produced by local stations. With the satellite technology available now, local news teams can also receive worldwide reports and even send their own correspondents to a political convention or a summit meeting. What surveys are showing is that the strength of the networks is not necessarily their ability to bring in pictures, but the expertise of their journalists. The local station in Paducah can ship its anchor to Reykjavík, but it is unlikely that he or she will have the knowledge and expertise of a network newsperson who has covered a specific beat for a long time. Such people bring a knowledge to the news that the local stations can't top.

The public wants to know more, and in spite of layoffs and budget cuts, accusations of bias, insularity, and shallowness, there are a few hopeful signs that TV news will continue to grow and become more thorough and valuable than ever.

FRED FRIENDLY

To the delight of some and the annoyance of others, Fred Friendly remains the conscience of television news. He's one of the upholders of the old H. L. Mencken dictum that the purpose of journalism should be to comfort the afflicted and afflict the comfortable. Depending on to whom you speak,

Below: Sharing a brief lull in the Today *sh[...] [w]ith Dave Garroway was one of the key factors in the success of the program i[...] ['] Fred Muggs, a chimpanzee whose antics enlivened the* Today *procee[...] [m]orning viewers.*

Hugh Downs (second from left) hosted [...] 71. During those years he was assisted by Jack [...] w from the very first Garroway broadcast, new[...] [W]alters, who began her career at Today *as a scr[ip...]*

he's either a supreme defender of the First Amendment or a royal thorn in the side.

He was working as a radio producer in Providence, Rhode Island, in 1948, when he got the idea to put together a record album of radio news history. He took his notion to one of the best-known and most credible voices of broadcast journalism— Edward R. Murrow. That began one of the most worthy partnerships in television news: Murrow as correspondent, Friendly as producer.

Together, they created the series, *See It Now,* in the fall of 1951. "Edward R. Murrow and I were new to television," he said. "We were products of radio journalism. But we did know that we had this new instrument, and we wanted an opening that would be a statement of what we were trying to do.

"That same autumn of 1951, the first coaxial cable across the country went through to San Francisco. It occurred to us that for the first time, mankind could see the Atlantic Ocean and the Pacific Ocean side by side. No one had ever been able to do that before. So we talked it over, and we built an opening."

One camera showed the Brooklyn Bridge and the Manhattan skyline. Another camera, a continent away, showed the Golden Gate Bridge in San Francisco. The two live pictures were placed side by side.

"Here's the Atlantic, here's the Pacific Ocean," said Murrow.

We're the first ones to be able to use this instrument. We hope we learn how to use it with those pictures on the first program, and we hope we never abuse it. I hope we never get too big for our britches." It's as good an epitaph as anybody could have. It cost us a lot of money, three or four thousand dollars, which was a lot of money in 1951. And I can remember we kept it a secret because we didn't want the budget people, or top-management people, to tell us not to do it. And somebody said when they first heard about it, "Why didn't you just run a film of the two?" We said, "But that's not the idea. The idea is that we are shrinking the earth in those first three minutes of a new television series."

The effect on the audience of seeing those two oceans side by side was startling. We thought it was just a passing moment, but it's had a half-life of thirty-five years. People still talk about it because, I think, it was a metaphor that said that this is different from the pen and pencil, different from the typewriter; this instrument can teach; it can illuminate; it can inspire—otherwise it's just "lights and wires in a box," something Murrow said subsequently. And that all came together with those pictures: the words were right, the pictures were right, and the technology was exploding right in front of your eyes. You said, "This is television—what a promise!"

Television can show you the Atlantic and the Pacific, and television can show you the face of the moon. But it can also show you the face and heart of man. And perhaps what it does best is the latter. When used properly, it is still the best lie detector—although it can be fooled—still the best way of transmitting to the public where the truth is, if people will see it. It's very hard to lie to the camera very long.

David Brinkley first attracted national attention with his pointed, slightly irreverent anchor work during NBC's coverage of the 1956 political conventions, the first time he was paired with newsman Chet Huntley. The two gained fame as the co-anchors of The Huntley-Brinkley Report. *Brinkley left NBC in 1981 for ABC News, where he anchors the successful Sunday program* This Week with David Brinkley.

Murrow's abilities and innovation were the keys to *See It Now*'s success. In its second season, the series traveled to Korea for a report in a style that we're very used to now—a personal look at a war and the people fighting it. Then, it was a first: a sixty-minute documentary called *Christmas in Korea*. "We were still trying to figure out how to use the camera," Friendly recalled.

Murrow, because of his experience in World War II, much of it in Britain, always found himself going to where there were soldiers. He loved people who worked with their hands, whether they were farmers or soldiers. He went out to Korea several times. And then we said, "Why don't we do an hour program—not just a half-hour—from Korea?"

We sent five camera crews with big thirty-five-millimeter equipment. Each camera weighed two hundred and fifty pounds. Five cameramen, five sound men, heavy equipment, lighting equipment, storage batteries, sound equipment, and five reporters.

The camera equipment then was not what the equipment is today. Today you can zoom; you can dolly. We could zoom, but not the way it can be done today. We had to change lenses—lenses were great big things. Even for me at my size—we could barely carry that camera across a mountain. It was very primitive. But I think fancy-pantsy tricks by cameras take away from the story anyway.

Murrow and the crews stayed there for ten days or so, shot fifty thousand feet of thirty-five-millimeter film, and sent it all back. My colleagues and I edited it down within a matter of two days, as I remember it, to a one-hour program that began with a marine digging a foxhole in Korea. It was the first time the face of war was seen in living rooms. A sort of broadcast prologue to Vietnam, taking a point of view very sympathetic to the soldiers eight thousand miles away on Christmas Eve. White Christmas: a lot of sadness, a lot of poignancy. It was a view of war: how cold it can be, how hard it is to dig a foxhole—and Murrow being there. Murrow used the word *communications*. I remember when he got back, he said, "Fritz"—I hated that, but that's what he used to call me—"it's a great communications instrument. It transported the whole country to Korea."

What Murrow and *See It Now* will be most remembered for is the courage to tackle Senator Joseph McCarthy.

The disease called McCarthyism had been around for three or four years. People would come to Ed and to me and say, "Why don't you do something about that?" And Ed, laid-back, would say, "Well, we will. But we can't do it until we find the little picture that will do it. What do you want me to do, make a speech? Want me to do a sermon?" He not only hated that kind of television, he thought it had no place.

We found it first in 1953 in the story of a single air force lieutenant, Milo Radulovich, a twenty-two-year-old who was cashiered because his father, mother, and sister were allegedly Communists. We did that, and Milo Radulovich was restored to active duty.

Then we began collecting material on McCarthy: thousands and thousands of feet of film, every speech, every hearing—everything. By March 1954, we decided we had enough to do a very critical examination of this man who was guilty of character assassination and was making

AVID BRINKLEY
WASHINGTON

Americans believe that their leadership and their neighbors were Communist agents.

CBS had given us a half-hour of airtime. It was ours, not the sponsor's or the company's—we could do anything we wanted. We went to them and said, "We're doing a program about McCarthy. How'd you like to buy an advertisement in the major newspapers so people will know we're doing it?" They said, "No, thank you." I think they were willing to have it be Murrow's responsibility, but they didn't want to brag about it. So Ed and I went out and bought and ran quarter-page ads:—TONIGHT, A REPORT ON SENATOR MCCARTHY. And at the bottom, because every ad had to be signed, it said MURROW AND FRIENDLY. And I still remember that the ad in *The New York Times* cost eighteen hundred dollars and *The Washington Post* a little bit less. A lot of money in those—and these—days.

A week later somebody very high in the company said to me, "You may have cost us the network." They meant that the pressure from McCarthy's allies, from the government, and from advertisers would cause the web—the collection of 180 stations that made up the network—to disintegrate. Public opinion was against Murrow in the first weeks after the program.

The chairman of the board of CBS, William S. Paley, was asked by Murrow the night before the program, "Do you want to see it?" He said, "No, it's your responsibility. You got it right?" Ed said, "I think we got it right."

Paley said to him, "If I were you I would announce that McCarthy will have a half hour of time to answer you."

And then that night or that morning, I guess, Paley called up Murrow and said, "I'll be with you tonight, and I'll be with you tomorrow."

We figured the only way to show McCarthy's technique of smears and half-truths was to show what he did: character assassination. We showed Reed Harris, who was the subject of a hearing, a former Columbia University student who had been kicked out of college when the campus newspaper had been critical of the administration. McCarthy used that on him, fifteen years later, to destroy him. We went back to show that attack on him, then we went back to show why he got kicked out of Columbia—because he wrote a book about the fact that football had become, at some colleges, a subsidized racket.

McCarthy accused Adlai Stevenson of something Stevenson was not guilty of. We showed the accusation by McCarthy, and then the real truth: that Adlai Stevenson, who had just run for President and lost, had nothing to do with that, was not a Communist, was not a fellow traveler. We took seven or eight charges by McCarthy, we put them on as they happened, and then we rebutted them—either with film or with Murrow saying the truth.

But for all the film and all of the showing of McCarthy's techniques of character assassination and Murrow's rebuttals, what emerged from that program—what made the difference—was the presence and integrity of Ed Murrow, remembered for his reports from the Battle of Britain. Looking into the camera, especially in those last three minutes, and saying, "We will not, we cannot live in fear of one another. This man has made us spy on each other; that's not what this nation is about. And whatever the threat of Communism, the answer is not turning on each other." The fact that a man of Murrow's stature could do that made other people say, "We don't have to sit back and listen to McCarthy any longer. We can write about him; we can attack him." Others had done it before, but this was Murrow, a powerful man because of television, and his reputation, taking a crack at this man who was a menace to all Americans—to all the world.

In the end, the death blow to McCarthyism was not our program. McCarthy destroyed himself when some of his hearings were televised.

As they went on, you could see McCarthy almost having a nervous breakdown on television. And Joseph Welch, the conservative Boston lawyer who was the counsel for the Army said, "Senator, I will say no more. I never thought I would see such cruelty. How cruel you are to attack a man who isn't even here. These hearings are over." And McCarthy just sat there, humiliated in front of the nation.

I think the end was not gradual after that. He turned to drink, and several years later died of cirrhosis of the liver. A dark mark in the history of this country.

See It Now ended in 1958, and Murrow's disillusionment with commercial television eventually sent him away from CBS to Washington, where he served as John F. Kennedy's director of the United States Information Agency. Shortly before his de-

Although he never anchored a nightly television newscast. Edward R. Murrow was the first television journalist to demonstrate the ability of a powerful TV reporter to have an effect on the events he covered. On his documentary series See It Now and CBS Reports, Murrow demonstrated the impact television reporting could have on everything from the plight of migrant workers to the political demagoguery of Senator Joseph McCarthy.

parture, there was one other Friendly-Murrow collaboration, working with producer David Lowe. The documentary, *Harvest of Shame*, about the nation's migrant workers, became another high point in television journalism. "I can remember Ed's ending to that program," Friendly said. "It still resonates. He said, 'Those are the people out there who make us the best-fed people in the history of the world. They don't earn a living. They have no constituency. They can't do anything to help themselves. Maybe we can. Good night and good luck [Murrow's trademark sign-off].'"

Friendly stayed on at CBS News, eventually serving as president for two years, watching and evaluating some of the key political figures and events of the sixties.

Television is not an X-ray machine. It can't see my ribs, my heart, my lungs—but it can see truth. It can tell when somebody is a liar. It can measure integrity. It's not foolproof, but most of the time it will determine whether somebody is lying or not.

For a long time Richard Nixon fooled the camera. When he made his speech in 1952, when he was running for vice president, and it was reported that there was a slush fund. He defended himself, not by talking about the issue, but by appealing emotionally: talking about the fact that he was just a plain man, he said, with a wife who wore a plain coat, and his daughters had a little dog named Checkers, and he wasn't going to give that up.

He was making an emotional appeal to the American public. And because the American public loved Eisenhower and wanted him for president, they took Nixon as a vice-presidential candidate. He got away with it that time. But then in 1962, when he lost the California governor's race, he made his "You're not going to have Richard Nixon to kick around anymore" speech, which was another nervous breakdown right on television.

In the end, a combination of Watergate and his response to Watergate caused the American people to finally make the judgment that he was not the man he said he was. And when he said in that Saturday night speech, "I'm not a crook. I'm not a crook," I think the verdict of the American people, and of history, was the opposite of what he was saying.

The years of the Kennedy Administration coincided with the maturation of television network news.

John F. Kennedy [had] a new, cool way of using television. He had great attentiveness; he could stand up in a news

The power of demagogic Senator Joseph McCarthy, as he spearheaded a ruthless search for Communists in government, was challenged by journalist Edward R. Murrow on a historic edition of his CBS News series, See It Now. *The program, which revealed the truth behind McCarthy's accusations, was a major step in the destruction of McCarthy's reign of terror. To McCarthy's left is young staff aide Roy Cohn.*

conference like a whiz kid and tell you all kinds of information that no president and few politicians ever could. I remember him most from an interview that I produced that was on all three networks. It was just before the Christmas of 1962, in the Oval Office. He always looked younger than you thought he was going to look. I remember him being quite reflective but saying, "This job is tough, tougher than I thought it would ever be."

I don't think anybody had ever thought of using television that way before. He knew that he couldn't kid the camera, that he had to be himself. And of course the Bay of Pigs in 1961 taught him a little bit of humility.

I think Kennedy was a television natural. At the beginning he was awkward, when he was a congressman reading off cue cards, eventually off TelePrompTers. He was so frigid at the beginning. Most people were scared of television, *are* scared of television. . . .

If you had to say the moment television news became the way that people got their news, I suppose you would have to say it was the early sixties, when nightly news first went to a half hour. Martin Luther King and the civil rights marches in Montgomery and Birmingham, children being barked at and bitten by police dogs,

And then the Vietnam War, the living room war. "War is hell," General Sherman said after the Civil War. Those were mere words until Vietnam—you *saw* that war. I think if Britain had seen World War I on television, it might not have lasted as long as it did. The television war went on for twelve years,

Television helped destroy the political career of Senator Joseph McCarthy in the fifties, after he launched a crusade against alleged Communists working in the United States government. The televised Army-McCarthy hearings in 1954 revealed McCarthy's shoddy tactics in unrelenting detail. He was censured by the United States Senate and died three years later.

CBS News Correspondent Howard K. Smith does a live report from Central High School in Little Rock, Arkansas, in September 1957, when Federal troops were sent to enforce a Supreme Court ruling against segregation in the public schools. A reporter doing a live stand-up from the site of breaking news was a complicated technological novelty then. Today, it's standard procedure.

and half of it was on television every night, half of those years. The war became an electronic war; the television became an electronic soapbox; the presidency became electronic, for better or worse. The electronic hearth was where history was being made, and this country will never be the same again. I don't think the world that has television will ever be that way again.

Coverage of the assassination of President Kennedy was equally critical, Friendly said.

Those four days of massive television coverage of the Kennedy funeral held the nation together. A nation which had a forty-year-old president shot from under them was in danger of disintegrating in an emotional tantrum. It could have happened—riots in the streets. Lyndon Johnson, to his great credit, stepped into that vacuum.

I think it was broadcasting's finest hour. And I think it may have saved this country; at least it got us through that period, until we had a succession to the next president. There's no way of understating what three commercial networks—and public television, having just come into the world—did

during that time. People at all three networks made the decision: no commercials, and more important, no entertainment programs. Television was for those four days the sinew, the stabilizing force, the gyroscope that held the country together. This nation has its faults, this industry has not always delivered on its promise, but for those four days, after Lee Harvey Oswald pulled that trigger, television performed as journalism very seldom in its long history has ever been able to.

WALTER CRONKITE

He began his journalism career working for the old United Press wire service, did his required time in radio news, and joined up with CBS in 1950. Now only semiretired, there has never been another anchorman like him—the avuncular presence that assured audiences every night that the world was still spinning, if occasionally slightly off its axis.

Walter Cronkite anchored the *CBS Evening News* for almost twenty years. He also served as the correspondent who guided us through national events and crises—from political conventions to wars and assassinations. His enthusiasm for America's manned-space-flight program was contagious ("Oh, boy!" he would exult at a lift-off or man's first trip to the lunar surface). It almost seemed that if Cronkite wasn't there to cover an event, the event just hadn't taken place.

"There is a natural curiosity on the part of all of us to be present at the scene of great events," he said. "That is pure television; that is the one thing that is strictly unique to television—that ability to go there at the time it is happening. The satellite has given us that capability around the world. Whether it's a tragedy or whether it's pageantry, a scheduled event or an unexpected one, that is what we are about. . . .

"I think the turning point was the return of MacArthur from Korea and his arrival at the airport in Washington. Those who had TV sets tuned in. As more and more people got sets, it became more and more the national phenomenon for everybody to tune into their TV set at the moment of crisis."

At no time was that truer than during horrible days following the assassination of John F. Kennedy.

"I was actually standing up and leaning over the teleprinter at the very moment that the bulletin came in," he remembered.

The first bulletin was that shots rang out as the motorcade passed through Dallas. Then, of course, events began tumbling in on us: The motorcade had veered off and was on the way somewhere, and then the motorcade was on the way to Parkland Hospital. We got on the air very shortly thereafter.

We got on with audio bulletins on the TV network within a very few minutes, just whatever it took me to run around the corner into the audio booth. We did not have a warm camera in the newsroom. Ever since then, we have always had a warm camera there.

I was on audio only for maybe ten minutes until we got the camera warmed up and in the studio, and then we got onto TV. My first reaction was "Good God!"—for humanity, for the American people, for John Kennedy. I didn't have any idea of course in the first moments how badly he might have been hit. The second reaction was: We have got a terrific story—we have got to get mobilized, get going.

I think that we all sense constantly a responsibility for our words, particularly when it's all extemporaneous, as this was. There was no script for any of it. It was all ad lib; it came as the pictures developed.

How can one keep ad-libbing over so many hours? "We have a superb research department at CBS News," Cronkite said. "They develop material very quickly overnight. There was a lot dumped on my desk about previous funerals of heads of state,

Jacqueline Kennedy at the White House entrance with her children, John junior and Caroline, waiting to join her late husband's funeral procession. Behind them are the president's brother and sister, then–Attorney General Robert Kennedy and Mrs. Ethel Smith. The Kennedy assassination led to some of the most extraordinary moments in television history. The networks suspended all regular programs for four days, covering the biggest news story of them all.

previous assassinations of heads of state, the way the funerals were handled, the presence of family members, and so forth. There was a lot of research material available—not written in a form to be broadcast, but I went through the material whenever I had a moment to get an idea of where we might go with something. So I wasn't led only by the pictures.

"We have a very close liaison between the anchorperson and the producers and directors of the broadcasts; if I have an idea of something we might pick up that either has occurred to me at the moment or that I have from the research material, we work together on that. So it's not just following the picture and doing cut lines. There is an integration with production to give it a rounded essence."

Cronkite's ability to reflect the emotions of the American people also came into play in his reporting on the Vietnam War. As our attitudes toward the war were changing, so were his.

I think that the first impression I had that things weren't quite what they were represented to be in Vietnam was on a visit, I believe in 1963, when I went up to Cam Ranh Bay and saw the vast effort being made to build a port at a time when we were being told that the limit of our involvement would be—and I don't remember the numbers exactly, but let's say 110,000 men, or something like that. Well, clearly, the facilities at Cam Ranh Bay were meant to take care of a half a million men or more. Checking back, I found that the supply line was being filled all the way back for a huge buildup. That's when I first realized that we were not getting the full story from our administration about our intentions in Vietnam. My doubts began at that point.

The other impressive thing was that as you got around Saigon in those days and talked with the officials involved—the pacification officials or the military officials or the AID [Agency for International Development] officials, you got different stories from each group. There wasn't a single cohesive story about what was happening in Vietnam. That made you wonder on what basis Washington

During the November 1963 weekend of the Kennedy assassination, one unbelievable event followed another. As Lee Harvey Oswald, the accused assassin of Kennedy, was being moved from the Dallas City Hall, he was shot and killed before television cameras by nightclub owner Jack Ruby. Within one hour of the shooting, four out of every five television sets in America were turned on.

was making its decisions. Up to that point I had felt we were right in being in Vietnam; I felt that it was a case where we had come to the aid of a nation that, while not a democracy at the time, had hopes of becoming one, and if we were going to preserve the ground for a democracy there, in an area of the world that was threatened by an imperialist takeover by another ideology, we had to be there, had to give them some help. We then got desperately overinvolved. The American people were not told the extent of the involvement.

As it was with so many Americans, the 1968 Tet offensive was critical in affecting Cronkite's view of the fighting in Southeast Asia.

Here was a major offensive that we had been told they [the Vietcong and North Vietnamese] were not capable of mounting, and they did mount it, and at first it was very effective. So as soon as it broke, we [at CBS] discussed the matter, and we decided we would do something rather unique and rather daring and risky. I would step out of my role as an impartial newscaster and go out there and do a sort of first-person impression of Vietnam and attempt to cut through all of the confusion of the moment.

It may have been a very immodest and egotistical exercise for us at CBS News to assume that anybody could or should do that, but when I got out there I felt that this did indeed show that the Vietcong and North Vietnamese supporters had a lot more strength left than we had been led to believe. It was obviously a much longer war than we had ever dreamed it would be, it was going to require more forces and a greater American commitment than we had ever been told it might take.

I came back and made some rather strong conclusions about it. I concluded that we ought to say that we had done the very best we could, we tried, it didn't work, and get out. . . .

I learned only later that Lyndon Johnson apparently said, "Well, if I've lost Cronkite, I've lost middle America," or something of that kind. I don't believe that was the deciding matter at all. I think it was just another drop of water in a great torrent that was overwhelming Lyndon Johnson at that point.

Many would disagree.

A few years after LBJ resigned, Cronkite interviewed LBJ for a television special looking back at the Johnson presidency. Johnson remembered Cronkite's Tet broadcast. "He said I was wrong, of course. He believed he was right all along. . . . There were some moments when he grabbed my lapel and pulled my nose close to his, and when you get our two noses together, you have quite a feat! He felt that I had gone overboard."

Cronkite's position brought him into contact with many of our leaders. Nowadays, he can afford to be

a little more candid about some of them. "Richard Nixon looked on television as he was seen to be by so many Americans, a little devious," he said, "lacking perhaps in sincerity. It came across as hiding something, telling you one thing while doing another with ulterior motives perhaps. I don't think this is just hindsight that makes me say this. I believe that that's how he was seen at times, a little shifty-eyed. . . .

"In one-on-one, he wasn't quite that way. He was much more direct and much better than he was in an attempt at a public speech—far better."

Interviewing politicians like Nixon was one of the hardest parts of Cronkite's job:

They are going to do everything possible to avoid their errors showing up on camera or their indecision showing up on camera, so it's not easy. You just have to keep digging and try to be as conversant as you can with the subject, so that when you don't get an answer, you know it and can come back at it from another angle.

Part of the problem of interviewing politicians on television is the time element. You're covering a lot of ground, and you just don't have the time to keep coming at him or

224

her at enough angles to get the facts, where you really can achieve something.

I think another aspect of it is that we have become a little too confrontational in our interviews, so that the subject is ready to be combative and, by gosh, isn't going to let the interviewer in there. I think if you approach this differently—if you are trying along with him or her to help the public understand what the problem is, you are likely to be more successful. That's been my policy, and as a consequence of it, I've sometimes been referred to as a soft interviewer.

Politicians recognized Cronkite's power, not only as a newscaster and opinion leader, but as a potential candidate himself.

I've been visited by official delegations from both parties, as a matter of fact, both wings of both parties, for all kinds of offices, everything from mayor to Senate to the presidency itself.

I don't think I could be elected, because I've got very strong feelings, positions that people wouldn't know I have until I get out on the campaign trail, and then it's a little late—you are going to lose awfully large segments of the population.

Besides that, what really bothers me is that not one of the delegations that has ever called on me has ever asked me first what I stand for. They've never presented me with a menu of major items that election year and asked my position. They've only talked about how easy it would be to get me elected. My name is already well known; the fund-raising would be simple. They go into all the technical details of getting elected, but never what I stand for. Now that is highly cynical. It indicates one of a couple of things that annoy me a great deal. Either they think it's not going to matter what I think—they'll handle that part of it—or they don't think it matters what a person stands for as long as they are popular and have some of this thing called charisma. That's terribly cynical. That can't lead to a very efficient democracy, it seems to me.

What *can* help lead to an efficient democracy is the reporting that Cronkite and his colleagues, at

Tom Brokaw worked his way up from local television news to the post of White House correspondent, host of The Today Show, *and now, one of the three top correspondent jobs in the country: anchor and managing editor of* The NBC Nightly News with Tom Brokaw.

their finest, can provide. The best informed of the men and women who work as network correspondents can shed light on events and issues, even under the enormous time constraints of the evening news.

TOM BROKAW

On the day Richard Nixon resigned the presidency, August 8, 1974, a network correspondent was standing on a box in Lafayette Park, the White House over his shoulder while he talked.

It was Tom Brokaw, doing his job and doing it very well, telling the nation what was about to happen—just the facts.

Now, Brokaw is one of the Big Three—the anchormen of the commercial networks' evening newscasts, watched by some forty-four million Americans every weeknight. In his position as anchor and managing editor of the *NBC Nightly News with Tom Brokaw,* he finds himself in one of the most visible positions in the country.

Brokaw worked his way up through the ranks of local and national television news and has one of the strongest journalism backgrounds and reputations in network news. He was born and raised in Yankton, South Dakota. . . . "I grew up in a part of South Dakota where we didn't get television until—well, I didn't get television until the mid-1950s. I was in high school by the time I saw it on a regular basis."

Brokaw began working in broadcasting at a local 250-watt radio station:

The signal reached just about to the end of the street. . . . I started when I was fifteen. It was magical to hear the sound of your own voice and a better job than sacking groceries. I learned a lot there. I have given credit for what

skills I have as an ad-libber—for being someone who does not panic—to that station, because there I was at fifteen, with fuses falling out of the transmitter, things breaking down, having to gab my way through all kinds of experiences.

It was very instructive, and also, I suppose, the beginning of my addiction. I thought more conventionally, and I think my parents did as well. I came from a working-class family. My parents wanted me to go to college. I think they expected—and I expected—that I would grow up to be something conventional, like a lawyer, and have an office and do a nice white-collar kind of job. But it was that early experience with the radio and the news ticker, the chance to share with people in the audience what was really going on . . .

In August 1963, two hundred thousand demonstrators—and millions more via television—watched as Dr. Martin Luther King declared from the steps of the Lincoln Memorial, "I have a dream." Television coverage of King's speech and the entire civil rights movement was an essential element in the fight for racial equality.

Television was an invaluable ally of the civil rights movement, bringing the story of the efforts of Martin Luther King and other civil rights leaders to the entire country. TV captured such moments as the climax of Dr. King's march from Selma to Montgomery, Alabama, in March 1965.

College did not go as smoothly as Brokaw expected. "I had a meteoric high school career. I was a high school star. I went off to college and I found out that you couldn't get along on just a smile and your easy charm.

I kept drifting back into radio and television because I could always get a job there. That was a problem as well, because it was an easy out."

Brokaw dropped out of school. "I went to work for a television station full-time when I was twenty years old, and I discovered how desperate life would be if I didn't get my ass back in class. So I went back and got squared away, completed my political science requirements for a degree, and worked at the television station in the meantime."

Brokaw got married and graduated from the University of South Dakota. He and his wife, Meredith, headed for Omaha, Nebraska, and a job at station KMTV in 1962. "I landed in one of those rare places in the American television spectrum where the newsroom was run by a man of old-fashioned news values. He kicked my copy back to me and looked over everything we did. We were wholly competitive with the newspaper in that town in terms of breaking stories and knowing what was going on. It was very exciting.

"I think some of my friends from college would come down there and wonder, 'What the hell is he doing there? He's making no money and is out chasing fire trucks, going to City Hall, staying up half the night, working on stories.' I learned a great deal there. It turned out that that station cranked

In June 1963, Buddhist monk Quang Duc doused his robes in gasoline and set himself on fire to protest alleged persecution of Buddhists by the South Vietnamese government. Horrible pictures such as this, transmitted to America by television, slowly fed increasing American discontent with our involvement in Southeast Asia.

In 1975, shortly before the fall of Saigon, American television viewers were horrified by footage of Vietnamese children burned and running in terror from bomb attacks during the final days of fighting.

out a lot of very good people who are in the system around the country now."

The station was small enough that everyone did everything, including run the camera. "I was terrible, awful," Brokaw said. "It was a sixteen-millimeter Bell and Howell. The running gag is that Brokaw got to be an anchorman because he was so rotten with a camera."

From Omaha, Brokaw moved to Atlanta and fifteen months as the anchor of the late evening news at WSB-TV. During Brokaw's brief time there, Julian Bond was denied a seat in the Georgia House of Representatives, the Klan marched in Atlanta, and Martin Luther King, Jr., was preaching at his father's church. "It was a real privilege to have lived in Atlanta in those days, because you really saw the best and the brightest of the South coming to grips with this terrible, terrible problem of racism in a courageous fashion."

In 1966, NBC sent Brokaw to KNBC-TV in Los Angeles. He was the anchor of the late evening newscast there, as he had been in Atlanta, but he was also carving out a reputation for himself as a good political reporter. One of his first assignments was Ronald Reagan, then running for governor against incumbent Democrat Pat Brown. "I used to ride around on the bus with Lyn Nofziger and Reagan out in Orange County, which is a sanctuary of conservative thought. He'd speak at coffees and teas and so on. . . .

"They kept him carefully sealed off from the press, by and large. You couldn't get very close to him. He was not at ease as a candidate in those days. He had a real mean streak about him. He really felt that he was on a crusade. The fact of the matter is, in fairness to him, I think the press in California was pretty much loaded against him. Pat Brown was very popular, particularly with report-

ers. And Ronald Reagan, actor—he got no respect, as they say. He really didn't, and I think that it irritated him. Moreover, he had come from an environment in which he had been pretty well protected by studio press agents. . . .

"All that happened in the sixties came to rest in California," Brokaw said, explaining why it was an exciting place for a TV newsman starting to hit it big. Brokaw covered everything from the free-speech movement at Berkeley to the assassination of Bobby Kennedy after the California primary in 1968. His politically savvy coverage of the California delegations at both the 1968 and 1972 Democratic National Conventions helped him win attention from the network news bosses. He enjoyed working the floor at the conventions. "I think it's the best job in the world," he said. "It's better than being the anchorman in the booth, I think. It's jungle rules, you live by your wits, and it's physical. I think if there is one job for which I am suited, it is that job.

It was Brokaw's work at the 1972 Democratic convention that led him into national big time.

I really had the California delegation wired. I was feeding stuff up to the booth all the time, and we were getting one beat after another on CBS and ABC. I just kept cranking this stuff out for them, having a lot of fun. At the end of the week, we had this big party, and John Chancellor took me aside and said, "You know, you're going to have to decide one of these days whether you want to keep that good life in California or be a grown-up and come back and be a network correspondent."

[NBC News President] Dick Wald came out at one point. We had a long lunch, and he said, "What do you think about the White House?"

I said, "I think that's very fast water to jump into." I felt confident I could do it, but, you know, Dan Rather was a .400 hitter there.

Wald said, "Well, why don't we send you to London for a

An AP photographer and a Vietnamese cameraman working for NBC News were present for one of the most horrible and indelible images of the 1968 Tet Offensive in Vietnam: A Vietcong suspect was captured and summarily executed in front of the cameras by South Vietnamese National Police Chief Nguyen Ngoc Loan.

year and then bring you to the White House? That will get you some credentials as a network correspondent."

I said, "That makes a lot of sense. Besides, Meredith will move real easily to London from the beach. I'm not sure she'll move so easily from the beach to Washington."

Then they called back and said, "No, it doesn't make any sense; you're going to do the White House thing or not. You need it; we need you there."

In 1982, he became co-anchor of the *NBC Nightly News* with Roger Mudd. Mudd left a year and a half later, and Brokaw has held the sole anchor spot ever since.

What's a typical day like in the life of a network anchor? "There isn't a typical day, first of all," Brokaw said.

I suppose that a day here begins at home at about six-thirty, when I get up, reading into the day by listening to the *Today* show and *Sunrise* and National Public Radio and then going through *The New York Times, The Wall Street Journal, The Washington Post,* and *USA Today.*

I try to get some thinking done at home. I check with the news desk, and then I get in here by nine-thirty. For much of the morning, I do what I call the business of being an anchor: correspondence and speaking and being interviewed.

About eleven-thirty in the morning, I begin to shift into a different gear, to start thinking in a more focused way about what we're going to do that night. At noon, I do a little promotional piece, and then I generally go off for a walk, go buy a book, run. I try to do some exercise every day.

I come back at about one-thirty and then wade into the minutiae of the news—not so much the bigger stories, be-

Television brought the Vietnam War into our living rooms on a nightly basis. New, lightweight cameras could go anywhere. They produced close-up, sometimes sensational images of war, images that would be a factor in gradually moving American public opinion from general support of the war to disapproval.

cause I have a good sense of where we're going with those. I try to get a sense of what else we ought to be dealing with to flesh out the evening program.

At about two o'clock or two-thirty, the executive producer and I will sit down and say this is what the day looks like. We have these fragmentary conversations in code most the day through, so by the time we get to that meeting, we have a pretty strong sense of what shape the program is likely to take that night.

I should also add parenthetically that on most days I will have looked at two or three things that have been prepared—longer features, longer investigative features, stories that are going to fit with something that's breaking in the news that day.

We assemble everybody around four o'clock, and we say to them this is the fashion in which we are going to do the program tonight; this is the rundown; these are the pro-

duction values. I hand out the writing assignments. I write two segments every night, and the writers write the other three. . . .

Then we all go into what I call the crash-landing mode. We start banging away at it, and the copy comes through me, and then it goes through a news editor. I'll make changes and catch things, and he'll make changes and catch things. He'll catch things in my copy as well.

Then, at six-thirty, we go on the air.

The Statue of Liberty appears on the screen, a John Williams theme song swells, and the title—*The NBC Nightly News with Tom Brokaw*—appears on the screen. Still as calm and modulated as that 1974 day standing on a box in front of the Nixon White House, Tom Brokaw delivers the news.

Television covered America's involvement in Vietnam right up to the bitter end in April 1975, when helicopters airlifted personnel from the roof of the American Embassy and the last Vietnamese evacuees crowded onto ships at the Saigon waterfront.

LAWRENCE GROSSMAN

Larry Grossman was focused mainly on advertising until 1976, when he became the president of one of his major clients, the Public Broadcasting Service. In 1984, in a move that surprised a great many people, he became the president of NBC News. It wasn't the first time that someone without a journalism background has wound up as the head of one of the major network news organizations. "I got a wonderful note from Dick Salant, who had an extraordinary run as the president of a news division [CBS]," Grossman said. "He said that when he first got the job at CBS, he had been a lawyer and not a journalist, although he had always been interested in it.

"When Frank Stanton and Bill Paley asked him to take on CBS News, he was sitting there holding his head in his hands. Ed Murrow came in and patted him on the knee and said, 'I didn't have any background in news either, when I started being a correspondent. The most important attributes are concern about public service, caring about people, and a determination to do the job. Don't let anybody put you off in terms of, Why aren't you a newsman?' I was mightily comforted by that."

Like Salant, Grossman has always been interested in the news—fascinated by it, in fact. "As a

Hundreds of antiwar demonstrators were injured in clashes with the Chicago police and the Illinois National Guard at the 1968 Democratic National Convention. Wise to the power of the television medium that was covering the violence, the demonstrators chanted, "The whole world is watching! The whole world is watching!"

young man working in advertising at CBS News, I used to go up every week and ask Fred Friendly for a job in the news department. That's the only thing I really wanted to do, and he always turned me down."

As NBC's vice president in charge of advertising, he was in steady contact with NBC News from 1962 until 1966, when he started his own agency. And as the head of PBS he demonstrated the management skills necessary to administer a news division of some twelve to thirteen hundred people and a budget of between $250 million and $300 million a year.

Indirectly, it was Grossman's involvement with

public TV that led to his job at NBC News. He knew Grant Tinker from the days when they both worked at NBC, Grossman in advertising, Tinker in programming on the West Coast. When Grossman became president of PBS, Tinker was busily running MTM Enterprises.

A couple of years after I started at PBS, I was really dismayed by the fact that we could not get any of the major Hollywood figures to produce programs for public television. While there was always a lot of handwringing in public about how terrible commercial television was in terms of outlets for creativity, and "If only we had the freedom blah-blah-blah . . . ," the fact is that none of them were offering any of their stuff to us. We didn't have any money to speak

Just moments after the networks reported Senator Robert F. Kennedy's victory in the 1968 California Democratic Presidential primary, they were back on the air to report the shocking news that the senator had been shot.

of, but we created an atmosphere, or tried to, in which the best programming or the best experimental efforts could go forward.

I was coming out to Los Angeles, and in desperation, I called Grant and said, "I want to talk to you about what we can do with public television." We went out to lunch, and all the two of us talked about was NBC and how sad it was that it was such a mess and how great it had been for us as young people growing up in the business. I came back and told my wife that if anybody offered Grant the job of program head at NBC, as long as Fred Silverman was gone, he'd probably leave MTM to take it.

On the day that the announcement of Tinker's appointment as NBC chairman came, he called Grossman. "We stayed in touch from then on," Grossman said.

Every time I got really depressed about problems at PBS, I'd come in and find he had more problems than I did. . . .

One day he called up and asked if I'd come over to see him. He knew of my overall abiding interest in news, even though I had never worked in it. But certainly at PBS, we put a lot of emphasis, at least in the years that I was there, on public-affairs and news programming.

I guess they were having problems with news. Grant asked if I would come over to NBC News, which was flattering and exciting. Something I'd always dreamed about, but a wrenching choice, because by then, PBS was in very good shape.

There were a lot of agonizing questions in my own mind about leaving public television, but I had been there for eight years. It had been a tremendous struggle, but very satisfying.

Grossman decided to move on.

How did he learn the ropes? "I came over a month or so ahead of time and watched a lot, went around, asked a lot of questions, visited the affiliates, asked what their priorities were, visited the bureaus before I actually took on the responsibility, made it my business to talk to all the key people in news. They're very good people here. I just worked my way in."

He described his responsibilities. "My job is not to produce programs," he said. "That's what we have producers for. I do not determine the lineup of each program. My job is to help set the priorities in terms of what our coverage is, what the emphasis of our programs should be, and to manage the news division, both in terms of the personnel and the budget. On the programming side, it's to make sure that we're operating according to appropriate priorities, to critique and to figure out what our new initiatives should be in programs and coverage of themes, specials—that kind of thing."

Grossman wholeheartedly believes that his news division is doing it better than the competition.

But I don't think there is a fundamental differentiation in three very good, very strong, very expensive, and very dedicated news organizations. I say that without meaning to sound Pollyanna, but it's true.

We have some things that I think characterize what we at NBC do. For example, a very fundamental belief that if a reporter is reporting a story he should be where the story is. Otherwise, the anchor reads the information. Our correspondents actually do the reporting and the on-the-scene work—as opposed to the kind of parachute journalism that goes on sometimes.

I'm sure you'll hear the same thing from the others, but we place a strong emphasis on the basics: Get the story, the coverage, in a very aggressive, competitive way.

At least in the years that I've been here, we have made a staggering investment in new technology—satellite, computerization, half-inch videotape. I think we're way ahead of everybody on all these scores, with a view toward being able to move where the news is—whether it's the Philippine revolution, or week-long trips to Australia, China, the Soviet Union and Vietnam [as the *Today* show has done]. We take advantage of the new technology to get out of the studio and move close to where the news is happening. That has been, I suppose, a kind of trademark of what we have done

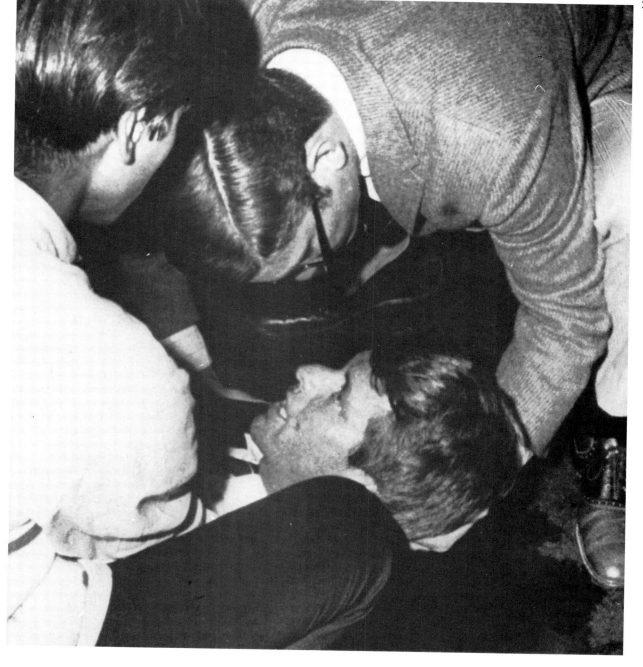

Violence spread from the streets of Chicago to the inside of the convention hall during the 1968 Democratic National Convention. Several journalists, including CBS's Mike Wallace, were roughed up on the convention floor.

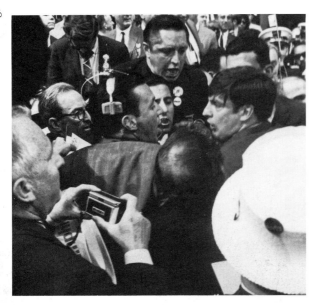

in the last couple of years, a lot of it stemming from my background in satellites at PBS. PBS was in the forefront of using satellites to transmit network programs.

The fundamentals remain the same: clarity, good writing, fairness, and a sense of doing what's important. But with the new stuff, we can bring the world onto the screen.

Grossman's presidency at NBC News has brought about a fundamental change in the way the network covers news. "There are two philosophies," Grossman said.

My predecessor, Reuven Frank, who is one of the great news people of television, came to it as a producer. His philosophy, which is a very legitimate one, is that each program is its own entity and enterprise and should be allowed to do its own thing. If you don't like the program, you change the producer. The executive producer is king of that domain.

My philosophy is more of a teamwork news division, an NBC news–wide operation. Programs are very separate, but there is also a great deal more integration. We don't have a specials unit that is separate from the rest of the

enterprise. If we're going to do a special, the theme should be integrated as much as possible into the *Today* show and the *Nightly News,* so that the special doesn't get just its one hour on the air, a blip of critical acclaim, and then disappear.

As another example, he cited NBC's trips to the Soviet Union and China. "We put together our travels so that everybody participates—the effort is to clarify and open up, provide a greater understanding throughout the NBC News schedule."

As far as local news competing with the network goes, Grossman said,

Everybody's got that completely cockeyed, in my judgment. To understand what's happening, you have to know a little bit about the history of television news, which is not all that long. I would divide it into three eras.

The first era was totally network news. That's all there was: Ed Murrow, Huntley-Brinkley. You knew more about what was happening in Moscow, Paris, Rome, London, and Southeast Asia and Korea than you did about what was happening in Queens, Manhattan, or Newark, New Jersey. There was no real local news.

Illustration: 1968—after the race riots broke out in New York City, Paterson, Newark, New Jersey, and Bridgeport, Connecticut—I had my own company, and I put together a group of television people, an integrated group and some Wall Street people, and challenged the license of WPIX, Channel 11, which was owned by the New York *Daily News.* They had no TV news there of any respectability. We said that we were going to have a station in New York that would explain New York, that would have an hour of local news every night. The first issue raised against us at the FCC was the unreality of our news-programming proposal. Everybody knew that if you did an hour of local news a night you'd go bankrupt, because nobody would watch.

Then, starting in about 1970, you had an era of a tremendous explosion in local news, as stations realized that it was cheaper than buying entertainment programming, more reliable, important to their image, and very commercial. Advertisers would buy it because people would watch it.

North Carolina Senator Sam Ervin, chairman of the Senate Watergate Committee, formally opened the Watergate hearings on May 17, 1973. Gavel-to-gavel coverage of the hearings throughout the spring and summer taught a remarkable television civics lesson. The hearings provided an unexpected boost to public television, which successfully rebroadcast the hearings at night.

You had a very quick growth, which accounts for the twinkie, blow-dried stuff. There was no tradition, no journalistic background, no sophistication.

Now, in the 1980s, which I would describe as the third era, oddly enough, you have a much greater—and I think much healthier—balance between network and local. What's happening on the local side is not expansion, which is over, but a consolidation of local news.

He points to a decision by WABC in New York to move the network's *World News Tonight with Peter Jennings* from seven P.M. to six-thirty, replacing it at seven with the game show *Jeopardy.* The significance of that decision was, Grossman said, "to cut out a half hour of local news. . . . In most markets, the concentration is on improving the quality of local news, developing a journalistic tradition—a tabloid tradition, but a good tradition.

"So what we're seeing now is a much healthier balance, an expansion of network news and a sorting out of what our roles are." He referred to the

White House chief of staff until his resignation in
1973, H. R. "Bob" Haldeman was one of the many
witnesses whose testimony made the 1973 Senate
Watergate hearings the most compelling daytime drama
on television.

News Mission Study, an NBC-commissioned research paper on what people want of local and network news: the networks for national and
international reports and local stations for local
news and national and international headlines. As
a result, Grossman said, the networks' job is to get
away from being a headline service. "What we have
been doing over the last couple of years, which is
one reason why I think we've been succeeding, is
to provide more insight, perspective, and context
with the major stories—fewer, longer stories, with
a leading correspondent reporting on the scene."

That, Larry Grossman believes, is part of the
reason why NBC News has been number one in the
ratings.

ROBERT SIEGENTHALER

Over his twenty-seven years at ABC News, Bob
Siegenthaler has held a succession of jobs and been
an eyewitness to much of our modern history. Currently, he is the vice president of news practices,
which he describes as "a multi-umbrellaed title. I
suppose the most analogous parallel would be in-
spector general in the army, somebody who looks
independently into situations to see whether policy
is being followed in the way we gather and report
news. If I detect we are departing from policy, I can
take some action to correct it." Siegenthaler tries to
head off trouble before it happens and investigates
alleged transgressions in ABC News's reporting.
His mandate includes everything from making sure
that investigative reporters are not "pursuing a trail
that is not well-substantiated" to explaining to a
producer covering the Jim Bakker story the difference between a *tryst*, an *encounter*, a *liaison*, and an
affair. He is a stickler for the proper usage of the
English language.

Siegenthaler was born in Pennsylvania, but con-
siders himself an Ohioan. He grew up in Cleveland
and attended college in Cincinnati. He was interested in journalism right from the start. "I was
always on the school papers," he said. "I was editor
of the high school and college papers, and I was
very interested in radio. I wanted to go into radio
reporting." After he graduated from college, he got
a job as a reporter on the Cincinnati *Times-Star* and
did some free-lance work in radio.

The service intervened. "When I came back from
the army, television was dawning, and I figured that
it was the coming force. Also, the newspapers were
going out, one by one, including my own. . . . So I
moved into television."

He got a job at WIIC, the NBC affiliate in Pittsburgh, now WPXI. He was there for three years. "I
started as a writer. Then I was a street reporter, and
I produced the six and eleven o'clock news—the
standard local experience."

He left Pittsburgh in 1961, moved to New York,
and joined the staff of ABC News as a writer. It was
at a point when ABC News was undergoing major
changes. ABC had been "languishing" as a news
organization, Siegenthaler said. Jim Hagerty, who
had just finished his job as White House press
secretary to President Eisenhower, was hired to
take over. "He hired a whole bunch of us," Siegenthaler remembered, including John Scali, Bill Lawrence—who was hired away from *The New York*

John F. Kennedy and Richard Nixon were both confident as they shook hands before the first televised presidential debate in 1960, but once they got in front of the TV cameras, Kennedy's assured performance and Nixon's discomfort gave the Kennedy campaign a powerful boost.

Times—and Paul Greenberg, who is a vice president at NBC News. Hagerty "got the management to make a commitment to upgrade the news.

"In the formulative stage, we had a lot of people who were very bright, but there was no infrastructure, as at CBS or NBC. Our library was nonexistent. The camera crews were contracted out from a company called Telenews for the first couple of years. We had a reputation for being slow off the mark.

"That changed rapidly as we got going." With the Kennedy administration in office, there was a lot of news to cover: Kennedy's trip to Europe in the summer of 1963, for example, including his famous *"Ich bin ein Berliner"* speech. "I was on that trip," Siegenthaler said. "We had extensive coverage there. The first time, really, that anyone could remember ABC as a full participant in the traveling circus."

Siegenthaler believes that a watershed moment

for ABC News had come almost a year earlier with the Cuban missile crisis of October 1962. "We really had it in place by that time," he said. He remembers preparing graphics about the radius of missiles launched from Soviet submarines off the East Coast.

At the time, Siegenthaler was working on an eleven o'clock national newscast that ABC produced. In spite of the possibility of nuclear war, he said, "We were totally focused on the job. I never remember being concerned for my safety. I don't think it occurred to me at the time we were discussing nuclear threats. Unconsciously, I must have thought if they blew up New York, somehow network headquarters would be spared," he said, laughing.

Siegenthaler was working with ABC News's special-events unit on November 22, 1963. When news of the Kennedy assassination arrived, he and Paul Greenberg were dispatched with correspondent Roger Sharp to Dallas. "We were told there was a plane leaving at four o'clock. We made a pell-mell drive to Kennedy [then Idlewild] Airport, driving on the median of Queens Boulevard. We made the plane. The president was dead. We did not know that Oswald had been captured. I think that must have happened while we were in the air.

"We got into this maelstrom in Dallas. Police headquarters was full of reporters. We were doing stuff at the scene. They were parading Oswald back and forth in the jail." With President Johnson and the body of Kennedy back in the capital, Siegenthaler was sent on an overnight flight back east, this time to Washington. Like the other two networks, ABC had decided to undertake nonstop coverage.

"I remember landing in Washington, going into the bureau, and somebody said, 'We're going to start broadcasting right away.' I said, 'Broadcasting what?' They said, 'That's why you're here.' We got guests and began." He worked all Saturday, into the evening. Then, for the next forty-eight hours, producers spelled each other in the Washington control room, a few hours on, a few hours off. On Sunday, Siegenthaler was on a common phone line shared by all three networks to exchange information and coordinate "pool" coverage,* when news came that Lee Harvey Oswald had been shot. "Somebody on the circuit said, 'They just shot Oswald!' I thought, 'That can't be—on a weekend of strange things, that can't be.' " His disbelief disappeared as he hastened to get pictures of the shooting on the air.

Siegenthaler's final memory of that bizarre four days in November: The ABC Washington news bureau was right on Connecticut Avenue, just around the corner from St. Matthew's Cathedral where Kennedy's funeral mass took place. ABC's control room faced directly onto the street, and Siegenthaler vividly remembers the sight of the world's leaders walking from the White House up Connecticut Avenue to the church. "We all stood up and did our best to peer between the people on the side-

---

*Pool coverage is the way in which the three commercial networks, PBS, and CNN often cover major events, such as congressional hearings and inaugurations. Logistically and economically, it would be a nightmare for each network to have cameras covering the exact same events. The networks take turns providing the cameras and engineers and the other participants share the cost in exchange for the pictures.

When a huge event covers a lot of locations, responsibilities are divided up. For example, when Pope John Paul II visited New York City in the fall of 1979, each New York television station had specific assignments: The ABC, CBS, and NBC affiliates provided cameras for certain stages of the trip; WPIX provided the coverage of the Pope's mass at Yankee Stadium, where their cameras were already in place for the Yankee home games.

walks to see de Gaulle, Haile Selassie, the king of Spain. . . . It was quite an emotional experience, being in the control room, switching, and actually watching it out the window, simultaneously."

Siegenthaler was the pool producer for several of the flights in the Project Gemini series, including the mission when astronauts Neil Armstrong and David Scott went out of control and were forced to make an early landing in the Pacific. "That was an exciting evening. . . . They had docked with an unmanned Agena rocket and suddenly went out of

control. Armstrong undocked, thinking the Agena was the culprit, but the Gemini capsule was still spinning around. He blew the retro-thrusters in order to stabilize it, but he then had to land, because he had no backup, no way to get out of orbit if he didn't get out of orbit then. There was no recovery vessel except some destroyer that was on its way with the mail to Wake Island.

"I always thought that was one of the reasons they chose Armstrong for the first moon landing, because he was so cool in sizing up that situation. As I remember, he had only a matter of a few seconds to make a judgment before he blacked out—they were taking so many rolls and such G-forces."

Siegenthaler worked coordinating ABC coverage for the moon missions. He and his opposite numbers at NBC and CBS spent a lot of time in Houston to get "book learning" on the Apollo missions. "I can read an Apollo flight plan like a real expert, because we went to a lot of trouble to learn about the experiments and the time line of the flights and the orientation of the spacecraft toward earth views, so when they turned the cameras on from the space-craft, we could put in the proper graphics. . . . It was a very, very challenging time and rewarding. I felt I was involved in a worthwhile project and I learned a lot. I learned a lot about celestial navigation, for example." He said that many of the astronauts and the flight controllers helped the producers under-stand every step of the moon missions.

He was also on the scene for many of the events in the civil rights movement. "I produced the cover-age of the 1965 march from Selma to Montgomery, Alabama. We did the daily report, feeds to the main newscasts, and then it culminated in three hours of live coverage as the marchers reached Montgomery and went up the hill to the Capitol. George Wallace

President Jimmy Carter and Republican presidential candidate Ronald Reagan shake hands before a nationally televised debate in 1980. All too often, the substantive discussion of issues in these debates has taken a backseat to the candidates' TV images or their ability to make a quick quip.

was up in the statehouse." Siegenthaler had been expecting support from production and engineering staff who were at Cape Kennedy for a space launch, but the launch had been delayed. "Nobody from Florida ever came up, including the mobile unit. We got a very mangy rented mobile unit somewhere and put it on the grounds of the statehouse." Ever willing to experiment, he tried to get a microwave shot from an airplane of the marchers entering Montgomery. "It was successful—that's the good news.

The bad news was that it was successful for less than sixty seconds."

There are two assignments of which Siegenthaler is particularly proud. In 1972, he was the pool producer for Richard Nixon's trip to China. "Sixty-six people were assigned to the pool—twenty-two from each network." To keep a mob scene from engulfing the Chinese, the two governments and the networks agreed that all state events and other scheduled parts of the Nixon trip would be pooled.

Armed police drop into position at the Olympic Village in Munich, 1972. The hostage taking of members of the Israeli Olympic Team at the 1972 Summer Olympic Games and their subsequent massacre was one of the most gripping events in television news history. ABC, which had the TV rights to the games, rallied its sports and news departments together to cover the tragedy as it unfolded, live.

The beauty of it was that because everybody wanted to go, we got the cream of the three networks' crops. It was like Noah's ark, and it's always very satisfying to have an all-star group.

There was a certain exotic quality about going where no Westerner had been since 1949, and there was the challenge of going to a place where broadcasting was not very far advanced. We were there five weeks prior to Nixon's arrival, and we built a television station. A CBS designer designed the layout, NBC or whoever designed the inside stuff, and an ABC guy was the chief engineer.

We flew a 707 full of gear in and set it up. You could have run it as a TV station in any of the top-hundred markets in this country. It was worth millions of dollars. We used it for Nixon's five-day visit, took all our equipment, put it back on the 707, and left. The building still stands. I don't know what they use it for.

There was a real sense of pride. Everything worked. Nixon arrived, the press plane, all the people came in, the correspondents, and here we had delivered unto them a broadcast point. They went out and did whatever they wanted to, brought it in, and transmitted it. The station ran twenty-four hours a day for those five days.

The other assignment that he recalls as being particularly challenging was the House Judiciary Committee's impeachment hearings in 1974. Again, he served as pool producer. In order to get shots from behind the committee members, he said, "We built a treehouse outside. We had a little trouble convincing Congress that it wasn't a bad dream of ours. We put the skeleton work up the outside of the building, took the glass out of the windows, pointed the cameras in, shielded them in black and nobody knew they were back there. It worked out pretty well."

The potential challenges were more editorial than technical.

I was determined that there would be no influence on the coverage. Everybody was very sensitive to the historical

nature of it. We were going to cover the Rodino impeachment committee whatever they were doing.

There was a school of thought that television had gotten Nixon, and so I remember telling my director, "You've got to be careful of the editorializing of shots. We're going to play it right up the middle, not have a shot of anybody of one camp or the other going, 'Tsk, tsk, tsk . . .' or clapping his forehead in disbelief." This was going to be done in a decorous way. I gave that speech every day of the coverage. "Let's not be a part of the story. Let's just cover what's going on."

I was also very, very attuned, unnecessarily so, to undue pressure on us from the White House or Congress. We had a disagreement over whether somebody would be in the truck with us as a technical adviser. I had a strong rule that there was not going to be anybody in the mobile unit who wasn't in the pool. I was all fired up to do my [John] Peter Zenger number, but everybody took no for an answer right away. It surprised me. I must have expressed it forcefully.

In 1979, when Iranian students seized the American Embassy in Teheran, Siegenthaler was director of planning at ABC News. "It's a terrible

The 444-day Iranian hostage crisis led to such an increased demand for news that ABC News developed a late-night program, America Held Hostage, *just to cover the ongoing story. The program evolved into ABC's popular* Nightline, *anchored by Ted Koppel.*

The students who seized the American Embassy in Teheran in November 1979 knew how to use television to their advantage. The militants bargained with the networks for interviews and film of their American hostages. Friends in the United States monitored how the story was being covered by American television and reported back to the leaders of the takeover.

job, because you make plans and everybody ignores them." ABC News President Roone Arledge came up with the idea of doing a nightly newscast on the hostage crisis. "They said, 'Bob, you do this for a while,'" Siegenthaler recalled. "I did seventy-seven straight nights." The series, titled *America Held Hostage,* became the successful news program *Nightline.*

"It was a lot of fun, because with no mold and no expectations, we did whatever we wanted. I used to wait until nine o'clock to make up my mind about what we were going to run at eleven-thirty. My staff hated that.

"Since there was no group in place, I picked veterans I'd known from various years, and we

An ABC News camera was present in June of 1985 to capture a horrifying image. An armed terrorist held a gun on TWA pilot John Testrake during an interview from his plane, which had been hijacked to Beirut. Although one passenger was murdered, Testrake, his crew, and the remaining passengers were eventually released after days of negotiations and intensive television news coverage.

formed this little band for a short period of time. Little did they know . . ."

He enjoyed doing the show—it was a break from his planning job, for one thing, but it also offered an opportunity to do more than simply report the news. "I really am hung up on the idea that television can be a force for illuminating—I shy away from saying educating—but certainly illuminating facts and illuminating viewers on a subject. I thought we were doing that."

He thinks a lot about the need for television to present the news with a little more depth.

The focus pieces on the Brinkley show and some of the focus pieces on *Nightline* that set up the discussions are good.

I think there's a hunger in the viewership to be informed. Instead, it has now become the television wisdom that it has to be entertaining, and so entertaining it's not informative anymore. The scenes change rapidly to "hold your interest." I think there's going to be a time when the pendulum comes back to a more discursive style.

Reuven Frank [of NBC] is one of the few practitioners who still does a sixty-minute documentary with a story line, where it unfolds and it's interesting; you're learning things, and you have to bring something to it in order to see it. It's not going to be flash and dash and glitzy, and it won't have a rock track, but it will tell you something.

Like Fred Friendly, Siegenthaler vehemently believes that television is much more than a visual medium. "Any fool can point a camera at something," he said. "That's why a good correspondent

Coverage of the space shuttle program had become so routine that the Cable
News Network was the only TV news organization on the air live when the
space shuttle Challenger exploded just seconds after its launch on January
28, 1986, killing all seven astronauts on board. Within minutes, the networks
suspended daytime programs to bring news of the tragedy to a shocked
American audience.

One fifth of the world's population—720 million people—watched live as
American astronauts Neil Armstrong and Edwin Aldrin set foot on the surface
of the moon in July 1969, a remote broadcast from 250,000 miles in space.

is necessary. You need somebody to say what the significance of the picture is, or you'll never know. One picture may be worth a thousand words, but a picture without any words is not necessarily conducive to understanding."

BILL MOYERS

Of all the journalists working in television news today, probably Bill Moyers comes closest to following in the tradition of Edward R. Murrow: in-depth, thoughtful reporting and analysis that respect the intelligence of the viewer. Journalism that is not afraid to take a stand. A voice of the television industry, sometimes supportive and laudatory, at other times critical and discomforting.

Like Murrow, Moyers never anchored a nightly television newscast. In order to achieve the kind of serious journalism at which he excels, he has moved restlessly back and forth between public and commercial television. A former theology student, he sees television as a bully pulpit for ideas and opinions but has grave reservations about how it is being used today.

Moyers was raised in Marshall, Texas. He worked his way through college at a number of jobs, including newspaper reporting. He went to work for Senator Lyndon Johnson, and when Johnson became Kennedy's vice president, became involved in the creation of the Peace Corps, eventually being named deputy director.

Moyers was in Texas when Kennedy was assassinated in 1963. Rushing to Dallas, he got a note to Johnson saying, simply, "I'm here if you need me." Now the president, Johnson got Moyers on board Air Force One and into the White House.

Moyers served in a variety of posts during the Johnson Administration: special assistant, speechwriter, chief of staff, and finally, press secretary. The experience gave him an insight into the machinations of American political power unparalleled by any other television journalist.

Moyers left Washington in 1967 to become the publisher of *Newsday*. His on-air career began four years later in 1971, as the host of a public television series called *This Week*. A year later, *Bill Moyers' Journal* began.

It was in the course of working on the *Journal* that the distinctive Moyers style emerged: a combination of documentary essays on subjects ranging from racism in a New York City neighborhood to the immorality of Watergate, and "conversations"—one-on-one, lengthy interviews with such people as Archibald MacLeish, Barbara Tuchman, Henry Steele Commager, and Robert Penn Warren.

Bill Moyers left public television twice in his career to go to work at CBS News; the first time was in the mid-seventies, when he was named chief correspondent and editor of *CBS Reports*. He came back to public TV in time for the 1980 presidential campaign and returned to CBS in 1981, working on the production of several fine documentaries (including the extraordinary *The Vanishing Family: Crisis in Black America*) and providing commentary on *The CBS Evening News with Dan Rather*.

Although Moyers was making a salary some ten times greater than what he made at public TV, he was only getting about a twentieth of the airtime. The dilemma was multifaceted: A major commercial network offers much more exposure for a reporter's work than PBS does, but the network is disinclined to give that time—talking heads and full-length prime-time documentaries draw neither big profits nor large audiences. What's more, Moyers was disturbed by the turmoil at CBS News; the budget

Charles Kuralt anchors the CBS weekend newscast Sunday Morning, *but he is best known for his* On the Road *reports. For more than twenty years, Kuralt has traveled all over the country, seeking the offbeat stories that say something telling about the American character.*

250

Ever since it went on the air in 1952, the Today show has used television technology to take its early-morning viewers around the nation and the world. Anchor Bryant Gumbel and co-anchor Jane Pauley have taken the show to China, the Soviet Union, Australia, and on a 2500-mile train ride through the American heartland.

In January 1972, a confident Richard Nixon talked with CBS News White House correspondent Dan Rather. During the course of the Watergate affair, Rather would become Nixon's most visible and outspoken network-news adversary.

The executive producer Don Hewitt (center) and the reporting team that has made CBS's 60 Minutes *the most successful and profitable news program in television history: (clockwise from left) Mike Wallace, Ed Bradley, Morley Safer, Harry Reasoner, and Diane Sawyer.*

ABC's Barbara Walters is known for her ability to snag an interview with virtually anyone in the world. Particularly noteworthy have been several conversations with Cuban Premier Fidel Castro.

cutbacks and layoffs taking place in the wake of Ted Turner's unsuccessful CBS takeover attempt and changes in leadership at the network.

Finally, Moyers was unhappy with what he saw as an increasing tendency at the network news divisions to opt for the flashy image or the punchy one-liner rather than comprehensive reportage that attempts to place a news story in its proper context.

"I came into the fishbowl, which is the command post of the *Evening News*, one afternoon, and I noticed the producers and executives were watching a satellite feed from abroad," he said.

One of the foreign bureaus was sending a report, possibly for use on the broadcast that evening. A producer looked at it and said, "That's not news." Another producer said, "But it looks like news." The executive producer said, "Then we'll use it." And they did.

Now what's wrong with that? First of all, it wasn't the best essence of what we could get about reality. More importantly, certain people might look at that and make up their minds as to what to do as citizens about what they saw, or what to do as government officials about what they saw. If you pass off news that is not news, you're as guilty of defrauding the public as somebody who sells a can opener that doesn't have a point.

That's the danger in letting the manipulative techniques

While working for CBS News, Bill Moyers was involved in the creation of several notable news documentaries, including the CBS Report: The Vanishing Family—Crisis in Black America. *Moyers went into the streets of Newark, New Jersey, to talk with unmarried fathers and mothers about the deterioration of black family life in America.*

of entertainment and show business decide what you're going to put on the air as news. The willingness to fall back on the picture alone is at the heart of the malaise that afflicts commercial television. A picture by itself explains nothing. Journalism means going back, looking at that picture and finding out what it means.

Journalism is about things that are important. It requires analysis. It involves interpretation. It's not just simply showing us what can be shown. It's trying to help us understand the meaning of it. There ought to be ten minutes of reporting for every minute you show on the air. You should spend a lifetime at the Pentagon if you're going to explain an arms proposal. Reporting is not just getting a picture and writing a catchy, cutesy caption for it. It's connecting seemingly unrelated events.

There is a fundamental fallacy in the network news. The reason that they're all suffering and losing viewers is not because of the rise of local news, but because they haven't come to terms with that fundamental flaw that exists at the heart of the seven o'clock newscast. "Beware the terrible simplifiers," as one historian said. They have twenty-one and a half minutes for the news reports, not thirty. Commercials take almost a third of the time. You cannot deal with the complicated issues of our day in two and a half minutes of a tightly compressed, highly edited, flashy report in which the basic assumption is that you've got to keep the audience beating along or they won't stay with it. The cost of that fallacy is that because they're trying to do so much in such limited time and keep it hustling that they are oversimplifying and underrevealing the importance of what is being reported.

The other fallacy with the news is that if you operate wholly in a commercial environment, in which the purpose is to entertain people, then you reduce all subjects and all talk to the level of entertainment. Sports become entertainment. Religion becomes entertainment. Politics become entertainment. And the purpose of entertainment is to please and amuse people, to keep them moving and not thinking. So you have evening newscasts which are treating everything as conflict and entertainment. You get people speaking in "sound bites." Politicians learn to speak not in terms of issues or ideas but in terms of "what will get me seven and a half to thirteen seconds on the evening news." When that happens, you begin to get God as seen by the tele-evangelists. You begin to get great issues of arms control and civil war in Central America as interpreted on the evening news. You don't really get a complex view of the reality that we must think ourselves through as citizens in order to cope with the accountability and responsibility that democracy demands."

Moyers believes that the problems he sees in the network news are endemic of all commercial television. "Every manager or owner I know in commercial television now simply accepts television as a by-product of the merchandising process," Moyers said.

A graduate of the Chicago school of tough, street-smart journalism, Frank Reynolds, the late ABC News anchorman, was highly regarded for his reporting skills and passion for a good news story.

That changes how you regard the people for whom you're producing or creating television. They're there to be hustled, to be seduced, to be sold something that somebody wants to sell. It changes altogether your sense of your mission, your purpose or your obligation to the viewer. You're not thinking of that person's imagination, that person's spirit, that person's soul. You're thinking of that person's income standard and status in life, his or her ability to buy what it is you're selling, not of that person as a thinking, authentic, seeking, inquiring human being. He or she becomes just one more object manipulated for the sale. That changes the environment in which you create as well as what it is you create. That's the way commercial television is being run today.

Flip from one channel to the other and you will see there

the results of people who sit back in advertising agencies and corporate boardrooms trying to imagine what it is that will allow them to reach the largest possible audience. America's full of entrepreneurs and hustlers and merchants and salesmen and others trying to give people what they want. There is too little in America of the creative artist, the creative journalist, the person who's willing to take a risk and fail, to give people what is good, what is excellent, and what is necessary. I was raised on a little newspaper whose editor said, "We're paid every morning to come to work and try to help people know what's important in the world. We try to get it from the wires and from our own reporting and we try to put it together so that busy people have a sense of what's important. What they don't know could kill them—whether it's the Nazi invasion of Belgium and Poland or the Japanese invasion of Manchuria and the Philippines. Journalists are supposed to do that."

There's a certain amount of elitism in this. I apologize for it, but I accept it. Every society needs a disinterested class of people who try to say: This is important. We'd better all think about this together or we're going to wind up in a dead-end tunnel on the way to nowhere.

This same society needs a group of creative people who have the freedom to take the risks that give people the best in entertainment, the best in the performing arts, the best in drama, the best in thought. Otherwise, we'll accept the proposition that the way to make America great is to level it down, not to level it up. You must find a way to give the cranky and eccentric artist, the intuitive journalist, the writer, the producer, the creator of unusual, thoughtful, daring, and challenging television occasional outlets, or our society will simply sit back, amused and entertained, a vast crowd of passive spectators.

This is not to say that Moyers has not been moved by moments on television—both public and commercial. "I have been greatly enhanced by much that's been on commercial television over my lifetime," he said.

When I was a young man in college, I remember seeing a documentary on NBC called *The Tunnel*. It was about the effort of some citizens of East Berlin to tunnel under the wall

Robert MacNeil (left) and Jim Lehrer, the co-anchors of public television's MacNeil/Lehrer Newshour, *broadcast TV's first nightly, sixty-minute news program. Their emphasis on in-depth coverage of the news and use of live interviews has been widely credited with influencing commercial network news programs.*

256

that the Russians had put up to divide the city. It paid tribute to the desperate yearning for freedom, the human spirit daring death in order to be free. That stirred me in a way that I have not forgotten these thirty years later.

Because of television I've been to a World Series and political conventions that I couldn't attend. I was introduced to the ballet on television. I've watched examples of human heroism—we were all watching when that Air Florida crash occurred in the Potomac River a few years ago. We watched as some young man standing on the bank of that icy river dived in and swam out to rescue strangers.

Television subpoenaed the conscience of the nation, as Martin Luther King said in the sixties. It showed me Bull Connor's dogs.* It showed me how people then were willing to put themselves on the line for their rights. It's taken me to distant lands that I would never visit. It's brought into my home minds alive and alert that have touched my soul.

The root word of television is "vision from afar," and that is its chief value. It has brought to me in my stationary moments visions of ideas and dreams of imaginations that I would never personally experience. It has put me in touch with the larger world.

Despite all of the things that commercial television has the potential to provide—and has from time to time—Bill Moyers's continuing disillusionment with its current state led him to leave CBS News once again in 1986. Before he left, Moyers told *Newsweek* he put forward a proposition to CBS Broadcast Group President Gene Jankowski: resurrect the title *See It Now* (the Murrow series), give him a fifty-two-week commitment, CBS's worst time slot, and the best producers and reporters at CBS News. "At the end of one year, you decide the success or the failure," Moyers told Jankowski. "If it fails, send me a dollar in the mail. If it succeeds, give me any payment you want—no agents."

Jankowski declined and Moyers returned to public television, setting up a company, Public Affairs Television, headquartered at New York City's public television station WNET. Moyers's projects have been appearing at a fast-and-furious pace: a series of conversations about the Constitution, three-minute reports on the history of the Constitutional Convention, programs with Mortimer Adler and Joseph Campbell, documentary essays on God and politics, and an essay on the Iran-*contra* scandal. On public television, Moyers said, "if you can raise the funds, there's almost no limit to the kind of artistic or journalistic endeavor you can attempt. It's been a place where the creative journalist or the creative artist could run to the limit of his or her imagination. I think the most important part of public broadcasting is that it assumes the best about the viewer. It treats you as if you were a citizen, not a consumer. It assumes that you have an imagination and want it stoked, that you come to the experience of television to be engaged and not just indulged."

There is still a great deal lacking in public television, Moyers said.

*T. Eugene "Bull" Connor was the safety commissioner of Birmingham, Alabama, who used police dogs and high-powered water hoses on civil rights demonstrators in 1963.

We're a young medium and we are fragmented into hundreds of stations. Public television is like an army without tanks or troops. You can't go very far, very fast. Public broadcasting has not had that centralized, fundamental, perpetual source of funding that enables the artist, the producer, the journalist to plan far ahead and to promote so that we can reach a larger audience.

On the other hand, I don't think public broadcasting ought ever to aim for the large mass audience. Once you go for the largest possible audience, you go for the lowest common denominator, and you start thinking of the country the way commercial television thinks of it—as one great, mass homogenized audience—instead of thinking of America as it always has been, a variety of constituencies, each of whom is looking for something authentic which, in its total, adds up to a sum greater than its parts.

Public broadcasting is designed to serve the person who discriminates. Notice I didn't say the schooled or the elite or the educated or the privileged, but the person who discriminates, the person who knows "I need news for one thing and entertainment for another," who knows "I like drama for one reason and documentaries for another." I think public broadcasting is suffering because it's now in search of the largest possible audience, instead of seeking out those people at every level of our society who are discriminating in the use of their leisure time.

Let's face it! Television is for leisure time. There's nothing wrong with sitting back and being passive about your leisure time and wanting to be entertained. But the word *leisure* is at the root of our word education. There are many people out there who want to use their leisure time for their own edification and their own illumination. Public broadcasting had better serve those people who use their leisure time to improve their lives and their minds and their roles as citizens, or we'll be failing our main purpose, which is to be an instrument of education in the best sense of the word.

The problems of funding and the dangers of the lowest common denominator have created a programming paucity on PBS in precisely the area of Moyers's greatest interest: news and public affairs. As he would admit, it allows a big-name journalist like himself to produce a very special kind of pro-

gramming, but few others get that same opportunity. "We're not doing enough public affairs programming," he said.

WNET, the flagship station of all public television, no longer has a public affairs department. It has a performing arts department, a drama department, an acquisitions department, but no public affairs. That's because public affairs, the free and open exchange of ideas, opinions, values and conflicts are very controversial.

When's the last time you heard the people speak on public television? When's the last time you heard a really good debate on immigration from the people who are living with it down along the border of Texas, instead of from senators and congressmen with ties on, being very careful to select their words wisely? The great, raucous mob that is democracy rarely gets heard. There's too little of the conversation of democracy. There's too much that's about other countries and not enough about America, too much that's produced in other countries, not enough produced in this country. You can't get a sense of the vast and vagrant currents that run in this country by watching public television.

There's this great chasm between those of us who are in the industry and those people who depend on television as their window to the world. They often are invited to look through the window. They rarely are invited to come in the door and participate, to make public television really public.

Many are wary of public affairs programs. "Real journalism and real public affairs programs have an edge to them," Moyers said. "They tell us what we don't want to hear. They show us under the rocks, they let the light shine in. Corporations don't want to pay for them. They're controversial. I know of one corporation that pulled its funding from my series because I did a debate on Big-Business Day, when big business was being challenged a few years ago. I know another corporation that threatened to bring the house down on WNET for an unfair—by

Newsreel film of the quadrennial Democratic and Republican presidential nominating conventions was broadcast on television as early as 1944. By the fifties and sixties, gavel-to-gavel coverage was the norm on the three commercial networks. In 1980, however, they decided only to provide live coverage of convention highlights.

its definition—picture of its operations in a foreign country."

Neither, Moyers said, is the money for such programs forthcoming from other sources—including the viewers. "Too many viewers are getting a free ride on public broadcasting," he said. "You wouldn't think of stopping at a kiosk on the corner and picking up a magazine without paying for it, would you? And yet people are tuning in to public television all the time, bringing that video magazine into their homes without paying for it. We don't have a central source of uncontaminated funds, funds that come with no strings attached in order to provide the journalism and public affairs on which a free and informed citizenry depend. That's a real failure on our part."

It is the way of people like Moyers to call us out on our failings, to remind us of how much there is to do, the broken promises and the unfulfilled possibilities of television. When you have a vision of what could be, it's hard to accept what gets by on a day-to-day basis. "Saul Bellow's character Herzog says in Bellow's novel that the people who come to evening classes are only ostensibly looking for culture," Moyers said. "They're really in search of clarity, meaning, and truth. People out there, he said, are hungry, they're dying." It's no metaphor, he says. "They're dying for want of something authentic at the end of the day. Television *can* give them something authentic. It can put them in touch with other, real human beings. Out of this society of individualized atoms—all of us living inside our own walls, behind our own doors, watching our own screens—it can create a sense of community. It can empower us, energize us, make us see that we, too, are a part of the whole enterprise and have a place in it."

There's reason for optimism, Moyers said. "Most of the time, commercial and public television hasn't lived up to expectations. But you know what? We're only sixty years old, twenty-five years old in terms of our knowledge of the techniques. I think we're probably just about twenty-five percent down the road to our maturity. I still believe that in response to the driven urges of people, television will rise to the occasion of becoming a theater of the imagination, of civic acts of imagination, that make us all part of the play."

9. SPORTS

In the early days of television, technology was limited. TV was more suited to sports action on a small scale. Boxing and wrestling were ideal events to cover.

rom the very beginning sports have been enormously important to television, and television has had a decided impact on sports, even down to the color of the uniforms. Television veteran Burke Crotty remembers persuading the boxing commissioner to have one boxer wear white trunks with black stripes and the other black trunks with white stripes, so that the early, primitive cameras could get a decent picture.

Even then, television could get in the way. "I recall doing a track meet," Crotty said.

We didn't have enough light to get a picture with the iconoscope camera, so I had spotlight operators go to work in all the spotlight baskets in Madison Square Garden. They focused on the runners, and we discovered that as the lights came up, the runners speed up and the timing of all the races went to pot. We had to cancel the races, put out the lights, and let them run them all over again. We never did cover track until we got better cameras and we could function without having that extra light.

In the early days, the cable that runs to the camera was almost two inches around. There were thirty-one conductors in there, and the slightest strain on that cable would break one or more of those conductors. We rarely ever went out to what we called a setup, to put out the cables and so forth, without breaking some of these conductors. We'd have to sit down, find the breaks, patch them, and put them back together.

It was especially troublesome at the horse races. At Belmont Park, we were not allowed to lay a cable on the ground. They had to be run through the trees to the camera positions and back to the truck. We always had broken cables. The result was that we had to be there at three o'clock in the morning to set up to do a job at three in the afternoon. Many's the day I started with one camera because that was the only camera cable they had that was not broken.

Crotty also claims at least partial credit for one of television's most popular sports. "I made an ar-

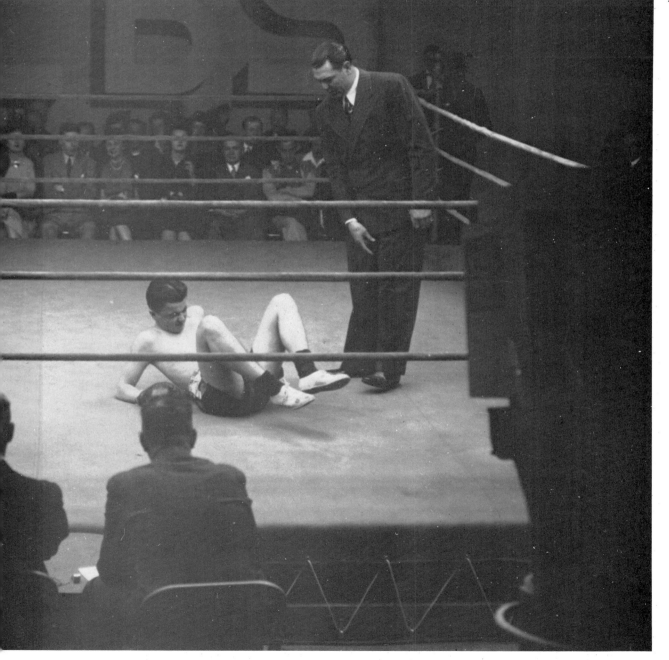

Two NBC cameras side by side cover a football game during the early years of the network's sports coverage. Breakdowns were common. According to director Harry Coyle, "You always had to have two cameras on the fifty-yard line because the equipment was unreliable. You had to protect your basic shot."

rangement to put wrestling on television one night in 1940," he said.

The chap I worked for in those days was furious when he heard about it. He walked up to my desk and said, "How many of these did you agree to do?"

I said, "Six." I had agreed to do six nights of wrestling from a hall out in Brooklyn.

He turned to me and said, "Get out of it. I won't allow it on my air."

Well, I didn't know it was *his* air, but he made that pretty clear in a hurry. I went out to the promoter, who looked at me and said, "I will let you out of five, but one you will do."

I said, "I won't do it."

He said, "You go talk to your lawyers." So I went to the lawyers, and the first chap said to me, "Well, who was there when you agreed to do this?" I told him, and he said, "That settles it; you had witnesses. You will do it." And I did it.

It was going to be on a Thursday night. Thursday noon, the man I worked for came to my desk. He said, "You do a nice job tonight, and don't come in tomorrow."

I said, "What do you mean?"

He said, "You're fired after this show."

So I went out and I did it, and the next morning I was sitting at home, and after a while the phone rang. It was this man. He said, "The least you can do is get in here and answer some of the phone calls!" It was the most successful thing we had ever put on the air, up to that point, and so we wrestled for ages after that. For five or six years, wrestling was one of the very favorite programs on television in America.

Many people bought their first television sets just to watch wrestling and other sporting events. Local saloonkeepers installed TVs to lure sports fans as customers. There was another reason why sports were so common on television. "Sports weren't very expensive in those days," CBS chairman William S. Paley said, succinctly. "We had to be very careful about how we spent our money. We weren't over-burdened with money, so we did a lot of sports."

Today, televised sports are a bigger spectacle than ever, a staple of the networks and cable, with entire channels—ESPN and SportsChannel, for example—devoted to nothing but sports programming. The technology has become astoundingly sophisticated. Tiny cameras and microphones can be placed on the yachts competing for the America's Cup, inside a car racing in the Indianapolis 500, even on the head of a runner in the New York City Marathon. Freeze frame, slow motion, instant replay, colorful graphics—many of the techniques developed by television sports producers, directors, and engineers are now used by television news divisions as well.

This increase in technology and the depth of coverage are two reasons that the costs of sports have skyrocketed. Another factor is the cost involved in buying the rights to professional games. In 1987, the three commercial networks and ESPN paid $1.4 billion for the rights to carry National Football League games through the 1989–90 season.

We may have reached the point where we are oversaturated with televised sports. The network sports divisions are not the profit centers they once were—the audience is becoming fragmented—and advertisers who used to depend on the sports audience—car manufacturers and breweries, for example—are looking elsewhere for places to sell their products. Beer drinkers watch MTV too, and cars aren't bought only by guys sitting around watching the ball game.

But the confrontational, black-and-white, good guy/bad guy nature of a game means that sports will always be a part of television. Television critic Ron Powers said, "Sports is the most successful programming on American television," because "it has all the elements of drama, of storytelling. It taps into a very ancient and primitive hunger on the part of the audience." Sports producer Don Ohlmeyer added, "Sports is entertainment. Sports is not the Holy Grail; it is not doing brain surgery; it is not wiping out hunger in India. It is flat-out entertainment."

HARRY COYLE

Images emblazoned in a baseball fan's memory:

- The Yankees beat the Dodgers in game five of the 1956 World Series—Don Larsen pitches a no-hitter, and catcher Yogi Berra jumps into his arms.
- Carlton Fisk hits a twelfth-inning homer in game six of the 1975 Series, giving the Red Sox a 7–6 victory—he watches the ball in flight and waves his arms, willing it into fair territory.
- The incredible comeback of the Mets in games six and seven of the 1986 World Series.

If you watched these games on TV, the images came to you courtesy of a director named Harry Coyle.

Coyle has worked in the TV business for more than forty years. NBC Sports Executive Producer

With just a handful of cameras transmitting to a few thousand viewers in homes and saloons, NBC broadcast a baseball game from New York's Polo Grounds.

Michael Weisman describes Coyle as the "Abner Doubleday of televised baseball." He said that Coyle has "set the standard by which all baseball coverage has been measured and will continue to be in the years ahead."

Baseball is Coyle's specialty—he was made NBC's coordinating producer of baseball in 1984—but it is only one of the many kinds of sporting events he has covered. He has directed twenty-six

Rose Bowls, twelve U.S. Open golf tournaments, and twelve NCAA basketball championships.

He was born in Ridgewood, New Jersey, and raised in Paterson. He was working as a project engineer at Wright Aeronautical when World War II began. He enlisted and became a bomber pilot with the Eighth Air Force, based in England. He flew B-24 Liberator bombers on over thirty-five missions, bombed Berlin, and was shot down twice. At

the end of the war, he went back to his old job.

Television was something new. "I saw an occasional telecast," he said. "Of course, nobody had sets. They were all in bars. It was still experimental."

A friend who had been registered 4-F during the war had a job at the Allen B. Du Mont Laboratories in Passaic, New Jersey. At night, he worked at WABD, Du Mont's TV station in New York. Six months after Coyle had returned to work, his friend told him there was a job open at WABD as a cable pusher. Coyle took it. His parents weren't crazy about the decision. "I was making $150 a week in my job at Wright Aero, and I went to work in television for $41.40. But the job I had was going no place up, maybe down, in fact, because Wright was a war contractor. It was obvious that television was the thing of the future."

It was a rough-and-tumble time. "Everybody did

Even though he was at the game, veteran NBC sportscaster Lindsay Nelson kept his eye on the TV monitor as he telecast basketball coverage live from courtside.

everything. There were no firm jobs. Advancement could be overnight." Coyle worked on the crew for about eight months and then went into production. He had a lot of studio assignments, but primarily it was "remote production—outside work. I covered MacArthur's return to New York, when he had the big parade, the 1948 political conventions in Philadelphia, inaugurations in Washington. If the Knights of Columbus were having a big affair at the Waldorf, we'd go there and cover the speeches. We used to cover the Easter parade up Fifth Avenue. Put a mobile unit out, interviewed people, things like that—man on the street."

And sports:

Sports is very important today to the network but it's only a part of the network. You have prime time, news telecasts, *Today* shows, *Tonight* shows, soap operas, sports. In the

early days, sports had a much larger function. Sports was the main factor to entice people to buy sets. That was due to the Joe Louis fights, the Army-Navy game, and in 1947, they started with the World Series.

People thought we were wonderful just to get a picture from Yankee Stadium to New Jersey. It was the crudest thing you ever saw. If you tried that today, people would say, "What are you, nuts?" As the equipment changed, people got more demanding as to what they'd accept as a good show.

Today, you hardly ever see a show lost. There might be a microwave or satellite failure or something like that; but to see a show go to complete black is unheard of. Well, in the first year we were doing remotes, if we were doing a two-hour boxing match, we'd be in black or have a slide up with two boxing gloves half the time while we tried to repair the equipment and get back on the air.

Coyle was not a huge sports fan, but he chose to concentrate on sports television for two reasons. For one, he missed the excitement of his war experiences: "It was hard to settle down." Television was "action and aggressive and everything else. It wasn't a nine-to-five job.

"Second, I noticed even in the early days that there were phases. Western shows were popular for a couple of months, then history shows. I felt sports would *always* be important, like the news. It would be a sure thing.

"It paid off. I've been in the business forty-one years. Never lost a day's salary."

Coyle became a director at Du Mont. "I'd say the first directing I did was boxing and wrestling. From there I went on to baseball and football and everything else."

In the beginning, he said,

Creativity was just as important in sports as anyplace else. Only it wasn't recognized like it is when you see a play or a movie. Actually, the innovation and creativity in sports were more demanding because nobody had set up any procedures. Who knew what to do? What kind of camera shots to take, what procedures, what sequence of continuity? It was all trial and error.

You were working with a lot of equipment that was put together with rubber bands and gum. To try something new, you had to create the ability to do it. Don't let appearances on screen fool you. There was a lot of blood behind it and thought and long hours.

We had a lot more injuries, because we did everything ourselves. We climbed up on roofs, we did our own microwaving.

Coyle remembers pieces falling off buildings and hitting crew members, feet going through tar-paper roofs, ladders falling: "One time, we were over at Seton Hall University doing a basketball game, and a bunch of us were going to put a microwave on top of the gym to send the signal back to New York. We asked them how to get to the roof." They were pointed toward a door. "Actually, what we were going into was a huge exhaust thing. Two of the guys almost passed out. . . . Everything we did in those days was rickety and temporary."

Cameras were on the primitive side, too. "In boxing, in the old days, we usually used two. Maybe three, if we got extremely lucky. In baseball, we started out with three, went to four. Originally, football was three. You couldn't extend your cameras too far in those days. We didn't have boosters or stuff like that. If you extended the cable too far, the signal would get too weak. So you could go maybe three hundred feet. Today, you can go three thousand feet. In fact, that's what held up the positioning of the center-field camera in baseball. I wanted to put a center-field camera in maybe a year or two before we actually did it in 1955. We didn't have the ability because the mobile unit most of the time was behind home plate. That was too far a run."

The same applied to football:

Below: TV sports coverage, 1946—Bob Edge, the sports director of CBS's New York affiliate, then called WCBW, provided the commentary at a basketball game broadcast live from Madison Square Garden.

As television technology improved, the coverage of sporting events could become "up close and personal," allowing viewers to see athletic performances as never before.

We started with two cameras on the fifty-yard-line. One camera maybe on the left, one camera maybe on the right, depending where you were. You couldn't be too aggressive in spreading your cameras too much. You always had to have two cameras on the fifty, because the equipment wasn't reliable. You had to protect your basic shot. Many times, you'd start with four cameras and end up with two. Emergency procedures were not emergency procedures—they were commonplace!

That's the way it went for years and years. Then you'd add a piece of equipment, the lenses would get better. The original remotes we did with one camera and one lens. We nicknamed it Dr. Cyclops. When we sent him out to do the first boxing and wrestling, we didn't fill the whole screen with a picture. It was just a circle. Then we went to the turret cameras, with four lenses on them. And the next move was to get the Zoomar lens. The pictures got better and better.

Coyle moved to NBC Sports as a staff director in 1955, and he continued to watch the extraordinary changes in sports coverage. As far as cameras go today, he said, "We have an unlimited amount—depends on what's needed. Each one of our mobile units has anywhere from seven to ten cameras on board. If we need twenty or thirty cameras, we just bring in three mobile units and marry them. It's

easy to get up to twenty-seven cameras, doing a pregame, postgame this and that. On the World Series, counting the dressing rooms, the blimp, and stuff like that, I get as many as eighteen cameras and twelve tape machines. Plus a million other toys: electronic graphics, 'slo-mo' . . .

"I counted—on most of our larger trucks, when the director sits there, he is looking at fifty-two monitors. When I do a World Series, all fifty-two are filled."

How does he keep track? "Have you ever looked in the cockpit of a big airliner?" he asked.

There's instruments all over the place. When I would walk into the cockpit of a B-24, there were about a hundred instruments, on the ceiling, all over. You learn with experience that with one sweep of the head you can tell which instrument is out of place. The same thing goes with fifty-two monitors. You don't ever try to look at fifty-two monitors at one time. But you know the monitors you're going to look at in a given situation.

When you direct a large show, especially in sports, you don't really have time to make a decision in a lot of cases. It's got to be an instinctive call. And you always put the same cameras in the same spots, whether it's fifteen or four. You start with your basics. When you do a World Series, maybe you add a lot, but your basics are still in the same spot.

We had about fourteen cameras working on game six of the World Series in '86. People don't realize it, but the instant live stuff was pretty much the same as a regular game of the week. I don't care if it's thirty cameras.

Baseball, Coyle said, is "a director's game for coverage, but it's the producer's job to follow through and come up with the insight and the inside stories, see all the little things, work with the announcers. They're equal responsibilities. The director has to be quick and take the right shots. But without a good producer, you're not going to get the great success.

"Some producers can find a story and see what's happening, little things like what's happening on the bench, the theme of the game, the reason why

A key behind-the-scenes man, Roone Arledge came to ABC in the early sixties and helped turn that network's sports division into the finest in commercial television. As the sophistication of television techniques increased, Arledge was one of the first to realize how they could be utilized to the advantage of TV sports. Slow motion, instant replays, isolated cameras, computerized graphics—all are essential to the Arledge philosophy of sports television—coverage that gives both fans and the uninitiated an unprecedented view of the action.

Professional sports commentators team up with professional athletes to provide expert coverage and analysis. (From left) ABC's Jim McKay and Howard Cosell had the assistance of champion jockey Eddie Arcaro for their broadcast of the 1978 Kentucky Derby.

With jockey Chris McCarren in the saddle, Alysheba wins the 1987 Kentucky Derby. Horse racing is a TV sport in which the actual contest is so brief, the bulk of the program is devoted to the pregame show and the victory ceremony.

274

the game's being won or lost—or maybe one of the guys is having a rough time with the manager. With some producers, that goes right over their heads."

Being involved in sports television means a wearying life on the road. "For a period of my life, I traveled every week, except vacations. You're on the road a tremendous amount of time. Because you have to give these figures on New York State income tax, I can remember out of three hundred and sixty-five days in a year, working maybe forty-eight days in New York.

"It's not bad now. Last year, I had a hundred days out of the state."

Coyle admires the new technology but believes it can get in the way of the game.

A jubilant Chris McCarren after he won the 113th Kentucky Derby—the run for the roses—riding Alysheba in 1987. Television sports technology has become so advanced, viewers could see and hear an interview with McCarren as he was still riding back from the finish line, just seconds after his victory.

For every producer and director, that's one of the greatest pitfalls you have to watch out for. We can do anything you want to the picture. We can put twelve pictures up on one TV screen. But what for? You know what I mean? We can do anything, but the only way that a new innovation should be applied to live sports is if it's a plus factor for the coverage. If it's just done to show the people that we have this piece of equipment, it's the wrong approach.

I'm not saying not to use it. We can put mikes on every ball player there is. We've got cameras the size of your thumb we can put in the catcher's mask, if they'd allow us. We can spin the picture; we can turn it upside down; we can use more special effects than you ever thought of. But how far can you go before you're losing what you primarily should be thinking about?

You must remember the basic reason you're out there: You're out there to bring all the action of a ball game in correct continuity to the public. That's the basic reason for being there. When you do a ball game, you're not doing *Star Wars*.

"The basics," Harry Coyle says, "stick to the basics."

ROONE ARLEDGE

Discussing Roone Arledge's impact on television sports, *Sports Illustrated* commented, "It is not too much to say that Arledge established sports TV as an industry."

No one has had a greater impact on the way we

276

see TV sports today. ABC Sports was not the first network to employ such technological innovations as "slo-mo" or instant replay, but under Arledge the network became the acknowledged leader in using the "bells and whistles" of video wizardry to create a greater understanding of the game.

It was Arledge who thought to point the cameras into the stands from time to time, to give the viewers at home a sense of kinship with the fans at the stadium; Arledge who developed the up-close-and-personal theme, creating a stronger viewer bond with the athletes they were watching by telling them something about the players' personal lives; and Arledge who turned television coverage of the Olympic Games into an art.

He has been with ABC since 1960, first as a vice president of the sports division, then as president, and finally as president of both the sports and news divisions. Since the Capital Cities takeover of the network, Arledge has relinquished the sports presidency, but he retains the title of group president of ABC Sports and News and responsibility for the news division.

Among his many programming innovations at ABC Sports were *The American Sportsman* and *ABC's Wide World of Sports,* which began in 1961.

"*Wide World of Sports* grew conceptually from necessity in those days," he said.

Baseball, always a fairly but not universally popular sport on television, was on all three networks, but because of the baseball league rules only forty percent of the country could see it. So we were looking for a better, year-round activity. *Wide World of Sports* grew out of that. The basic concept was that around the world people go to see events in large numbers and get very emotionally involved, but in many cases Americans either know very little about them, or have very little interest in them.

Our thought was that if, through a combination of techni-

The Roone Arledge philosophy of television sports can especially be seen in ABC's coverage of the Olympics. Imaginative graphics and profiles of the athletes are offered, giving the viewer a personal, insider's look at the competition and what it means. Pictured here is Olympic discus thrower Mac Wilkins.

278

Bjorn Borg sinks to his knees as he wins his fifth successive men's singles title at Wimbledon in 1980. One of the primary goals of TV sports producers today is to capture emotional and dramatic moments like this one, moments that once were solely the domain of sports photography in newspapers and magazines.

Players like Billie Jean King helped turn tennis, once considered a game for the elite, into a popular TV sports attraction. Television attracted many new players to tennis and opened a second career to competitors like King, who is an articulate and intelligent TV sports commentator.

cal ability and reportorial skills we could define what it is that they're attempting to do in sports around the world, as well as why it's important to the fans of these sports, then the American people would become interested.

That was proven to be true. In fact, techniques such as slow motion, stop-action, instant replays, and freeze-frames, which today are universally part of sports television, grew out of that period of trying to explain some sports that we didn't think people would understand and attempting to make the television screen have the capability that the motion picture screen and the magazines have to capture and freeze a dramatic moment—or to discover whether

someone's foot was in or out of bounds, safe or out in a baseball game.

As familiar to the American public as the phrase "up close and personal" is *Wide World's* opening montage, with its pledge to bring us "the thrill of victory, the agony of defeat."

To some extent, we were in the storytelling business when we wrote the opening of *Wide World of Sports.* We talked about the human drama of athletic competition, which basically was what we set out to capture. Our theory was that it is just as important if you're a young Russian high jumper trying to reach a certain height, or a water-skier trying to jump farther than anyone has ever jumped before. In your context, in your life, and to other people who are interested, that particular event is just as important as Jesse Owens trying to get four gold medals in the Olympics.

We had to identify that drama and make the viewer understand the context in which it takes place—something of how it feels to be there and what kind of person is attempting to do this, whether we like him or don't like him, whether we hope he makes it or he doesn't make it—what is it he is trying to achieve. And if the viewer has all of that information, then he is ready to experience the feat itself.

Another Arledge idea was *NFL Monday Night Football.*

We were very interested in having professional football as part of our sports presentation. At one point we had broadcast the American Football League, which we had helped to establish. But then it got a huge offer from NBC, so we were out of professional football for a while. Pete Rozelle, who was then and still is the NFL commissioner, and I had talked about the possibility of playing on Monday night. The idea actually came from baseball: A man named John Fetzer had tried to sell us a package of Monday night baseball games. However, we didn't think baseball had enough universal appeal with regular season games. But I was very taken with the Monday night idea, and Pete was determined to make it happen.

He had a problem: Both the other networks had to pass on

TV brought a popularity to professional football that it had never before experienced. The horizontal, across-the-field nature of the game, along with its constant, often violent action, made it a natural for the television screen.

it before we could do it. It came down to the final day, and NBC decided to pass on it. Over the objections of our affiliated stations—who thought it was going to cost us college football, which they thought was more important—and over the skepticism of most of the advertisers, we went ahead with it. And it was successful almost from the beginning, partly because we treated it somewhat as entertainment.

We knew that going in on a regular weekly basis for a football game—opposite, at the time, CBS's very, very strong Monday night schedule and NBC's movies, which were then at the zenith of their popularity—you couldn't compete with just a sports event itself. You couldn't depend on every game having great significance. And you certainly couldn't depend on having every game be close and highly competitive. So on those other nights, we had to have something to make people stay tuned and be interested.

The first person I hired for the games was Howard Cosell. Howard, a very controversial character, had done radio interviews, boxing, including Olympic boxing for us, but he had not done football. And he didn't fit into any of the standard categories: He was not a play-by-play announcer, nor was he an expert commentator who, having played the game, could articulate its nuances. He was a

The Super Bowl is super in more ways than one. Not only is the game the ultimate event in the professional football season, it is television's most expensive advertising buy. Thirty seconds of commercial time, during the 1987 championship, when quarterback Phil Simms led the New York Giants to a 39–20 win over the Denver Broncos, cost $600,000.

With cameras following every moment of the action, both on the field and in the stands, TV sports producers attempt to turn each event into a story with a beginning, middle, and end—the agony of defeat or the thrill of victory—in this case, the triumph of New York Giants Brad Benson (number 60), Phil Simms, and their teammates over the Denver Broncos in the 1987 Super Bowl.

reporter and a columnist, a dispenser of opinions, a motivator of discussion, and a stirrer-up of action.

In combination with him I hired Don Meredith, who had been a quarterback of some distinction with the Dallas Cowboys, but not one of the all-time great players. He is a man of a southern, country kind of humor; he and Howard were natural foils for one another. That provided an element of entertainment to tune in for, regardless of how good the game was.

It worked. It was the third or fourth game in the season, which should have been very competitive: St. Louis and Dallas at that time were the two best teams in their division; they were playing in Dallas, and the Cowboys were just awful. Don Meredith, describing what it was like to be a losing quarterback in Dallas, became the butt of Howard's sarcastic humor all during the game. The badinage between the two of them became something that the American people really loved. The chemistry worked. I recall the game ending something like thirty-three to nothing, and it was up against a big Johnny Carson special and something else. It should not have done well at all—but it did do very well. We knew from that time on that it was going to work.

Sometimes, critics felt that the Arledge flair was being flashed a little too far, with coverage of so-called "trashsports" and such "nonevents" as *The Battle of the Network Stars.* Arledge denies this.

"I've never accepted *trash* as a valid adjective to apply to sports," he said.

These events grew from a competition that we had on the air for a while called *The Superstars,* which started off as fun and ended up as fun. It was never intended to be taken seriously. We took away the seriousness by not allowing athletes to compete in their specialties.

To take such activities as serious sporting events and to compare them with anything else misses the point. It's like comparing a soufflé with a roast duck. We weren't pretending it was anything other than what it was. I was troubled by people judging us by the fact that we would put on a program like that. That's analogous to criticizing a great

When batting superstars Mickey Mantle and Willie Mays joined the major leagues in 1951, team owners were alarmed at the effect television was having on stadium attendance. Today, American and National League owners and players are dependent on the revenues generated by the sale of broadcast rights. Games are scheduled around the demands of TV, and teams have even changed cities to take advantage of lucrative television package deals.

newspaper for running recipes and crossword puzzles on Sunday.

We think of such programs as a little garlic in the stew. The *Wide World of Sports* includes crazy little nooks and crannies where people do strange things. For example, the demolition derby, where people bang cars into each other until only one car was left standing. It was a crazy, foolish, but interesting little event that we'd devote something like ten minutes to out of an hour and a half once a year—or arm wrestling, where literally the strongest men and women win. You could see the same thing in a barroom.

He also vehemently rejects the thought that "the thrill of victory, the agony of defeat" phrase might be considered overblown.

I think it's an apt description of the emotional clash that takes place in a sporting event. I do think that if we hadn't come along with it someone else would have. However, all around the world others have contributed, with us, to this "we're number one" kind of attitude that anyone who

With the close-up camerawork and storytelling abilities of TV sports, viewers could share New York Met Ray Knight's excitement and elation as he hit a home run in the final game of the 1986 World Series.

finishes second, no matter how nobly, has somehow failed. I think it has gone far beyond anything that I approve of, recommend, or admire. I particularly find that with the Olympic Games. I don't know how you deal with it. It's one thing at a college football game, with two traditional rivals cheering and yelling and ridiculing each other and waving banners and all that. Carried over into the international field in the Olympics, where nationalism plays such a major part and politics is so prevalent, I think the elements are there for all sorts of dangerous things we can't even imagine today.

Arledge is fully aware of the effect television has had on sports financially. "American football could survive without television coverage, but it would have to restructure itself financially from top to bottom," he said, "although I don't think we've done very much to the game itself by televising it, that is, any structural changes in the game. But certainly the financial and economic structure of all sports—the Olympics are probably the most dra-

College basketball, like the 1987 NCAA championship in which Indiana beat Syracuse by one point, has become a staple of the TV sports schedule, but according to NBC Sports Executive Producer Michael Weisman, the popularity of sports is cyclical. NCAA basketball is not as big a ratings success as in past years. That could easily change, Weisman said. Professional NBA basketball was in a slump just a few years ago. Now it is once again popular.

matic example—have been affected by television far more than they should. If television money was suddenly extracted from sports around the world, the whole edifice would collapse. On the other hand, it would rebuild itself. There'd just be lower salaries, and they'd start all over again."

What's the appeal?

I think the fundamental appeal of sports on television is the same as it is in the stadium or anyplace else. It's an artificially contrived set of circumstances designated to test people under pressure, to do feats that in themselves are not worth very much, but which given a set of rules, become very important. Television particularly magnifies the human dimension of these people's achievements under those stressful conditions.

In terms of impact on viewers, sports on American television is incredibly important. Something like the recent 1984 Olympic Games probably moved more Americans and were seen by more people than almost anything I can think of. And that's been true of prior Olympics. These are periods in which sports has a universality. There's a large and continuing audience of Americans, as there are people all over the world, who watch sports almost as a tribal rite.

MICHAEL WEISMAN

Michael Weisman is very young to have done all that he has. Thirty-seven, he has risen through the ranks of NBC Sports more rapidly than a Sid Fernandez fastball. He was NBC Sports's youngest producer at the age of twenty-seven and was named executive producer at the age of thirty-three. He is a child of television, not afraid to use the latest techniques to tell a story.

His first memory of television sports is "running home after school at three o'clock, all the way downhill" to get home to watch the World Series. Usually, he made it in time for the fifth inning.

Directing those games was Harry Coyle, who twenty years later would become his colleague.

Sports was always an interest. "Like most young kids, I was a ball player," Weisman said. "I played Little League and enjoyed sports, like most of the kids in the neighborhood." But television was an even bigger interest, especially because Weisman's father had started out as a reporter with the Reuters news agency and then moved to ABC-TV as a show publicist. "He had shows in the early sixties like *The Untouchables, The Pat Boone Show,* and *Naked City.* I remember in the fifth and sixth grades, bringing in eight-by-ten glossies. It made me a little bit of a celebrity in my neighborhood. So it was glamorous for me growing up to be somehow associated with television."

Weisman's first job at NBC Sports was in a newly created position, assistant to the producer; the year was 1972. "At the time, we had Saturday baseball, Sunday football, and Monday night baseball. Each of those shows had a separate producer. But there was only one assistant. So what would happen was that I'd be assigned to the Saturday baseball game; after the game, the producer of the show would go home, but I would go from the Saturday game to the Sunday football game. The producer of that would go home, and then I would go to the Monday night baseball game." It was the kind of grueling schedule you can only keep up when you're young. "It was great," Weisman said. "I was twenty-two years old, traveling from city to city, going to all these games, and loving it." His energy and skill led to a rapid series of promotions: associate producer, producer, coordinating producer of baseball, and finally, executive producer of NBC Sports under NBC Sports President Arthur Watson.

Being an sports aficionado is an enormous plus

for Weisman, in more ways than one. "Enthusiasm is a key element of what we do," he said. "We even tell the announcers sometimes: If the announcers don't seem to care, why should the viewers at home care? If they're sitting there on the fifty-yard line and the feeling is conveyed to the viewer that they'd rather be someplace else, the viewer is going to think, 'This couldn't be a very important game. Why should I watch this?'

"I also think that when you're a fan, you're curious about things. A lot of the so-called innovations that I've brought to our telecasts were largely because of the fact that I'm a fan and I'm curious. We know that there are assistant coaches up at the top

Black American athletes at the 1968 Summer Olympics in Mexico City used the internationally televised stage of the games to make a dramatic protest. After winning medals in the 200-meter event, sprinters Tommie Smith (center) and Juan Carlos mounted the winners' platform and stood with their heads bowed and their fists clenched in the black-power salute during the playing of "The Star-Spangled Banner."

Personalities are as important to television sports as flashy technology. An appealing competitor, Soviet gymnast Olga Korbut gave a performance at the 1972 Summer Olympics in Munich that brought new popularity to the sport of women's gymnastics. But television sports can capture the tears and tension as well as moments of athletic triumph. Here, Korbut is comforted by a coach after a disappointing performance cost her an Olympic medal.

of a football stadium sending plays down to the field. We know they exist; we've seen a million shots of them. But what goes on up there? I said, 'I'd love to put a microphone and a camera and see what goes on up there.' Sure enough, we did."

Another key to success: "I care about the sports. If there's a sports-journalism story to do, if there's something that's a little upsetting to the viewer, it's going to be upsetting to me as a fan. So we're going to do a story about the lack of black coaches, or the fact that franchises are moving too easily, or that a player is unhappy and perhaps not performing well."

You also need a touch of the showman.

Basically, what we do is entertainment. It's relaxation, escapism. When we're doing a Saturday afternoon baseball game in the middle of July or August, people are watching it because they're fans. Very often, it's on as background noise. I picture these people sitting in mid-America: It's ninety degrees wherever they are, and they're watching the game of the week, half-snoozing on the sofa, maybe a can of beer in front of them, reading the newspaper as the game's going on. Or maybe it's the Sunday afternoon football game: It's bitter, bitter cold, and the game is on. People are huddled up in their houses, looking at the game, cheering and eating lunch.

So it's mostly entertainment. I don't kid myself. That's the primary reason people watch it. But I do have a sense of responsibility that there are certain stories—no matter how unseemly, boring, or negative—we have to address. We have an obligation to address issues. There are people at home who would rather just see the highlights of the week, the great catches and the errors and the funny things that happen in baseball. But we have an obligation to do what we think is right.

I asked Weisman about his reputation for innovation. "The best type of innovation is one where everybody wins," he said.

People recognize that it's something different, and they also recognize that it makes the telecast better, and the production people recognize that it makes their jobs easier.

An example is the ten-minute ticker. We started that in football. For as long as I can remember, the big complaint from our football audience—as at all the networks—was that there were not enough other game scores. We would tell our producers every year: more scores, more scores, more scores. It used to frustrate me that you'd see a score,

10–3, in the second quarter, and the next time you'd see that score it might be 48–47. What happened?

In the truck, the producers would be turning around to the production assistants and saying, "Have you done the scores? Give me the scores."

So I came up with the system called the ten-minute ticker. As close to every ten minutes as possible, the guys in the truck know to update the scores—made their lives easier, and it made it better for the viewers, because they know that every ten minutes they will get all the scores.

"No words necessary—just pictures" were all a TV sports commentator had to say when millions of American television viewers shared the joy of the United States hockey team's victory over the Soviet Union at the 1980 Winter Olympics in Lake Placid. The win came at a time when American morale was low; the nation was mired in the Iranian hostage crisis, and the game took place just weeks after the Soviet invasion of Afghanistan.

When the young, inexperienced South African runner Zola Budd tripped American Mary Decker at the 1984 Summer Olympics in Los Angeles, she shattered Decker's hopes for a gold medal in the women's 1500-meter race. The agonizing moment was seen over and over again in slow motion and freeze frame as TV sports analysts tried to determine how the accident had occurred.

A simple solution and one that has caught on. Another innovation of Weisman's got him more publicity than he bargained for. Weisman announced that during the network's coverage of Super Bowl XX that there would be one minute of silence during the pregame show.

There's such a lot of hype about the Super Bowl. It's such a long sports day. We had a two-hour basketball game, a two-hour pregame show, the three-and-a-half-hour game, and then a half-hour postgame. I said, "God, that's a lot of sports in one afternoon. It would be kind of nice after all this selling and all the hype coming up to the game, if we could kind of take an intermission. Relax and let everybody catch their breath." So I said, "I'm going to do that. One minute of just nothing."

We didn't even put out a press release, but it made front-page news. They called it "the bathroom break" or "the run for the toilet." Then people got outraged: "Nobody's telling *me* when to go the bathroom." It's kind of upsetting to me that after fifteen years in the business and all the Emmys and stuff, when my career's finally written up, I will be known as the Minute Man.

I think the reason it got played up so big was probably a combination of factors. One, it was the Super Bowl, and anything associated with the Super Bowl was going to be played up very big. Two, some people thought it meant one less commercial. Anything to do with commercials gets people excited; they have strong feelings about them. Three, there was probably some bathroom humor there. Those things combined to make it a much bigger story than we imagined.

Is there a thin line between innovation and gimmickry?

We did a show last year on our football pregame show called "Surprise Saturday." We said, "We don't want the producers or anybody to know who the guests will be on the show. The four announcers will bring in their own surprise guests." You can call that gimmickry, but I call it fun, interesting. Sure enough, a lot of people tuned in.

We prefer the word *innovation*. I find that usually the people who call it gimmickry—particularly at the other networks—are the jealous ones who just do the same thing week in and week out. They think that's the only way you do television. One of my mandates as executive producer is to challenge people to look at how to do things differently. Don't accept the status quo.

In boxing, for example, we started a gimmick or an innovation that I think is a public service: It struck me that whenever you go to a fight, you're constantly concerned with how much time is left in the ring, particularly if your guy is getting beat. The way the networks handled fights for years was to put the clock in to start the round, and then take it out. I said, let's leave the clock very small in the lower right-hand corner and just let it count all three minutes. People said, "You can't do that. It's too distracting." But it worked.

We started something called "Due up Next" in baseball. We thought, hey, who's coming up next inning? Put it up as you go into the commercial. Now, every local station, every network does it. When we first did it, it was a gimmick. But television is very much a copycat business.

Not all of his ideas work. Something dubbed "instant preplay," for example, that was tried during an Orange Bowl game.

I said, "Hey, let's tell the viewer before the play"—thus, "preplay"—"who the isolated camera is going to be on."* If we told them the isolated was going to be on the linebacker number fifty, they can choose to watch or not watch the linebacker in the wide shot, as they wish, knowing they're going to see a replay of him afterward. So in the wide shot, the actual play, you could kind of keep one eye on number fifty and see him get knocked down. It makes the viewer more involved in the broadcast—"I can't wait to see this replay." They're curious now on the close-up to see how blocking techniques took the guy out of the play.

It was misunderstood by the press, because after the

*The isolated is a camera that focuses on a specific player or part of the field during the play. You don't see the shot during actual play. It's stored on videotape and used usually for an instant *re*play.

Some would argue that attending an athletic event in person is the next best thing to seeing it on TV. No one in the stands could witness a moment like Greg Louganis's back three-and-a-half sommersault at the 1984 Summer Olympics as they could via television—augmented by extraordinary close-ups and slow-motion instant replay.

Orange Bowl, they said, "NBC guessed right on only thirty-three percent of their instant replays." That wasn't the object of it: to guess who was going to be involved in the play. It was to let the viewer in. But we never did it again.

Weisman wants his viewers to see and hear everything. "We sometimes feel frustrated, because the technology is there to let us mike people and to get cameras everywhere, but obviously, the leagues, to protect their sports, put limitations on us. We approached major league baseball about miking the umpire and putting a camera on the umpire's mask—small cameras here and small cameras there. The leagues stop us, maybe correctly so. I think if they would allow us to do some of these things, it would remove some of the mystique, which may or may not be advantageous. It depends on how you look at it."

It's all part of the process of telling a story in sports.

I try to remind people that doing a sports telecast is not unlike writing a story: the tease being the headline, the opening camera shot as the opening paragraph, and then you close it in the end; you finish the story. I tell our people, whatever you started with at the beginning, make sure you go back and conclude it.

I'll give you an example. CBS did the first fight with convict James Scott from Rahway Prison in New Jersey, a maximum-security prison. He was an undefeated light heavyweight. He won; CBS closed the show by saying, "So James Scott is now 17–0, the fight was in the prison, he's that much closer to winning the championship."

I produced a James Scott fight. The day before, we went to the prison. I asked James to put on the robe he would be wearing and the shorts. He threw the hood of the robe up on his head. We taped him walking through the corridors of the prison and into his cell and slammed the door. So we had that piece of tape.

When the fight ended, [NBC Sports commentator] Marv Albert said, "James Scott is now 18–0, but for inmate number 642-849"—we're showing the barbed wire, the police and guns, and the walls—"it's back to cellblock D, building three." Here's James, slow motion in the corridors of the prison, music, back to his cell, cell door slams. We went off the air.

That was the essence of the story: This is not just another fighter who won at Madison Square Garden or Sunnyside or wherever. He won; that's great; he's on network TV, but now he's back to that cell, and that's where he'll be.

Among his other duties, Weisman is looking down the road at a major assignment: executive producer for NBC's coverage of the 1988 Summer Olympics in Seoul, South Korea. "I've assigned a coordinating producer for the Olympics, because it's a year-round job day in and day out. I could not, in effect, oversee the sports division *and* the Olympics for two years. I will make all the on-the-spot decisions, in addition to the key decisions leading up to the games as to who the hosts will be, the talent we use, and the key production assignments. But I've assigned Terry Ewart as coordinating pro-

ducer, and we're going to have a huge production and technical staff, something like six hundred people. It's a major undertaking for just two weeks of broadcasts. Day after day, they're preparing for the Olympics. I'm losing sleep over it, but they're preparing for it."

The price for the Seoul games was lower than expected, and that's a good sign, according to Weisman:

particularly when you compare it to the winter games, which ABC bought. The Calgary [Alberta, Canada] games went for $309 million, and they will have approximately seventy-five hours of programming. We paid $300 million or less for the summer games and we will have 179 hours of programming. So there it is. We paid relatively the same, but we'll have at least twice as many commercials and opportunities for commercials. Plus, most people would say that the sports that you have in the summer games, by and large, are more attractive to the American audience than the winter sports and get higher ratings. The other benefit, of course, is that it's a springboard, an opportunity to highlight your new fall programming and personalities. That's a tremendous advantage.

The projection is that NBC, although not making a fortune, will make a profit on the '88 Games. So it was a good acquisition.

Why were they able to get it so inexpensively?

The market has changed. Historically, I think the summer games every four years have tripled in rights. That wasn't the case with this one. It was closer to double or less than double. I think it was just a matter of all three networks recognizing that it had gotten so expensive not only to produce, but with the rights, it was strictly the economic law of supply and demand. It's carefully planned what you can take in from commercial revenues and sales of miscellaneous properties relating to the Olympics.

It's still a lot of money! We're talking like it's chump change. It's $300 million just for the rights. It's another $100 million or more for us to produce it. When you make that

The closing ceremonies of the 1984 Summer Olympics in Los Angeles. ABC Sports paid $225 million for the TV rights to the games. For two and a half weeks, 188 hours of Olympics coverage filled the television screen.

kind of bid, you're gambling on the strength of the dollar, gambling on the American economy. NBC has economists and money people who make those kind of projections: what the dollar will be worth, how much sales people project, how much per commercial they can sell, what kinds of ratings you will have.

He doesn't think there's a glut of sports on television.

You go through cycles. The NBA is a great example. Eight or ten years ago, people said the NBA was dead. The NBA didn't have a contract with any of the networks. It wasn't getting good ratings, so you didn't see the NBA. Four years ago or thereabouts, CBS started producing the NBA games again. It's a huge success, terrific ratings, terrific profits.

College basketball has now gone through a period where most people feel there's too much on. All three networks and cable are doing it. Ratings are going down. What's going to happen with NBC is we'll do less college basketball. What happens when you do less college basketball is that eventually people want to see more.

You try to stay a step ahead. But really, the marketplace and the public determine how much sports there is, and if there's too much. For me, there's never enough.

Weisman does not believe that professional sports would collapse without television. "What would happen is that the players would certainly have to make a helluva lot less money. But professional sports existed before television. Instead of making two million dollars, players would have to make thirty thousand. And they would get by just on people coming to the games.

"Newspapers are a major source of interest. In some ways, more so than television, because you read your daily newspapers about the Yankees and Mets. If there wasn't television, as long as the newspapers and magazines were still around, you'd still go to a Yankee or Met game. I don't think sports

The raising of the Olympic flag was one of the simpler events of the Hollywood spectacle that opened the 1984 Summer Olympics in Los Angeles. Television executive producer David Wolper put on an extravaganza that featured thousands of balloons and streamers, hundreds of singers and dancers, and eighty-four pianists playing George Gershwin's "Rhapsody in Blue."

would fold. They were there before television and they'll be there after television."

But without television, Mike Weisman would be very unhappy. For him, the attraction of televised sports is that "it's live and unpredictable, with real elements of human drama and emotion that you don't necessarily get in scripted, preplanned shows. We go into every telecast as if it won't be like anything we've ever done before. We're always on the edge of our seats, getting ready to react to whatever happens live. I'm obviously a fan."

Obviously.

10. BEHIND THE SCENES

As the coolly logical Science Officer Spock, a citizen of the planet Vulcan (although his mother was an earthling), Leonard Nimoy was one of the most popular characters on the science-fiction series Star Trek.

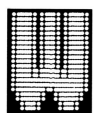hen television people talk about the "creative end" of the business, they are usually referring to the producers, writers, directors, and performers. But there are hundreds of people necessary for the success of a television show—all those names you see rolling by during the closing credits. Craftspeople with vast technical expertise—from cinematographers and production designers to the people who create the music, costumes, hair, and makeup. It is a collaborative medium, and each is responsible in one way or other for the overall look and feeling of a show: the plush legal firm of *L.A. Law*, the music-video look of *Miami Vice*, the peeling paint and soiled walls of the station house on *Hill Street Blues*.

Much of their jobs immerse these people in the day-to-day tedium associated with any kind of work. There's an old Hollywood joke: The most exciting day in your life is your first day on the set; the most boring day in your life is your second day on the set. But whether these people are working on the number one series in the country or on a pilot that's headed for the network slush pile, they take enormous pride in what they do. They are eager to talk about what they are responsible for and how they fit into the complicated production machine that cranks out hundreds and hundreds of hours of TV every year.

GERALD FINNERMAN, ASC

Gerald Finnerman, ASC (American Society of Cinematographers), is the director of photography for *Moonlighting*, a show that spares no expense to get its very special look. Finnerman is a man who

(From left) Leonard Nimoy (Science Officer Spock), William Shatner (Captain James Kirk), and James Doohan (Chief Engineer Montgomery "Scotty" Scott) were leading cast members of the science-fiction series Star Trek. *It developed a cult following that made it more successful in syndication and as a popular series of motion pictures than it had ever been as a network show.*

Cinematographer Gerald Finnerman became totally involved in virtually every aspect of the program, including the scripts, the series' unusual lighting, and the set design.

was brought up in the old school of cinematography, and he's proud of it. He brings an artistry and a meticulousness to his work that has been one of the key factors in making *Moonlighting* successful.

"I'm second generation," he said. "My father was one of the original members of the union, Local 659, International Photographers Guild. He came into the business in 1928. I grew up in the business.

Since I was five or six years old, all I can remember is the motion picture business.

"Although I didn't major in photography in college, I always wanted to be a cameraman." Finnerman attended Loyola University and majored in abnormal psychology. In 1950 he took a job at Warner Brothers, where his father was on contract as a cinematographer. Soon, he was working as his

father's assistant. When his father died at the age of fifty-five, Gerry Finnerman found a mentor in one of Hollywood's finest cinematographers, Harry Stradling, Sr., who had been a close friend of his father's. He worked for Stradling for eight years and was his camera operator when Stradling won the Academy Award for *My Fair Lady.* From Stradling, Finnerman learned the old-fashioned style that has served him well in creating beautiful television pictures. "Color wasn't very popular in television until the sixties," Finnerman said.

At that particular point, everybody said, "Well, you have to take a light over the lens and flat light color. Light everything." Even the networks wanted you to light everything. Color would take care of itself—the shades of reds, greens, and blues would all take care of themselves and blend, and you'll have a nice-looking picture.

But the old timers, like Harry Stradling, James Wong Howe, Ernie Laszlo, Charlie Lang would always go back and say, "In the forties, when I was shooting black-and-white, you could only get dimension one way." And that was by cross-lighting and halftones. They stuck to the ways of the thirties and forties and still continued to light color as they would black-and-white, which wasn't as safe, but it certainly was pretty. They were the ones who were getting the dimensions when everything else was being flat lit. . . . So I pretty well stuck to the theory of cross-lighting, trying to get dimension. . . . That's the way I was taught.

That style is passé. There are very few cinematographers today who could light a black-and-white show.

Significantly, Finnerman was nominated for an Emmy for *Moonlighting*'s black-and-white episode, "The Dream Sequence Always Rings Twice."

Finnerman's first television series as cinematographer was another landmark television show—*Star Trek.* He got the job by default. Stradling's son, Harry Stradling, Jr., was also a cinematographer, the director of photography on *Gunsmoke. Star*

Trek's producers unsuccessfully tried to persuade him to join them. When he refused, they asked Stradling senior to try to convince his son. Stradling knew his son's decision was firm. He suggested they promote his camera operator, Gerry Finnerman. "I went over for an interview with Gene Roddenberry [*Star Trek*'s executive producer]. They said, 'We'll give you one show to do, and if we like it, we'll give you another show.'" Finnerman was hesitant, but Stradling senior was reassuring. He was about to start shooting the motion picture *Funny Girl,* with Barbra Streisand. If Finnerman didn't succeed at *Star Trek,* he could rejoin Stradling on the *Funny Girl* set.

"He said, 'You're a smart boy. You know what to do,'" Finnerman recalled. "So I went over in May, and I started. I was on the show one week, and they were oohing and ahhing, and at the end of the week, they came down and offered me a three-year contract at, I think, eight hundred dollars a week. That was a lot of money in those days. I couldn't believe it."

Finnerman approached *Star Trek*'s unusual science fiction format with a basic philosophy: "the idea or vision of that third dimension. That was not seen on any of the other shows." It was difficult at first.

I did have trouble with the network [NBC] at the beginning. They were hesitant to accept the fact that people were in shadows, or half-lit or silhouetted, or that colors were used on the hair. But Mr. Roddenberry was very nice and supportive, and said, "I don't care what they say. I know what I'm seeing on the screen, and I like it. You just keep doing what you're doing."

A lot of it came by accident, because in those days I was searching, and a lot of it came from a certain amount of ego or arrogance. When somebody tells me I can't do anything, by God, I'm going to do it! The network would say,

"You're not to use any colors." We were on a different planet every week, and I would look at this huge set that was supposed to be the planet—I couldn't envision a different planet without a certain warmth or coldness, depending on the script.

It's like music. Photography is like an opera or a symphony. We all know that when we're tired and we sit down at night and we start listening to Wagner or Tchaikovsky, how involved we get, and how the juices start to flow. That's how I feel about photography. Certain romantic scripts, I make romantic with color and shadows. We had some scripts that were brutal, and I made them brutal—cold.

Whatever was in the script, I tried to encompass. I took my time. I read the scripts. I tried to know the characters as well as the actors did. Finally, you really *do* know them almost as well as maybe the actors and the writers. A director will come through, and he's there for a week or two, and he's gone. But we're there all the time, you know, and pretty

soon you get to know Captain Kirk or Spock or whatever show you're doing. . . . It's a feeling you get that comes out on the screen.

Another program for which Finnerman won an Emmy was a TV movie based on the life of show business impressario Florenz Ziegfeld. "It was really a woman's show," Finnerman said. "In real life, Ziegfeld was a womanizer, and we had four beautiful women in the show." As a result, Finnerman gained a reputation as a "women's cameraman," much as George Cukor had a reputation as a women's director. It helped lead to Finnerman's current job with *Moonlighting*. What does women's cameraman mean? "In this day and age, it's very important for every star to look as good as they can or better," he explained. "There are techniques whereby they can look better. As cinematographers, we approach each individual like a plastic surgeon. Each one has flaws; each one has scars. . . .

"Each one has a different kind of nose. Cybill [Shepherd], for example: She can look very bad if you put the light on the right side of the camera. She has a slight indentation in her nose, and when you put the light right of the camera, it just bends her nose like a banana, so you just have to watch it.

"It's sometimes difficult for the men to understand, because it seems like we take so much time on the women. But everybody on the set is treated equally."

Finnerman was not involved with *Moonlighting*'s pilot, but shortly after it was completed, he was approached by the show's producers.

They came to me and said, "We have a show that is unique. We want a different look. We want the look of the black-and-white of the forties." We all sat down and had a meeting, and they said, "We want this incorporated and this and this. Can you do it?"

I said, "Yes." And then I said, "It would be nice if we could maybe get away from those lousy-looking zoom lenses. They suck the background of people to you and not you to the people." I also said, "It would be nice if we could go through long master shots [the wide shot that includes all the characters in a scene], seven, eight, nine pages, like Hitchcock." We're throwing ideas back and forth. We sat for about two hours, discussing the concept of the show. I mean, I'm still discussing, and I didn't know whether I had the job. But I threw everything I had into it, saying, "Yes, I saw your pilot. I think I can do a better job on the lady. I think, overall, I could give you what you want." When we finished, there was satisfaction on everybody's part. Right away, we're saying, "Hey, let's get rid of all the television gimmicks."

I went back home and they had already called my agent. I was tickled. This seemed to me to be a terrific thing. I signed to do the series, and it started.

Finnerman's background and training appealed to executive producer Glenn Gordon Caron, who is a certified movie nut. Finnerman cites Hitchcock, John Ford, Fred Zimmerman, and Preston Sturges as primary directorial influences. *Moonlighting* is shot more in movie style than television style. The long master shots, for example: "They don't do that in many shows that I've seen," Finnerman said. In other programs "it's a lot of quick cuts. Bring the characters in and three close-ups. Take them out and three close-ups. Take them over, sit them down, and talk for eight pages. We don't do that. This show never stops moving."

As for his own role:

Without a doubt, the cinematographer on a television series, dealing within the parameters of a producer's wishes and specifications, not only sets the style, but he sets a show—sets the movement, sets the lenses. And usually the directors who come in will adhere to the parameters of the show. It is not very easy when the star of the show is as knowledgeable as Cybill Shepherd and is saying, "I don't want the camera dropped on me. Don't shoot up on me."

She's absolutely right. You don't do low shots if you want a lady to look pretty. She's very camera-conscious. I know she likes to get her coverage done first because she gets tired in the afternoon, and it shows. You put makeup on during the day, and you add to it. You don't take it off and put it on and take it off and put it on. So by the end of the day, after twelve hours, we watch her very carefully. We use different diffusion; we use different lighting if possible; we go from hard lighting to soft lighting.

Diffusion, the process by which you film through a somewhat opaque filter to soften hard edges, is a minor sore point on the *Moonlighting* set. Cybill Shepherd's shots are diffused, and if you look closely at *Moonlighting*, you can see the difference between the way she is filmed and the way costar Bruce Willis is shot. According to Finnerman, "Women have to be diffused. I don't care who it is . . . Somebody took a pretty good shot at me [in a magazine article] for overdiffusing Cybill. I went to my producers, and they said, 'You just keep doing what you're doing. We love it, the network loves it, and she loves it.' I can't go by the opinion of one man who may need new glasses. I have to defend myself by saying, 'Yes, we use diffusion—we use heavy diffusion—but I don't consider it jarring.'" Case closed.

Finnerman sees his relationship with the director as key. Younger directors often have not been exposed to the old techniques that he learned: big dolly shots, cross-lighting, etc. "It bewilders them." He feels that unlike other series,

there's no formula for this show saying that somebody walks in the door, we take them over to here and then over to there. I approach the directors and I say, "You work with the people, and you get the performance, and I will give you

the look of the show you want." Basically, they are much happier that way. It takes the pressure off of them.

They rehearse a scene with the people, and then they'll turn the set over to me. Then I will block the shot. I'll go so far, and if it works the whole way, I'll say, "Okay, we can do the whole eight pages." If there is a problem, I can stop and work it out—I feel I have omnipotence in that area.

We get directors who are not what you would call strong camera directors. Many of them have not done film, or many of them have done only two- or three-camera comedy shows. Sometimes they're not as confident or cognizant of screen direction, cuts, overlaps. It's my job to protect them, and I do.

It's different from doing a three- or four-camera comedy show on tape, where you can see the monitors and say, "All right, cut from the close-up to an over-the-shoulder, or cut back to the master." You don't have the ability to do that on film. . . . There are a lot of critics here checking performance and angles. It's a lot different, a lot scarier.

The cinematographer serves other functions with the director as well. Finnerman's college psychology training comes in handy. "We deal with an awful lot of ego, especially on a show that's as hot as this one is," he said. "You have to remember that you are the therapist between the director and the stars. There comes a point where the stars know their characters better than anybody else. They sometimes frown on a director coming in and trying to direct them before they've had a rehearsal. . . . This has happened a couple of times, and I can see the sparks start to fly.

"I try to be the buffer. I'll take a director aside and try to explain to them that it's best to watch what they [the actors] do, get their feel or their input, and then go from there, rather than come in and demand this or that."

Problem solving comes relatively easy to Finnerman: "I learned through a long period of going to a psychiatrist that there is more than one alterna-

Miami Vice's art director Jeffrey Howard applied his background in painting to the special look of the series. The fashion styles of stars Don Johnson and Philip Michael Thomas were only a part of an overall show design that was influenced by art, architecture, graphic design, and even music videos.

tive. It's never either/or; it's this and this and this. There are so many different ways to approach everything, whether it is photography, directing, acting, that nobody should be pinpointing one little thing. Give me a problem, and I'll change it. That's the way you have to think."

JEFFREY HOWARD

Art director Jeffrey Howard studied theater design, but he primarily sees himself as a painter. His artist's eye was in full evidence when he served as the art director for the first two seasons of *Miami Vice.*

Say what you will about that series' purported violence and overemphasis on the drug culture, *Vice* set a visual style that was unlike anything ever seen on television before. Working hand in hand with executive producer Michael Mann, himself no slouch when it comes to color and design, Howard helped devise the look that was copied in fashion, advertising, and graphic design. For his work on the series, Howard received the 1985 Emmy for best art direction.

He has distinct ideas about what makes his designs special. "I have a background in the fine arts," he began. "I started out as a painter, but I got a master's degree in theater arts because I decided that I wanted to do something other than paint to make a living. I decided to become a stage designer." Howard got his master's at Brandeis University. He moved to Hollywood in 1975 and got a job at CBS Television City working as an assistant art director on several Norman Lear comedies, such as *All in the Family, One Day at a Time,* and *Mary Hartman, Mary Hartman.* Then, "with two years' experience in videotape, I was able to jump into film and started working as an assistant

art director in movies. But I did several television movies along the way, so I was always maintaining my involvement with TV."

In 1980, Howard became a full art director on the movie *Private Benjamin.* Following that film, there was an actors' strike, and Howard found himself back in the television business, working on commercials at EUE-Screen Gems.

I did hundreds of commercials for Screen Gems over a period of about four years. At the same time, I was also doing a lot of painting in my studio at home: abstract paintings, concerned with breaking down the surface into collagelike pieces to create a sense of space, using color to play with emotional and psychological responses.

Doing the commercials, I was working with a lot of young directors, because frequently that's the only kind of work open to them until they can prove themselves. Some were from Canada, some from England—they were a new wave of directors who were interested in combining the beat of rock and roll with motion pictures through fast editing, quick cuts.

There was a tremendous emphasis on spectacle in commercials, a tremendous explosion in what computer animation could do, and growing appreciation for what television can do.

There was also at that time foment in the art world. Painting made a resurgence, the Bauhaus architectural style. It was also the beginning of postmodernism, which wants to throw out all the cool geometry in place of a collage effect—disparate things being mixed together in almost a haphazard way to create something unexpected.

So there were a lot of things happening in the arts and in the media. Television was ripe for something very special to come along. In fact, I think that in those early days the commercials really looked better than the prime-time programming. Programming had stopped incorporating anything other than the mainstream kind of information that was shared by all. It left out so much of the fringes in music, in design, in fashion and architecture—all that was sort of percolating on the side, waiting to be recognized. Television was playing it safe—the old lowest common denominator.

Gradually, in the early eighties, there was

a recognition on the part of the networks that they were losing audience for the first time. They were losing audience to cable TV. They were losing audience because people simply weren't watching TV.

Michael Mann certainly has to be credited for recognizing what a great world of culture was out there being unrecognized and not brought into television. The music has got to be one of the most important elements that he has been able to incorporate into prime-time programming—the combination of music and drama.

When you add music, you set the drama free. It becomes

also an operatic kind of statement. And it allows you to take license with the visual part of the show. It allows you to stylize in a way, because the music sets you free and puts you on another plane of representation.

Thus began *Miami Vice.* "The show offered a wonderful package," Howard said. "It brought something to television that was simply lacking, something that was out there that everybody was aware of, certainly. Everybody was listening to the radio, following their favorite rock music, buying crazy clothes, but you didn't see it on television."

Michael Mann would certainly agree with Howard's assessment and his belief that Mann's special knowledge of the criminal world was another reason for *Vice*'s success. "Michael Mann tapped into a whole world that hadn't been explored yet," Howard said.

The Mafia underworld was almost a cliché. In *Miami Vice,* Michael Mann was able to bring stories of political intrigue that were right out of the headlines and the biggest story of all right now, the huge traffic in illicit drugs. He was able to make an interesting equation between illicit activity and an illicit life-style—these criminals with unbelievable wealth and luxury. This was something that was very tantalizing, because the show is set up in such a way that we can participate in it through Sonny Crockett [the detective played by Don Johnson], who's only playing at being a criminal. It's a wonderful tease—bringing an audience into a world that they've never seen before. That's why the show looked different, because we tried to create a world that looked like you have to leave the earth to visit it. It was like another planet.

Of course, design is a critical part of that. We wanted to create a world that was new and alien and slightly threatening, but mysterious and beguiling and seductive at the same time. A world that was not completely Sonny Crockett's—he, after all, is a simple guy who was thrust into this unbelievable labyrinth of illicit behavior. . . . The dread and alienation which is a by-product of that look is something

that gives him the feeling that nothing lasts, that everything is surface, everything is illusory.

Miami Vice broke ground in the sense that it revealed the tremendous depth possible in visual language. Our culture is very visual. We are attuned to things and their importance as symbols. *Miami Vice* tapped into this language that speaks in terms of what people wear, what people drive, what people surround themselves with, and the effect that this might have on a person. It was a conscious attempt to funnel into mainstream television some radical positions.

Howard explained the relationship between what he was doing in his painting and his approach to *Miami Vice.* "I began to see the similarities between a TV screen and a piece of paper," he said. "They're both two-dimensional surfaces, and they both can be manipulated in a very graphic way. The collage-style paintings that I was doing could be translated directly into a use of design across the screen, by creating contrasts in the sets. I no longer began to think of a set as something that actors walked around in, but rather something on the screen that only had reality on the screen. Of course, colors played a tremendous role in allowing me to achieve that strong, graphic kind of presentation on the screen. . . . I remember wincing at one thing in particular in those old, hoary guidelines for art directors and production designers: Be very restrained in color; always use nothing but beiges or neutral tones."

Jeffrey Howard may not think of the set as something the actors walk around in, but he does feel that it's important that "every designer should be an actor in a way, because there has to be a motivation for the physical universe that's filmed, a motivation for the ambience, for the *mise-en-scène.* It is very much similar to the way an actor creates motivation for the way he enunciates his lines and the way he moves his body. Anytime I get involved with an actor's or a character's space, I'll study the lines like I'm the actor studying his lines; I'll look for the clue to why this person is the way he is. That's the beauty of our business—that technicians can also savor a little bit of the magic by becoming actors themselves in order to interpret a script. Every good designer does this."

Howard believes that *Miami Vice*, like the Hollywood films of the twenties, has made its design mark. "I see the impact just driving around major cities. One of the most gratifying things about my two years was to see it in Miami—I was able with this show to hold up a mirror to the city's own renaissance."

When Howard worked on *Miami Vice*, the pace was frenetic.

It was tough to have concept meetings on every show, because at any given time in episodic television, you're working on three shows. You don't have the luxury to sit down and thoroughly conceive every single detail, you know. It has to be done on the run, and it has to be done with a strategy—a total concept—completely in hand. You have to be able to invent on the spot, based on a gestalt, a philosophy that's agreed upon. The show is only successful if everybody is in sync and everybody is sympathetic, because if you have to stop and explain, you're going to get in trouble.

I was completely in sync with Michael Mann, so much so that I was able to carry on with very little input from him after the first couple of shows. The key thing was to set the whole tone, and that was done through discussions about aesthetic approach.

The pace is very difficult. That probably has very little bearing on the ultimate apprehension of the show by the audience. They don't see what went into making it. It's just part of the economics of the situation. The show is only licensed for so much [the license refers to what the network pays for it], and it requires that you work very hard to get it done. It happens to be the kind of pace that causes people to burn out after a couple of years. I don't think you can

do it for longer than a few years running. You have to be replenished in some way.

For Howard, replenishment comes from his art. One might think that he takes the aesthetics of television production design too seriously. But what is encouraging for the television industry is that there are people like him who are willing to devote their ideas and creative energy against often horrific deadlines to make a TV show look different.

CANDIDA CONERY

Candida Conery got started as most hairstylists do—she went to a beauty school. After a brief stint with the circus and a ten-year career working as a hairstylist on various motion pictures and TV shows, she is now the hairstylist for *L.A. Law*.

"A girlfriend of mine in high school was going into beauty school," Conery remembered. "So I enrolled too, because I sort of idolized her. You know, you get these very strange friends when you're in high school; years later, you never have anything to do with them. . . ."

Conery saw beauty school going hand in hand with plans for college. "I was going to college, and I was going to be a teacher." She got her beautician's license, and the money she made helped pay for tuition and books. "I went to college for two years and stumbled," she said. "I got bored. It was toward the tail end of the Vietnam War era, so I got involved in a lot of marches, and sort of forgot my schooling. I was also doing gymnastics at the time.

"So I burnt out a bit. Holding down two jobs and an apartment, trying to go to school at the same time . . . just went a little nuts. I sort of left school and hairstyling altogether.

To the casual viewer, details like a star's hairstyle may seem unimportant—until something is wrong. It can distract from a TV show's story, or an actor's performance. For L.A. Law *hairstylist Candida Conery, an inappropriate hairdo can mean calamity.*

"I joined the circus. It was an all-girls flying act. No contracts—it was absolutely hysterical, the best fun I ever had for about four months, all summer long.

"I always wanted to be a Jill-of-all-trades," she says, but hairstyling was one thing she knew would pay the bills, so she returned to it. She found a job in Beverly Hills and then rented space on Ventura Boulevard. "I was there for a number of years, really getting a good-sized clientele," she said, but she left to take another crack at show business.

I made up this incredible résumé that said absolutely nothing. My mother was an English teacher, and with her help

we just sort of expanded it—hobbies, sports, education. I sent it up to Universal, and kept calling them. There was a woman up there, Florence Avery, who was their department head. She was so polite. She kept saying, "Well, there's nothing now, but do call back." And I'd say, "Thank you very much," in my best businesslike voice.

The third phone call, she breaks down. She just goes, "Have I ever met you?"

I said, "No, would you like to?"

She said, "Yeah, get your butt up here." I went up to talk to her the next day, and we hit it off real well. I started working the next day and basically never stopped.

Her audition was showing she was capable of putting a space helmet over the coif of a female lead on the *Buck Rogers* television series. "It was a little night shot out behind the amphitheater at Universal," she said. "I put her hair in a bun, slammed the helmet on, and froze my patootie off—it was so cold up there." She passed the test. The next thing she knew she was working on one of the *Airport* movies—"twenty-fifth hairstylist down the road.

"I had worked from budget shops to Beverly Hills as a hairstylist, and now I was throwing myself into a completely new set of rules and standards," Conery said. "I was back at square one. I had to become humble real fast. That was a pretty rude awakening.

"It was surprising how much I didn't know, and how much I'd have to relearn." Why is it different from any other kind of hairstyling? "Hair is hair. You come into my shop for a haircut, I look at you, we talk, I cut your hair, we talk some more about styling and how you wear it for everyday."

But when working on a set with an actress, she said, "I've got to construct something that will last an entire day and look exactly the same. Six hours apart and possibly even two weeks apart, the actress could be walking from one room to the next and have to look exactly the same." In other words, two parts of the same sequence might not be shot at the same time, but they still have to look as if they're taking place in real time in the final product.

"So we take a lot of matching photos," Conery explained. "If we do it two weeks down the road, I've got to make sure you look exactly the same. That's the most difficult part of the job. What I really had to learn was the matching."

Mistakes can slip through, though. In an *L.A. Law* scene with one of the series' stars, Susan Dey, "I parted the hair on one side for one scene, outside a door. Then when she came inside through the door to a bar, it was parted on the other side. It was shot on two separate days." When the episode aired, she said, "I just gasped. My sister didn't notice."

Conery came to *L.A. Law* via a hairstylist friend who was working on the series' pilot. She joined him on the pilot, he left, and she was asked to stay. "They enjoyed my work, they liked me very much, and I enjoyed them tremendously." She said it was a different work experience from most of her previous movie and TV shoots. "The normal set of circumstances is us versus them, crew versus producers, above line versus below line. In this instance, our producers are wonderful people. They are thoughtful, kind, and appreciative. I think they're brilliant writers. I'm very pleased to be working with them.

"This is an unusual situation for me. I enjoy being appreciated. On almost every production you work on, the only time you ever hear from a producer, or anyone above the line, is when you're in trouble, when you've done something wrong. Otherwise, everything goes along, and it's fine, hello, good-bye."

As with the other behind-the-scenes members of

a production team, Conery works closely with the producers and the cast. Notes are written, and suggestions are made. The producers decide that Susan Dey's character should be a blonde—"We take care of it. . . . Jill Eikenberry came in, and I had a few suggestions from working on the pilot. We put them on film. We put Jill on film in a couple of outfits and some hair and makeup. We ran some tests, which they always used to do in the old days—run screen tests for different looks. It's not done so much now, especially on television. You don't have much prep time.

"You are creating another person, a being, an ego. You want to make them look the best they possibly can, not only stylewise, but colorwise and coordinationwise." In this case, Conery says, "I have to see the wardrobe, and I have to see the jewelry they're wearing. A lot of times, when I'm doing their hair, if the earrings aren't on, there's a balance that's completely missing.

"They usually have them dress and come back to me, so they're dressed when I do their hair. If there's a very high collar, the hair should go up, whatever is more flattering and natural. There's a 360-degree silhouette that you have to work with, around and around. At the end, I usually have them stand up on eye level with me and turn around, so we can see all the angles—something I had to learn real fast. When you're doing stills, you can place people in certain positions and angles, and you'll get what you want. But film is very cruel."

She prefers negotiation to fighting when it comes to determining a style, but she has strong likes and dislikes.

I will never force anyone to wear something that they truly aren't comfortable with, because first and foremost is their comfort as an actor. They've got to go out there and act.

They've got this whole other thing going on with them besides me. I'm a very small part of it. I'm there to support this person in their acting. There's a certain perimeter that I stay within.

You work with that individual until you are both satisfied. I tell you, most people know their own hair better than anyone else does. They've lived with it their whole life. When they say, "Believe me, my hair won't do this," I believe them.

Sometimes I will go ahead and try it just for the heck of it to see what happens, because maybe my technique of doing something might be a nice surprise for them. But if they have definite ideas, I try to stay within the structure they're requesting. I don't need to upset them. I know there are people in my profession who do strong-arm actors and actresses. I don't. I think it's dreadful.

She tries to be a diplomat. "The ultimate politician—there have been times when a woman said, 'I really want it up.' I have to look at her and say, 'Let me explain to you why this wouldn't look good up.' I put the feelers out to see how adamant they are about this.

"Actually, men are more difficult," she said.

They want the attention. Actors' egos are very fragile, and you have to have a tremendous ego to be an actor. That's not being derogatory. They just have to—it's part of the process of acting.

Men really want a lot of attention. It's more attention than anything else, because you don't have that much to work with—it's maintenance and upkeep. They have to be stroked and taken care of.

I'll do little extras for them. I'll use some shiny hair spray for an older actor. Richard Dysart [senior partner McKenzie]—for him I use an oil spray because it makes his gray hairs shine through. And even as short as his hair is, I'll blow-dry it for him in the morning, because it does help. It keeps the fuzzies down, and it makes me feel good. The same thing with Michael Tucker [attorney Markowitz]. I've gotten him a special little hair treatment thing that makes his hair thicker. I like doing that for them. It makes me feel good.

But she tries not to get too close personally. "You learn over the years to pull back," Conery said.

You don't give all. I'm a perfectionist to a degree. I want things to be right. I want people to be happy, and I want things to be logical. This is not a logical business.

I am with the actors and actresses in the morning first thing, and part of the process of getting them comfortable and ready for the day's work is saying, "How was your night? How was your weekend?" If it was just dreadful, possibly you talk about it. But I try not to get too personally involved. That's protection for me and protection for them. I don't want to know too much about them.

It's important that people realize the psychological impact that we have in the morning. People are very vulnerable at that time in the morning. We come in in the wee hours. We have prep time, the makeup people and hairstylists, to get ready for the actors coming in. It's like taking them into your arms, judging their mood. They may come in boisterous as all hell, but most of the time they come in very quiet and sedate, and you work up from there.

We prepare them for that day's worth of acting. If they have to do a scene that's just gut-wrenching, horrible stuff, you've got to know to definitely stand aside and let them have that space. Don't say a word. Maybe they want to talk, but most often not, because they've got to prepare.

You've got to know that instinctively, because it's very uncomfortable for an actor or actress to say to you, "I can't talk right now," because they have to come out of themselves to say that. You run across a lot of Method actors.

That is really one of our main functions: creating the character along with the actor in the morning, with the hair and the makeup and the wardrobe—putting it all together to present them on the set mentally and physically ready. It's very protective, you know. I have to keep people out of the trailer if it's not the right time for them to be bouncing in and out. It's an all-enclosed little atmosphere that you must create.

There are people who can throw actors off. I've witnessed it. A lot of the other crew members are not aware of what goes on in the trailer in the morning. Sometimes they'll come up and blurt something out. People will say things, not thinking. I just clutch my heart and go, "Oh, God." It's always a precarious situation.

On our show, more often than not, we're dealing with very well-adjusted human beings. They go out and do their thing. But there are some very heavy scenes, and we have to be quiet.

The actors are so damned good.

Conery said that watching them perform, "the makeup artist and I always end up crying ourselves."

She wants to stay in the business, but maybe in another role. "Having been at it for ten years, I now feel accomplished, I feel secure, and I'm now just starting to wake up and see the other things around me. What does a producer do, and what does a director do, from A to Z? I've taken a couple of courses. I'm fascinated by the entire process. Maybe I'll branch out into one of the other areas."

Conery already knows how to cope with pressure. "As far as disasters and crises go, we are used to having to just fix it at the last minute. Wing it; get it done. Things will be thrown at you left and right: 'Listen, we haven't got time for this, so we're going to switch this scene. So that means you've got to have those fifty Indian maids ready.'

" 'I've got to *what*?' "

Somehow, Conery says, you carry on. "They say you make an amazing amount of money. I say, 'Yes, it's going to pay for the most amazing funeral!' "

DAVE GRAYSON

Dave Grayson is the makeup man for one of television's most popular leading men—Bruce Willis, the hip-talking, wise-guy star of ABC's *Moonlighting*.

"I've been around, and I'm sincere," Grayson said. "I think Bruce Willis is a gigantic talent, probably, in my experience, an astonishing talent."

Makeup man Dave Grayson might have become involved in television much sooner if his main client John Wayne had accepted a TV role that was offered to him in the mid-fifties: Marshall Matt Dillon on Gunsmoke. *Grayson went on to do makeup for one of the hottest stars on television,* Moonlighting's *Bruce Willis.*

When Grayson says he's been around, he's telling the truth. He has been a Hollywood makeup man since the mid-forties and has powdered the faces of everyone from the Three Stooges to Glenn Ford and Kirk Douglas. His film credits include *The Blackboard Jungle* (with Ford), and *Seven Days in May, Lonely Are the Brave,* and *Town Without Pity* (all with Douglas). For years, Grayson was John Wayne's makeup man. At first, he said, "I didn't need TV. I did John Wayne on the road; I did his films, went to Europe with him, did his commercials. He did a great many personal appearances." In between Wayne assignments, and as Wayne worked less and less, Grayson got into television.

In the early days of television, Grayson remembered, "TV would have been like Devil's Island, compared to doing major films. I think the major studios all looked down on TV. They didn't get into it until it was well on its way. They thought it was a temporary phenomenon. They didn't see the potential of talkies, either. There were some very, very confusing years before the motion picture studios saw the potential of TV. They wore blinders. They tried CinemaScope. They had to divest themselves of theaters. . . .

"They didn't see TV as a source of revenue in the beginning," Grayson said, "but eventually, it saved their lives. . . . Our unions—the makeup unions and all the film unions—signed a contract to do TV, too, which was fortunate because it was a move from one type of filming to another. We lost nothing."

Grayson himself didn't really begin to get heavily into television work until the 1970s, when he began working on the series *Police Story.* "It was much easier to do film," Grayson said, especially if you were assigned to one performer. "There was a certain easy pace in doing a big movie. The schedule was long, and it was slow-oriented, and it worked around the star system. If a star wanted to go home at six o'clock, the star went home. A big movie was a luxury compared to TV."

There is very little difference between movie makeup and the makeup used for filmed television. The big difference was between black-and-white and color film. "In the very sensitive early film they used a black-and-white powdered look," Grayson said. "In my era, even in the early forties, in black-and-white films, we used a darker lipstick, essentially a red-based lipstick that was darker and brighter.

"As color film became more sensitive, makeup became much less difficult to do—it's a more natural look. A woman's makeup for color TV essentially is a natural makeup. If she wants to be stylized like they are in *Dynasty,* that's the look that a lady would have going out to a high-fashion party. But essentially, it's natural.

"For a man, too. Doing a makeup on Bruce Willis is not complicated. It's keeping him clean, keeping him powdered, and keeping him happy."

There are exceptions, of course. The stylized makeup Grayson mentioned—or prosthetics, the kind of effects employed in movies such as *Planet of the Apes.* Grayson had some fun with character makeup when *Moonlighting* did "Atomic Shakespeare," its *Taming of the Shrew* show. "We got into medieval beards and such things. It became more involved and more interesting."

Television makeup is also quite different in live or taped television, where Grayson's son works. "Techniques are different from live and tape TV to film TV because they use a great deal of light in the TV studios. They use much heavier makeup and more defined makeup—more highlights and shadows to compensate for all that light being poured in."

The brighter lights used for videotape production require heavier makeup. For a series like the videotaped Gothic soap opera Dark Shadows, star Jonathan Frid (who played a 200-year-old vampire named Barnabas Collins) needed especially dramatic makeup effects.

322

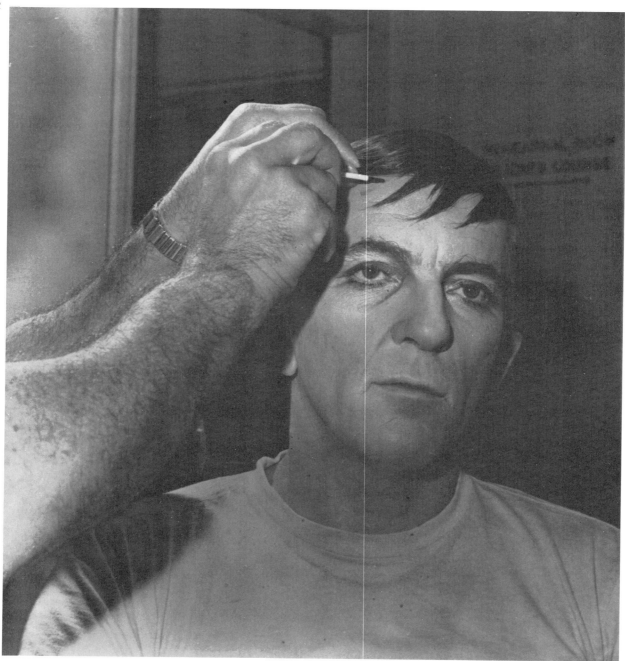

Because modern lighting for film is not as harsh as it was in the early days of television, shows can now be shot in a more realistic way. Performers in filmed episodic series don't have to endure the horrors of incredibly hot lights and heavy make-up.

Grayson started helping out on *Moonlighting* and joined the show permanently in the summer of 1986, working with the series' other makeup artist, Norman Leavitt. Given Grayson's background in the movie business and the *Moonlighting* crew's movie mania and their affection for the classics of the medium, it seemed a natural combination. "I'm not a TV watcher per se, but I watch this show," he said. "I think it's just a great show, the best-written comedy show I've ever seen."

He and star Willis have a good relationship, too. "I think I'm always motivated to do the best I can, regardless of whose makeup I'm doing," Grayson said. But he doesn't believe in "nurturing," as hairstylist Candida Conery does. "I've never felt

that," he said. "Of course, I feel an empathy for people I enjoy.

"After all, I have an ego, too. I've never felt that I had to nurture them and walk the dog or take care of the babies. I have a job, and I'm subject to the same pressures they are. They don't have to like me necessarily, but it helps. I don't have to like them, but it helps also. I've heard through the years— 'You're the first person in the world to see them, so you have to make them happy. You have to give them a positive view on life.'

"I'm sure a lot of makeup and hair people don't."

Television may be a collaborative business, but it doesn't have to consume your life. Dave Grayson is a pro. He just wants to get the job done.

11. THE BUSINESS

In 1946, troops were still coming home from World War II and women remained the mainstay of the assembly line. With the ban on the production of commercial TV equipment lifted, RCA went into full production of black-and-white receivers at its plant in Camden, New Jersey.

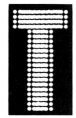he National Association of Television Program Executives (NATPE) came to New Orleans for their annual convention and took over the city as swiftly and thoroughly as a military coup. More than eight thousand people were in attendance. NATPE members are people with a lot of clout; they're the ones who buy and sell television shows, the ones who determine what you and I are going to see. You could barely take a step without being reminded of television's power to involve just about everyone. On the back of the front seat of a taxi was pinned a note: "Attention NATPE attendees: Your driver is a songwriter looking for a publisher. Any contacts in the entertainment field would be appreciated." Billboards on the way into town from the airport advertise a new talk show for the fall season with Geraldo Rivera—up for sale at NATPE. On the local broadcast of the *Today* show, mixed in with the commercials for used cars and cold cures, were spots for programs called *The Christian Science Monitor Report* and *The Wil Shriner Show:* "Come see us at NATPE Booth 848!"

NATPE's convention brought $10 million into the city of New Orleans, according to outgoing NATPE President David Simon. But that's nothing compared to the hundreds of millions that change hands between TV stations and program suppliers.

"Let's get out there on the exhibition floor and do some business!" David Simon yelled at the opening luncheon. Suddenly the theme from *Star Wars* pounded out over the public address system.

On the exhibition floor, program distributors were pushing everything from *The Best of the National Geographic Specials* to *GLOW—The Gorgeous Ladies of Wrestling.*

Many stars were there: the cast of *Who's the Boss?*, Pat Sajak and Vanna White from *Wheel of Fortune*, Sid Caesar, Carol Burnett, Lorne Greene, Lloyd Bridges, Curly Neil from the Harlem Globetrotters. People were dressed up like Gumby, the Incredible Hulk, GoBots, and Transformers. Young women in bathing suits and police hats patrolled the aisles, asking people, "Have you seen *Calhoun?*"— a new cop show. Paramount had a huge display area, designed to resemble a set from their new series, *Star Trek: The Next Generation*. The Walt Disney Company had built a huge silver replica of the Disneyland castle. Free food and booze were everywhere.

In many of these display areas, off to the side or behind a corner, there were tiny rooms, some not much larger than a telephone booth, used for potential customers to screen product. But these were also rooms in which deals were going down: Deals were being discussed and deals were being closed, executives in business suites were holding tight, little, intense meetings with station programming directors.

Trends come and go at NATPE. "A couple of years ago, everybody was going crazy with court shows," Hank Price, the director of programming and marketing at WUSA-TV, the CBS affiliate in Washington, D.C., said. "Court shows were hot; we had to have them. Year before that, it was game shows. We have a tendency to go in herds. Everybody likes something, something's a hit, and they all do it. The big hit this year is *The Oprah Winfrey Show*. So not only do you see everybody wanting Oprah Winfrey, you see a lot of the shows *like* Oprah Winfrey."

The other noticeable trend is in "first-run" programs, especially sitcoms. First-run means shows that are produced specifically for the local stations,

shows that have not previously been seen on the networks. They are also called "off-network" programs.

First-run sitcoms have their drawbacks: no track record, for one thing. "That puts the onus on the individual station to make a decision if it's going to be successful or not," Bob Furlong, from WCVG, an independent station in Milwaukee, said, "and take a chance on a program that hasn't been proved on the networks. . . . It's a test, and the station managers now have to make a serious decision."

But there are advantages to first-run, too. KMBC's Pat Patton said, "You don't have the long-run commitment to first-run," meaning that a station doesn't get tied down to something if it's a flop. "And, as a rule, the expense is not as great."

The interest in first-run is just one indication of the sweeping changes that have taken place in the way television is run as a business. "It has become a more competitive, more difficult business to make judgments in," Bob Furlong said. "Previously, if a station made a mistake, it was easy to correct. Competition wasn't as strong. Today, if you make a mistake, it turns into a serious situation."

"You have to be a lot more creative these days than you had to in the past," Jill Koehn, from WISC-TV, the CBS affiliate in Madison, Wisconsin, said. "Now the sales force has to be especially creative. Where basically, they could stay in the office and answer the phone, now they have to do a lot more knocking on doors. You have to be a lot more creative to make money now."

Commercial television is still a great business, from a moneymaking point of view, but the boom days are over. "We've been seeing a number of independents filing for Chapter Eleven," Hank Price noted. "But a well-run television station is always going to be a very good business."

Some see the current problems many stations are facing as a simple market shakeout. "From there on, it's very bright," Bob Furlong said. "I just think that probably the industry is maturing," Michele Ball, from KICU-TV, an independent station in San Francisco, added. "Stations can continue to do okay for themselves, but they have to be well-managed and watch the bottom line."

One of the primary concerns is the continually climbing costs of programs. "At some point, we're going to have to say, 'Whoa. Let's back off,' " Pat Patton said. "We can't keep paying the same incremental price increases for programming year after year. The syndicators are asking for thirty, forty, fifty percent increases in license fees. It can't continue to happen."

All of this, of course, is having an effect on the networks as well. Programming costs affect them, too, as do the encroachments of independent stations, cable and VCRs. "Barter" syndication is another factor, a system whereby for a cheaper price, syndicators hold back a certain amount of the commercial time in a show to sell to national advertisers. When Viacom starts distributing *The Cosby Show*, for example, it will do so by satellite, and will retain one minute of ad time for national sale, leaving local stations with six and a half minutes to sell. That's one less minute of national time that might have been bought from the networks.

Many of these new twists in the game are responsible for much of the chaos and shake-ups we're seeing in the three networks, all of which have gone through corporate rearrangements—two being sold to other companies. But in spite of all the aforementioned problems and threats, the station managers and program suppliers I spoke with did not foresee any of the three disappearing, as some critics have suggested. Hank Price, at Washington's CBS affili-

ate, has a certain interest at stake. "I think the networks' future is incredibly strong now," he said. "We were hearing three or four years ago that the networks were dead. Cable television was going to take over. The fact of the matter is, you have to be as big as CBS or NBC or ABC to have the national advertiser's base in order to make that work. You can't make it work if you have only three hundred thousand households watching. So I think the networks will be with us for the foreseeable future."

Michele Ball, an independent, agreed. "I don't think they're going to disappear, because they're so established, and they still command the largest share of the audience in terms of both over-the-air and cable television. I don't see erosion taking place at such a fast pace that it would cause the networks to disappear. I think they're going to see increased competition. They'll obviously never go back to the shares they were getting in the late sixties and early seventies, before cable took off and other diversification such as independent television came on the scene. But they'll still be a main force in the industry."

These people are not producers or writers or directors or performers. They specialize in a very different kind of creativity: turning television into profits.

HENRY SIEGEL

Henry Siegel is the chairman and president of LBS Communications, Incorporated, formerly known as Lexington Broadcast Services, one of the biggest companies in the syndication business now, handling such series as *Fame*, *American Bandstand*, and *What's Happening Now*.

"I enjoy watching television, and I enjoy the television business," Siegel said.

But actually, where I really began was the advertising business. I had a twenty-three-year association with an advertising agency, and through that association developed a special relationship with advertisers. So when I started this company ten years ago, it was with the barter business in mind. We sell a portion of our show to national advertisers, and the other portion, the local stations sell on a local basis.

We started with a series called *Sha Na Na* [a syndicated series that featured the nostalgic rock group, interspersed with guest stars and comedy bits]. Today, we're involved in everything from the *The New Gidget* show to *The New Monkees*.

First-run is the key factor. When we first started in the business, nobody understood what that was. First-run was shows people thought were a lesser quality than what currently was on network television. Now these shows have the quality and the prestige of the networks.

We were the guys—with MGM—who decided to continue the production of *Fame* [after the series was cancelled by NBC]. We put up the money, and we sold the advertising time. MGM produced and distributed. That was a major success. New episodes were produced strictly for the syndication marketplace.

However, as with virtually everyone in the business, Siegel does not see any threat to the networks, despite the syndication competition. "The networks are a very strong entity," he said. "Obviously, they do have problems. Not necessarily growing pains, but they're at a point now where they have to retrench and decide what business they really are in.

"There's no doubt about it—they are sick. Maybe they just have the flu. I think we'll see healthy networks, particularly in 1988, when there will be elections and the Olympics and all of those things happening. Eighty-eight will be a fantastic year."

He noted that in 1990, in all probability, restrictions will be lifted and the networks will be allowed to syndicate shows themselves. "There are millions of dollars that can be accrued there. If they decide to go into our business, they are going to be very strong competition."

Siegel said that there are advantages to bringing in business solely as a distributor; it helps keep production costs down. "We're able to effect some cost savings that the networks can't. We don't have eight levels of people looking at a script. We allow the producers to produce the show and deliver it to us because we trust in the production company. The networks agonize over everything from casting to scripts. If they cut down some of that level of decision-making, I think you'd see a decrease in production costs. Producers are willing to deliver less expensively if they don't have to make changes or late-night revisions. . . . An example being *Fame:* Based on these kinds of things, when we took *Fame* over, we were able to save over a hundred thousand dollars a week."

Siegel can afford to predict a rosy future for television broadcasting, and he does. "TV stations still are a very viable business," he said. "The doom-and-gloomers who are out there are really only a few people, but they're the ones, I guess, with the loudest voices."

He relishes the competitive nature of the business. "I've always been competitive—I have a twin brother," he said. "The television business brings out the competitiveness in you.

"We are a company that knows that you have to be in the competition out there, fighting for your time periods. That's the nature of our industry, the nature of our company, the nature of our country. There's always going to be somebody making money on something. Somebody else is generally going to try to get in there and take that business away from you. Competition is very important to the business."

BOB JACQUEMIN

It's really true—when you drive onto the lot of The Walt Disney Company, the security guard tells you to drive down Mickey Avenue and take a right on Dopey Drive. Office corridors are lined with Disney memorabilia, storyboards and, glass cases filled with toys. A memo announcing the Washington's Birthday/President's Day holiday features a cartoon of Mickey Mouse chopping down a cherry tree.

Disney has always been into television in a big way, ever since the days when *Disneyland, The Mickey Mouse Club,* and the Mouseketeers filled the air with relentless cheer and energy.

But there's serious business going on now. Disney has its own cable outlet—The Disney Channel—*The Disney Sunday Movie* on ABC, *The Golden Girls* on NBC, and it has become heavily involved in syndication through its Buena Vista Television division. Buena Vista is selling from the vast library of past Disney product for movies and TV and creating new programs unlike anything Disney has ever been involved with before: *Siskel and Ebert and the Movies,* for example, and a game show produced by Bert Convy and Burt Reynolds, *Win, Lose or Draw.*

The senior vice president of Buena Vista is a man named Bob Jacquemin, an expert in the mysterious ways of television syndication. He came to the Disney organization from Paramount, part of the exodus that occurred when Michael Eisner left Paramount to become the chairman and chief executive officer of Disney.

Jacquemin is a shrewd businessman and a man who's thought of in the syndication business as an innovator. While he was at Paramount, as executive vice president of sales and marketing for domestic television and video programming, he was involved with several new ideas that had a strong effect on syndication. One of them was Paramount's "guaranteed production" plan. Local stations are jittery about buying a series that is still in its first years on the networks. They are afraid that if the network were to cancel the series prematurely, the local stations would be left with an insufficient number of episodes to air five days a week for several months. Under the plan created by Jacquemin and his colleagues, Paramount guaranteed the stations that they would produce a sufficient number of shows, even if a series was canceled by one of the big three.

Entertainment Tonight is another example, the first syndicated show to be produced and aired on the same day—"day and date," as people in the business call it—and distributed to stations by satellite. At the time, many stations didn't possess the proper equipment. Paramount helped provide it. "I referred to our group as the Tupperware group," Jacquemin said, "because we were out selling dishes."

If you want to understand television as a marketplace, how it fits into the scheme of the real-life business world and how syndication works, Bob Jacquemin is the man to talk to.

"It was about 1960 that I got into the business," he said.

I went to work for an advertising agency in St. Louis and got into media buying: buying television time for Anheuser-Busch and Ralston Purina. Then I jumped the fence and became a seller for a national sales rep firm called Peters, Griffin, Woodward.

Walt Disney was one of the first Hollywood studio heads to recognize the economic potential of television. The Mickey Mouse Club, a daily variety show starring a group of talented kids collectively known as the Mouseketeers, was a successful children's show from 1955 to 1959. A quality family show that made extensive use of the Disney library of cartoons and movies, Disneyland gave an enormous ratings boost to the ratings of ABC when the series went on the air in 1954 and was an invaluable promotional tool for Disney's California theme park.

*Even though color television would not become the norm until several years
later, the producers of* The Adventures of Superman, *starring George Reeves,
looked to the future and began filming episodes in color in 1954. More than
thirty years later, the series is still a syndication success.*

Vintage television series like The Lone Ranger, *starring Clayton Moore as the
masked hero of the Old West, are still available to viewers in syndication. The
first episodes of the series, originally seen on ABC, were produced in 1949.*

I went from PGW to Tele-Rep, was with them for eight years, and left to go into business for myself. I did all the TV marketing for the Dallas Cowboys and put together preseason packages and worked with Tom Landry on a coach's show that was syndicated in some twenty markets in five states. I handled University of Texas football, too. . . .

Syndication started in the fifties. Basically it consisted of stations buying either off-network series or buying feature films.

A company called Ziv Television Productions was one of the forerunners of the syndication business. They would go into local markets and find sponsors. They'd go to the banks and savings and loans and car dealers, sell the program to a company, and then they would find an outlet in the marketplace. The advertisers were very much involved on a local level in syndication.

Then there was a long period of time when it was basically just licensing off-network series for cash—series that had been on the networks for three or four or five years. . . .

The camp, comic book adventures of Batman *(Adam West), assisted by his youthful companion* Robin *(Burt Ward), were a major television craze when the series premiered on ABC in 1966. Here, the Dynamic Duo are surrounded by four of their archest rivals: (from left) the Penguin (Burgess Meredith), the Joker (Cesar Romero), the Riddler (Frank Gorshin, later played by John Astin), and Catwoman (played here by Lee Meriwether, but also by Julie Newmar and Eartha Kitt).*

In the mid-seventies, syndication really started to come into its own. Previously, the networks were in almost total control of the industry. Cable was not a factor. But there was such a healthy broadcast economy in the seventies, it allowed the growth of stations to occur, and that growth was primarily in the independent station community. Couple that with the growth of cable and networks "stunting"—putting in a miniseries or a one-time-only special against an ongoing series—the cumulative effect was a breakdown of viewing patterns.

That's why local television has been able to grow. There were no longer just three viewing alternatives. The prime-time-access rule was another major development. That allowed for the growth of new programs that did not have the networks as their point of origination.

I don't think we're challenging the entire livelihood of the networks. It's another competitor. The more competition, the better you have to be. The winner should be the viewers, by giving them alternatives.

There are certain fundamental forms of programming that work in syndication: your off-network product, your feature film product, reality-based programs, Phil Donahue or Oprah Winfrey, talk shows, animation, game shows.

It's surprising that Disney, which had been active for so long in the TV business, had waited such a long time to get into the lucrative syndication business. "From what I can gather, in the sixties and seventies, management did not want to jeopardize the relationship with the networks," Jacquemin replied. "Make the network sale and keep the relationship strong and healthy. But when Michael Eisner and Frank Wells [Disney's president and chief operating officer] came in, the decision was made, yes, you can get into syndication, provided syndication and The Disney Channel work very closely during the transition period."

There was no conflict, Jacquemin said, because there was so much Disney product from which to choose.

Michael Eisner recognized that syndication is a viable business to be in. It's a very profitable business.

You pick up a trade paper and you read about Chapter Elevens and the problems in the business. In reality, I think it's a small sector of the broadcast community, and I think it's cyclical. I draw an analogy between our business and a bull market in the stock market. Growth has been meteoric. It has attracted a lot of outside investment capital. There has to be some settling in that process. It's a correction and I think we will be stronger for it.

We—Buena Vista—are part of the process of launching new shows. We're not in the process of renewing successful shows because we haven't been in business long enough. I hear a lot of people in the industry say it's real tough getting new shows on the air. When you think about it, there's a positive reason for that. A lot of the shows that are on the air are working! Why would anybody want to throw a *Wheel of Fortune* or an *Entertainment Tonight* or an *Oprah Winfrey* off the air if they're working?

We're producing better product. You look at the stuff that was produced ten years ago and we have made greater strides forward than the networks have in ten years. The definitive line between network-quality programming and syndication is blurring.

Costs are going up at a very high pace. But that too will settle out. We are a classic supply-and-demand business. When there is an oversupply of product, prices go down. When there is a scarcity of quality programming, prices go up.

The projections on *Cosby* for syndication are something like $3 million an episode. That's where the business really is now. The cost of doing business at a television station for programming is so high that you're not afforded the luxury of making mistakes. Ten years ago, you could buy a program, make a mistake, and correct it. Here, you buy a program in today's marketplace and if you make a mistake the consequences are staggering.

This was a business where the profit margins were forty percent. Then it became thirty. Then, independent stations were perfectly willing to make five or ten percent. Then it became, "Well, I'll break even for the first couple of years." Now you're seeing, because the cost of doing business has gotten so much higher, the stations that have just started up are the ones that are in the greatest jeopardy, unless they are well enough financed to weather any storms that come along the way.

In spite of the risks, Jacquemin is excited about the continued potential for expansion, including the current production of situation comedies exclusively for syndication. "It's a high-risk, but high-reward potential. Five years ago that wouldn't even have been considered.

"We're always going to look for new franchises in programming. That's the hardest part of our job. And it's also the riskiest part of the business. For anyone to come up with the next new show is always real, real tough."

You never know where the next hit is going to come from. "All you have to do is go back three or four years ago when ABC was talking about getting out of situation comedies, that they would never produce another one. And along comes Bill Cosby and you have twenty-eight comedies on the air.

Following the success of Batman, ABC rushed another longtime fantasy hero onto the screen. The Green Hornet was played by Van Williams (left). He was assisted by his Asian chauffeur, Kato, played by a man who would become a legendary star of kung-fu movies, Bruce Lee.

Lynda Carter starred as prime-time television's woman superhero, Wonder Woman, a star-spangled patriot who helped all good Americans fight the Nazi menace and other assorted evildoers.

Sitcoms are now alive and well on network television, which then flows comedy product into syndication and keeps this marketplace healthy.

"The common denominator of our entire business is the software, not the technology or the hardware. What's driving this business is not the new technology as much as the programming. The VCR and cable and direct broadcast by satellite will have an impact on us, but not as great as the impact of what you put *on* the air or *in* the cassette or *on* the cable.

"I feel I'm now at the essence of television, and that's the program."

ROBERT WRIGHT

Robert C. Wright came to NBC from General Electric as the successor to Grant Tinker. His previous

Bill Bixby played Dr. David Banner, a mild-mannered chemist who, because of a radiation overdose, was transformed into The Incredible Hulk, *a powerful monster, whenever he became angry. The Hulk, based on a comic-book character, was played by muscleman Lou Ferrigno. The series aired in prime time on CBS and is now seen in syndication, marketed as a show that's especially popular with children.*

position had been as president and chief executive officer of General Electric Financial Services. He began his career with GE as an attorney in 1969 and has moved in and out of the company ever since, alternating jobs in GE's various divisions with periods of time in private practice and a three-year stint as president of Cox Cable Communications in Atlanta. As a result, he wasn't without *some* experience in television when he came to NBC, but many were hoping that Tinker's successor would be someone within the company or at least within the broadcasting industry.

"There was a lot of apprehension about the change in command," he was quick to agree, "was and is." It will take some time to work through the apprehension, Wright said. "I think that the more isolated a business is, the more that's going to be the case. Even though this is sort of a contradiction, we're a very isolated business. We're in the middle of a lot of activity, but we're very isolated in what we do versus what the rest of the world is doing. We take photographs of steelworkers, but we have no particular knowledge of what steelworkers are doing. We report from the lofty position of not having to be a steelworker."

The programming is what fascinates Wright in his new job and what gives him a minor case of the chills. "Broadcasting has two very distinct elements to it," he said. "One is operations, which is something I am acquainted with: selling inventory, selling advertising, doing the things that are involved in getting material on the air.

"The fragile nature of entertainment programming is somewhat of a surprise to me. You don't see that at the station level. You are generally selecting from syndicated programming or programming that has a history to it. You can see the product. You already know what it looks like. What the local station manager has to agonize over is the selection of the local news anchor."

What amazes Wright about entertainment programming for the network is

making a big commitment to what people's tastes and attitudes are and how shows will be received. That is an extremely difficult and challenging assignment, and what I think makes network television such a risky and volatile proposition.

News is more or less pretty straightforward. Your ability to do it well, and to maintain quality, of course, is always an issue, but the process of how you do it is not a mystery. Sports is not a particularly mysterious situation, either. There, you're basically purchasing outside rights, so you're bidding, which is always a gamble, but you're bidding for a product which you already understand. You know what a baseball game is; you know what a football game is. It's a question of whether you think you're going to be able to sell enough advertising. So while it's very risky, it's the kind

By the time American kids turn eighteen, they will have seen 350,000 television commercials. One producer, Joan Ganz Cooney, decided to use the style and pace of TV commercials for education. The result—Sesame Street—revolutionized children's television.

of risk you get your teeth around and decide how dangerously you want to live.

Entertainment programming is quite a different issue. It's a much more complex, much more intuitive, and different from the kinds of businesses that I've been exposed to. There's as high a percentage of error built into it as anything I've ever been acquainted with, and it isn't all from the creative side. There is an awful lot of patterned thought that goes into it. I've been very impressed with Brandon Tartikoff and the people out in Burbank [the site of NBC's West Coast operations]. They really have very interesting schemes for the development of creative talent and the selection and positioning of programming. There are very different problems dealing with daytime, prime time, and late night; they have dramatically different audiences. The programming people have different, creative people who are interested in the different day parts. The ways you stimulate audience viewership is very different in those day parts, and I've found that to be a challenge."

Daytime programming in particular, Wright said:

The daytime challenge is a greater intellectual challenge than prime time. First of all, there is the question, Is the audience changing? Do we know the audience well enough? That has confused the issue a little bit. There is a belief that there's a lot of working-time viewing going on. We don't have a good handle on that. We're not even clear on what the nature of the home viewing is. Who is there? How attentive are they?

There are difficulties in defining the audience, and there are difficulties in defining the advertisers' objectives in reaching the audience. I think those two things together have made daytime programming a lot bigger issue for all three networks than it ever has been. The profitability in daytime programming has diminished. There has been a loss of viewership on the three networks, not dramatic, but enough, a steady erosion, a somewhat greater percentage than in prime time.

The formats have not changed. We have become more aggressive in our soap operas, but our game shows remain very similar to what they have been. NBC has made as many attempts to try to deal with daytime viewing as anyone. David Letterman was one of our more notorious fail-

ures when he was on daytime television. News is a factor now on daytime, but not enough of a factor for us to lay the gauntlet down and say to the affiliates, "We want to program a half hour of news at noon. Why don't you program the other half hour?" There's still a little uncertainty.

In the last two years, advertisers have taken the position that the audience is well enough known that they can afford to cut back on their actual dollars of expenditure for that audience.

Wright noted that advertisers are especially enamored of the current trend in fifteen-second commercials, known as the split-thirty, and that they like the idea that you can get more repetition of an ad's message if you tell it in less time. "I'm not sure that we see the same creativity in the

TV's cutest couple, Muppets Kermit the Frog and Miss Piggy, stars of both television and the movies, are all turned out in tux and ballgown to introduce a San Francisco Ballet production of Cinderella *for public television's* Great Performances *series.*

Sesame Street's Big Bird and Barkley the Dog traveled to the Great Wall of China for the first Chinese-American television coproduction, Big Bird in China, *in 1983.*

advertising community's dealing with the audience as they had years ago. The advertiser comes to us and says that the audience is the same as they were fifteen years ago. I say, 'But your ads are the same as they were fifteen years ago.' We're locked into a view of a declining audience and a lack of dollars coming in from the advertising side. I don't know what will happen with that, but we're willing to take more chances in trying to focus in on that audience. We're certainly looking for breakthroughs."

There have been other things that surprised Wright about the world of network television. "The business is more fragmented than I would have thought," he said. "Sports, news, and entertainment are really very different businesses. People grow up in them, stay in them. Some people change, but not many. If they leave NBC, they tend to stay in the same area someplace else. The vast majority of the people don't expect to cross-pollinate. We're not an enormous business enterprise, but we're not a tiny one either, and yet the people in each division are basically engaged in their own world."

That seems curious to a man like Wright, who has worked in so many different areas of business. He is also surprised about some of the ways in which money is spent—NBC's offices of Standards and Practices, for example. He noted that such an office only exists at the three major networks—none of the "developing" networks like USA or Arts and Entertainment have them.

I don't think it's wrong, but I was astonished at how we have historically accepted so much of the burden of dealing with social issues and dealing with the government, dealing with groups and the affiliates. We have just plain accepted an enormous burden. We have allowed ourselves to become the only practical interface for every special-interest group and as a result find ourselves defending ourselves against things that we're just airing, that we didn't produce

at all. We indemnify our affiliates for everything we put on the air. I mean it's crazy; what are we doing?

I just wish we could find a way to get some of the other parties involved in the benefits of this endeavor to share some of that burden, because it's a very substantial organization, a lot of difficulty and a lot of issues. I'm not proposing that we get out of it, but we've got to get a better sharing of responsibilities, whether it be on the advertisers' side or the affiliates' side.

The special-interest groups aren't going to go away. I do think that independent programming and cable is lessening some of that burden on us. Only the diehards now believe we control everything that goes on in television. I still see letters from people who somehow still believe that we control censorship over all programming. There are still people who give speeches, who say, "Television said this and television said that," not distinguishing unregulated cable from the affiliates or the independents. The generic labels are still around, but I think less people are using those labels, and that makes it somewhat easier to deal with.

The broadcast world has turned topsy-turvy in the last few years, and Wright believes that the only way for the networks to survive is through ingenuity in programming and fiscal responsibility at the same time.

I think there is no question that anybody in the network business has got to be very concerned about the relatively fragile nature of what they're trying to achieve. We have to do whatever we can to be as creative as possible in how we go about spending our money.

I was making a list in my mind of the relative economic performance of the seven or eight companies that are truly network companies. It gets a little arbitrary as to what you call a network—I'm using Fox as a network, for example. NBC is certainly the most profitable today, but the surprising thing is, it's a tie for number two. I don't think very many people have focused in on this, but ESPN, CNN, and CBS are all three tied. After that, you go down to a different level. The USA Network is more profitable than ABC. The Weather Channel is ahead of ABC. ABC is going to be below Fox,

NBC Entertainment President Brandon Tartikoff found himself taken hostage by Saturday Night Live *stars Joe Piscopo and Eddie Murphy when he hosted the series' season premiere in 1984.*

and Fox is a start-up company, so they've got enormous losses.

It is a very crowded, highly competitive, and well-staffed competition. For other than the specialized networks—ESPN and CNN—it's not clear how any of the participants will retain their position. CNN and ESPN have two ways in which they can make money: They can sell advertising, and they can raise their subscription rates for the cable systems. They would argue that they inherently are a more stable business than the broadcast networks are, and that they can get to a level of size maybe as big as we are, and they can stay there without having to do these big dipsy-doodles that we go through.

When Wright is asked what he thinks television lacks today, he says, "I think television is a marvelously responsive medium. I've always thought that the criticism of television not being a better driver of educational values sounds good but doesn't have a lot of merit." There is no reason, he believes, for a PBS-type program to be a part of the NBC schedule as well. "The assumption that if you put it on NBC more people would see it is really a specious kind of argument. If the audience that is watching the show on PBS is happy with it, my guess is that the audience watching it is predisposed to that type of viewing. They planned to see it. There's no reason to have to take that and run it over to NBC to somehow accomplish that.

"We spend a lot of time looking at trends. If we see programming trends on other television networks or services that we think would have merit to the larger audiences that we can deal with, we're not humble. We'll steal the idea. Actually, we don't have to, because the writers and the people who are doing it will come to us as soon as they feel that

they've got something that is going to be more in tune with our larger audiences."

For the most part, Wright thinks television is covering the bases.

I think cable today has done a lot of damage to the argument that there is a lot out there that people want to see and aren't. The whole thing has gone around in a circle. You take all those people who argued that there's a tremendous amount of audience out there that is unhappy with what's on television, and if you only show them what they want, they'll come and see it. Cable has given them thirty channels of programming. But their tastes haven't changed a bit from what they were before cable arrived. In a society where essentially nothing is prohibited from being on television—except for hard-core pornography—the basic tastes of people are the same. There aren't a lot of dramatic tastes out there that are unserved. People's desires may have changed, but not because of television. It's because of the way the generation has been moving, whatever direction that may be.

I think that seven years ago, when I was in the cable business, some of us had the view that people would only really be interested in watching five or seven channels of programming. While that kind of escaped the world, fundamentally, I think we're back to that now. The rest of it is sort of convenience viewing—the same kind of programming— just viewed at different times.

There's plenty of news, plenty of information on television today. And there is certainly plenty of entertainment, both new and old.

Wright thinks people are basically satisfied with what they're getting from television. TV is big business, but it is also show business, with all the craziness and unpredictability that that implies. Some of Robert Wright's rules apply, but the public's taste in entertainment can change far more radically than its taste in appliances.

12. THE FUTURE

*That Renaissance guy of the twenty-first century—the
computer-generated Max Headroom, talk show host,
cola huckster, star of his own action series, and
all-around man about town.*

*"Whatever is wrong in American life, you will find
wrong in television."* —HERBERT BRODKIN

*"It's not chancy enough; it's not bold enough; it's
much too narrow for the world we live in."*
—BARBARA CORDAY

*"The problem with television in this country is that
commercial television makes so much money doing its
worst, it can't afford to do its best."*
—FRED FRIENDLY

*"My feeling is that when something good happens
on television, it's extraordinary. It's miraculous."*
—JOHN FORSYTHE

*"The only way you can get any feeling out of a
television set is to touch it when you're wet."*
—LARRY GELBART

eorge S. Kaufman once said that ev-
eryone in the phone book should have
two occupations listed: "Plumber/
Drama Critic," "Lawyer/Drama
Critic," and so on. Today, everyone's
a television critic, and that's probably
as it should be, considering the enormous role that television plays in our lives.

It is in the nature of the hopeful critic to look
ahead, to always want something new and better.
Some look to the future in practical terms. Ask
television executive Imero Fiorentino and he will
tell you that "the next quantum leap" is "telecom-
munications for business not just entertainment,
teleconferencing—made possible by satellites and
smaller cameras that can handle lower light levels.
You use the medium to eliminate travel, time, and
cost—not only the money for tickets and hotels, but
the wear and tear on executives." Many companies
are involved in teleconferencing already. Fiorentino

predicts that within five years, eighty percent of corporate America will be using television communications.

Joe Flaherty, the vice president and general manager for engineering and development at CBS has said, "By the dawn of the twenty-first century, television will offer a diversity of services and a technical quality as different from today's television as the introduction of color was to monochrome experiments."

Flaherty is perhaps the leading advocate in this country of what may well be the next step forward in television, HDTV (high definition television). The standard American TV picture consists of 525 electronic lines. The HDTV picture will have some twelve hundred lines and offer a picture as sharp and clear as thirty-five millimeter film. In fact, a feature film in Europe and a Canadian TV series are being shot with HDTV equipment. The finished products will be transferred to film or standard videotape. Flaherty estimates that using HDTV, movies and TV shows that are currently filmed could save at least fifteen percent of their production and postproduction costs. "You can't tell the difference between HDTV and film," Flaherty said. "It's really quite amazing."

At home, HDTV will make possible big screen television of really good quality. What's more, movie theaters could be converted to HDTV with shows sent on a handful of lightweight videodiscs. "Very inexpensive to ship. In addition, once you're in the electronic domain, you can encrypt the signal. Pirates will have a real problem, because on every disc you can incorporate a unique address code for every cinema in the country. If someone tries to copy something, the theater can simply be cut off."

Flaherty sees other innovations in digital sound, including "surround sound—as close as you can get to reality. Time will tell whether people will want that every day in their living rooms, but it's very effective." And, he said, "There is a technical potential for three-dimensional television. Really high-quality 3-D TV could happen if there's an artistic need. Mind you, it's not cheap to produce, and it has not seemed to be a big success in the cinema over the years. But you may not need funny glasses to view it. Holography may be the answer."

"A close collaboration between art and technology is crucial to the future," Flaherty believes. "You can't collect an audience with test patterns," he said. "On the other hand, you cannot deliver a single syllable to the home without the technology.

"We have to concentrate on the future because it comes quicker than ever before," Joe Flaherty said. "That which we believe may never be is soon commonplace."

LES BROWN

Les Brown is the editor in chief of *Channels of Communications*, one of the most serious-minded publication around about the communications business. He has been covering the television business for more than thirty years. He grew up in Chicago, started writing and editing military newspapers for the army while stationed in Alaska, graduated from the University of Chicago, and started looking for a job in journalism. There were no positions available at any of the local papers, so he went to work as the Chicago bureau chief of *Variety*. He moved to New York as *Variety*'s radio-TV editor, and in the mid-seventies, joined *The New York Times* as a reporter, with broadcasting as his beat. He has been the top editor at *Channels* since it began in 1981 and is an outspoken media critic. "For years, we were expecting revolutionary change in the industry," Brown said, "but we never expected anything as convulsive as this," especially referring to the changeovers at the three major networks. "The expectation was that technology was going to drive the change, but all the technology served to do was to inspire deregulation. What really drove the change in the industry was business, and business was spurred by deregulation, so that's the role technology played.

"The existence of this technology—in a time of conservative administrations in this country and Britain who believe in free markets and liberal policies toward business—made it easy to argue for deregulation because there's no longer a scarcity of frequency. You've got cable systems that can bring in fifty-five channels, direct broadcast satellites, home video, all these other means of distributing television."

As a result, he said, "A lot of the regulation that was very well thought out was simply tossed out. For example, the antitrafficking rules that required the owner of a station to keep the license for a minimum of three years before selling it. When they threw out the three-year rule, a lot of speculators got in the game: Buy a station for $50 million, do something to jack up the ratings, and sell it for a $100 million."

The changes, Brown said, have affected the value system of broadcasting.

There is a shift from a responsibility to the public, as mandated in the Communications Act, to a responsibility to the shareholder. A lot of the people who believe in market forces and free markets and those kinds of things think that's the same thing. I think it isn't.

If your greatest responsibility is to the stockholder, then there are no values other than bottom-line values; the exploitation of children doesn't matter, the exploitation of sex and violence, propagandizing, selling airtime to anybody who might be irresponsible or have a radical point of view without a Fairness Doctrine, any of those things. Everything's fair as long as the station or the network makes a profit and rewards the stockholder. We have only to read the reports of the Wall Street analysts who cover broadcasting. They don't care anything about quality—that's an irrelevant issue to them. The guy who is most celebrated is the guy who makes the most money on the least investment. That's really what it's about.

It's a whole new breed of management, not only at the networks, but at station groups all over the country. We had a cover story in a recent issue of *Channels:* "Who Owns Broadcasting?" Faceless investment pools, investment bankers, financial wheelers and dealers, people who have very little respect for the work of television—none of them, as far as I can tell, has any of the qualities or the instincts of the impresario. I guess the sense is that they don't have to, that somebody else in the company will be in charge of the programs. That wasn't the case in the past. William Paley was a great programmer. Frank Stanton had those talents, even though he denied it. So did Leonard Goldenson at ABC, the Sarnoffs, Bob Kintner, and certainly, Grant Tinker—all those people who ran NBC over the years.

For all the budget-cut fears around the Big Three, he thinks they will keep their news organizations. "They'll certainly keep the evening newscast. They're already working at keeping it, changing it from being a headline service to something else, using the really knowledgeable journalists they have. Most of the journalists working for the networks are top of the line, expert in lots of areas. That's really what the networks have over the local stations by and large. The idea is to turn that expertise loose and really let it flex its muscles."

That may not be enough to save the networks in the long run, Brown said. "I want to make it clear that we're not talking about the near future, but the far future. It may be twenty years. But we could see a breakup of the networks. There could be lots of national services. Maybe they'll operate one or two days a week, or offer news on the hour or something like that.

"The whole system could become decentralized. We already see a vigorous syndication industry that is selling original programs, not just reruns. And advertisers are already taking some of their network budgets and putting it into syndication because it's cheaper and better targeted. There's a very healthy alternative to network television in barter syndication, and as that grows, the stations feel more and more comfortable buying programs that way. If they can make more money doing it, they're likely to break their ties with the networks, especially if the networks don't find some way to make themselves indispensable to the local stations."

The networks still control a majority of the viewers, but their share is down. "If you talk to network people, they'll tell you, 'That's it, that's the extent of the erosion, it will never get worse.' Bullshit. Who says? What if Ted Turner's WTBS gets hot or the USA Network? What happens on cable when all the cities are wired? When the major cities are all wired, five years from now maybe, and it's no longer suburban television, then it's possible to have a real national cable network, with a penetration that's significant in the population centers. When you have that kind of penetration, you can quadruple the billion dollars of advertising that went to cable last year."

The three networks owned the business. Ninety percent of the audience went to them. Now it's something like sixty-seven percent. The rest has gone elsewhere.

But that does not mean death. "I don't think the networks are doomed," Brown said, "but they really will have to establish their place. They can no longer take for granted that they have a place in this changing environment. In fact, what sort of works against them is their own success, the fact that they are less likely to innovate or adapt. The tendency is to go with what always has worked. All the other guys don't carry that baggage.

"The more the networks cut, the more they risk disaster, because the key to surviving out there is the programming. When you cut, you try to find cheaper programming, and you harm yourself."

The seriousness with which Brown talks about television is just one indication of the legitimacy that the industry has obtained. "You're not a cretin anymore if you talk about television," he said. "It's okay to watch television. Most of the dumb shows seem to be gone. I've been on juries in international competitions, and I can tell you that Americans have nothing to be ashamed of. We know how to make television shows, and we make them very well."

ARTHUR C. CLARKE

Arthur C. Clarke is a prolific author of science fact and fiction, the prophet of the communications satellite, and someone decidedly optimistic about the future. Now seventy years old, he has been dreaming about space travel all his life. He joined the British Interplanetary Society at the age of seventeen and is extraordinarily knowledgeable, as can be seen by reading any of his works, such as *2001* (and its sequel, *2010*), *Childhood's End,* and *The Nine Billion Names of God.* Born in Britain's Somerset, he now lives in Sri Lanka.

On the day of the moon landing in 1969, there with Walter Cronkite and astronaut Wally Schirra sat Clarke. It was appropriate for him to be there for several reasons, one of them the famous article of his that was published in 1945.

The war was obviously ending, and we crazy space cadets in the British Interplanetary Society were looking around for ways in which rocketry could be made to pay for itself in the hope that one day we would be able to build a spaceship and go to the moon.

I thought of the idea of using satellites for relaying television programs, and it seemed quite obvious to me that the one place to put such a satellite was in so-called stationary orbit, so that it remained fixed over the same spot on the equator. Then you just needed three of them around the world and you'd have a complete global television or radio or telephone distribution system, whatever you like.

I wrote this up in an article. The original title I had for it was "The Future of World Communications." When it was published in *Wireless World*, the editor changed it to "Extra-Terrestrial Relays." I wonder if that was the first time the word *extraterrestrial* appeared in print? Perhaps ET goes back to the *Wireless World* article.

Clarke said that his satellite idea "certainly wasn't ruled out as being ridiculous, because by the time the article appeared, the V-2 rocket had arrived, and the atom bombs at Hiroshima and Nagasaki had been detonated the month before. So people took this sort of thing very seriously. The idea was not laughed at."

However, he was very much surprised by the speed at which the communications satellite developed. "I was not surprised by the satellite itself—admittedly, when *Sputnik I* went up in 1957, it was a great shock—but I never imagined the communications satellite network would spread as rapidly as it has done.

"The spread over the whole world has been incredibly dramatic. People demand information and entertainment even before they need food. You see television antennas on small shacks where people can't afford to eat."

Clarke traced the evolution of communications satellite technology. "The first generation of satellites were fairly low powered, and therefore needed enormously large ground stations with dishes about thirty meters in diameter to pick up the very feeble signals. They could only be used as relays from one continent to another. But now, as satellites become more powerful, one can work with a dish antenna which could be only a matter of a few feet in diameter. Instead of costing millions of dollars, they cost only a few hundred dollars, and that makes it possible for the satellite to broadcast direct into the average home. That's DBS—the direct broadcast satellite. It's a tremendous quantum jump in a period of less than thirty years."

Clarke says dishes will continue to get smaller. The next step, he believes, will be a wristwatch-sized receiver that could pick up satellite signals. It may not work for television—at least, initially—but it will "enable you to have intercontinental telephony—person to person," he said. "Telephony is going to be revolutionized when people can talk to each other from anywhere in the world with a little wristwatch telephone."

In fact, Clarke has said that high-powered satellites will help the world and the human race become "one big gossiping family. We're seeing the beginning of a sort of global communications network," he said.

"In fact, I call it the 'electronic nervous system of all mankind.' Within a lifetime, it will be possible for anyone to talk to anybody. You won't even have to know where anyone is. You'll probably have some kind of code. It's rather important to know if they're going to be awake or asleep when you call. Now *that's* going to be a problem—time zones."

Actually, Clarke said, "It's far too early to assess

354

the global effects of TV satellites. It's as though one were trying to assess the impact of the telephone about ten years after it had been invented. We're just at the very beginning of global satellite communications, which are going to affect every aspect of human life. That's a question I prefer to answer in fifty years' time."

Clarke took a crack at it, anyway:

The TV satellite is going to blanket the whole world with all sorts of information. . . . One thing I'm rather pleased about, and this is something that many politicians are *not* pleased about, is that this will penetrate all frontiers. You cannot keep out communications from space, although attempts have been made to limit and restrict satellite communications. That's going to be totally impossible. Satellites don't recognize frontiers. No matter what the politicians say, this has already been settled by the engineers. Whatever the politicians try to do, they will not be able to prevent people listening to different sources of information. Ultimately, it will be impossible for any censorship to block out information, no matter what the governments may try to do.

Many of the enclosed societies are very worried about direct broadcast satellites. There has been a great argument going on in the United Nations about the free flow of information. You can prevent the reception of signals by jamming, but that is quite difficult, because you have to have your jammer fairly close to the satellite in orbit. You're probably breaking all sorts of regulations that every country has signed if you do that.

You can also encode or encrypt your transmission so that they can only be received by somebody with a suitable decoder. But there are some very, very clever software people around now, so for almost any coding devices invented, someone will invent a cheap decoder.

If the Soviet Union tries to prevent direct broadcast to its country, it won't have a leg to stand on because it is already direct broadcasting to half the world. In Colombo, [Sri Lanka,] I'm picking up beautiful signals from the Russian satellites. Excellent quality.

There are those who think that satellites might impose a kind of communications imperialism on the rest of the world, one that's highly American: "Coca-Cola imperialism." Clarke disagrees. "The communications satellite will establish one or perhaps two global languages," he said.

The probability is that it will be English, which in a sense already is the language of mankind—the airlines, shipping lanes. I think about a third of the human race understands English now to some extent. As communications satellites become more widespread and available, more and more people will learn from the "third parent," as someone once called the television set. They'll learn English as a second language, or perhaps French, or possibly Russian or Chinese.

Satellites will have two influences: They will enable a few nations or perhaps companies to have a very dominant role and to spread their ideas over the whole planet, which is not necessarily a bad thing. No one company and no one social or political system will be able to do this—we may have two or three Big Brothers.

I don't mind two or three, it's one Big Brother I object to.

Nonetheless, he is afraid that one effect of the communications revolution is to spread uniformity.

Just as in airports all over the world—you never know where you are. On the other hand, the opening up of many cultural channels will work in the opposite direction, so a balance will, I think eventually come about.

There will be lots and lots—thousands—of small-scale, limited communications channels over which perhaps a thousand people will be talking to each other: specialists, experts, professional groups, doctors and lawyers. They'll all have their own communications networks, and there will be so many of these all melded together, I think that the danger of uniformity or conformity is very small.

We'll have a multiplicity of possible services made available. How it's all going to work out in the long run, of course, only history will show, but we have an enormous potential here—most of it for good, some for evil. But in the long run I'm sure that the good will predominate.

Enormous benefits will be reaped by the more

impoverished nations, Clarke believes. "Television is not a luxury, it's a necessity," he said.

Especially for the Third World. I get very angry with people in the First World—the overdeveloped world—who are against improved communications for poor, developing countries that suffer from information starvation. You've got to have sources of information in these countries to tell the farmers what crops to grow, to advise them when the monsoon rains are going to come. Television is the most effective way of getting this sort of information over. I have lived through a revolution here in Sri Lanka and seen the advent of television. It has changed the whole atmosphere of the country. It's true there's an awful lot of junk—cheap American and British crime serials and so forth. I'm afraid that that's inevitable, but I think that, on the whole, even bad TV is better than no TV, because it does show people how other countries live—what standards of life are possible. In between, they learn a great deal about the world around them. If you share information, nobody gets poorer. It isn't like material goods.

I think the communications satellite may have a greater impact on the Third World than on the so-called "developed world." Europe and the United States already have elaborate ground communication and television networks, but much of the world—Asia and Africa—have never had any of this. They will leapfrog from smoke signals to the satellite. The new satellites will bring information into every village in Africa and Asia, news about the world, weather and medical information. In fact, the satellites may make it possible to solve many of the problems of the Third World.

The restless mind of Arthur C. Clarke is very excited about the possibilities for a better life and for peace.

I'm very optimistic about the possible uses of TV satellites. I believe that in principle, communication is a good thing. One can communicate badness, propaganda, evil, pornography, all sorts of things, but in the long run, the more communications we have, the better. To establish a peaceful global community, communications are absolutely vital.

There's an old saying that the pen is mightier than the sword. The communications satellite is mightier than the ICBM, because the communications satellite is going to spread ideas and concepts throughout the world more powerfully than even the written and printed medium have been able to do.

I'm very anxious that space technology be used for peace, not warfare. I coined the phrase "weapons for peace," referring to communications satellites, also weather satellites and earth resource satellites and all the others that are doing so much to protect this planet and to make the human race one global family.

You cannot have a modern society without television. It's as simple as that.

PHOTO CREDITS

p. 192 / PH
p. 194 / PH
p. 195 / PH
p. 196 / PH
p. 197 / PH
p. 198 / PH
p. 199 / PH
p. 200 / PH
p. 201 / PH

8. THE NEWS
p. 207 / TBA
p. 208 / CP
p. 209 / CP
p. 210 / CP
p. 211 / CP
p. 212 / AP/WWP
p. 214 / PH
p. 215 / AP/WWP
p. 216 / AP/WWP
p. 217 / AP/WWP
p. 218 / AP/WWP
p. 220 / AP/WWP
p. 222 / AP/WWP
p. 223 / PH
p. 224 / PH
p. 225 / PH
p. 226 / AP/WWP
p. 227 / AP/WWP
p. 228 / AP/WWP
p. 228 / WWP

pp. 230–1 / AP/WWP
p. 232 / AP/WWP
p. 233 / AP/WWP
p. 235 / UPI/Bettmann
    Newsphotos
p. 236 / AP/WWP
p. 237 / AP/WWP
p. 238 / Mark Godfrey/
    Archive
p. 239 / AP/WWP
p. 241 / AP/WWP
p. 242 / AP/WWP
p. 243 / UPI/Bettmann
    Archive
p. 244 / AP/WWP
p. 244 / AP/WWP
p. 245 / AP/WWP
p. 246 / AP/WWP
p. 247 / NASA
p. 249 / Bettmann
    Newsphotos
p. 250 / AP/WWP
p. 251 / AP/WWP
p. 251 / AP/WWP
p. 252 / PH
p. 253 / PH
p. 254 / PH
p. 255 / PH
p. 256 / PH
p. 258 / © Leonard Freed,
    Magnum Photos

9. SPORTS
p. 263 / TBA
p. 265 / CP
pp. 266–7 / CP
p. 268 / CP
p. 270 / CP
p. 271 / TBA
p. 272 / AP/WWP
p. 273 / AP/WWP
p. 274 / PH
p. 274 / AP/WWP
p. 275 / AP/WWP
p. 277 / AP/WWP
p. 278 / PH
p. 279 / AP/WWP
p. 280 / MSN
p. 281 / PH
p. 282 / AP/WWP
p. 283 / AP/WWP
p. 284 / MSN
p. 285 / AP/WWP
p. 286 / AP/WWP
p. 288 / AP/WWP
p. 289 / AP/WWP
pp. 290–1 / AP/WWP
p. 292 / AP/WWP
p. 293 / AP/WWP
p. 295 / AP/WWP
p. 296 / AP/WWP
p. 299 / AP/WWP
p. 300 / AP/WWP

**10. BEHIND
THE SCENES**
p. 305 / PH
p. 306 / PH
p. 307 / PH
p. 309 / PH
p. 313 / PH
p. 316 / PH
p. 321 / MSN
p. 322 / MSN
p. 323 / MSN

11. THE BUSINESS
p. 327 / PH
p. 332 / PH
p. 333 / PH
p. 334 / PH
p. 335 / MSN
p. 337 / CP
p. 338 / CP
p. 339 / PH
p. 340 / AP/WWP
p. 341 / WNET
p. 342 / CTW/
    Victor DiNapoli
p. 344 / PH

12. THE FUTURE
p. 349 / Cinemax
p. 355 / GTV

INDEX

ABOUT THE AUTHOR

Michael Winship, the writer and coproducer of the public television series, *Television*, began working in TV in 1974, when he joined the staff of NPACT, the National Public Affairs Center for Television in Washington, D.C. Shortly thereafter, he moved to New York City public television station WNET. As an associate producer, writer, and producer, Winship worked on more than fifty documentaries and news specials, including coverage of everything from the Iranian hostage crisis and Abscam to the 1979 American visit of Pope John Paul II. For WNET, he has also written *The Brand New Illustrated Journal of the Arts* and several popular music specials, including *Jukebox Saturday Night* and *Benny Goodman: A Musical Tribute.* Now a freelance television writer, Winship was the head writer of the Emmy award–winning series, *Smithsonian World,* served as a creative consultant to the National Geographic Society's television division, and has written for such other PBS series as *Media Probes* and the Children Television Workshop's *Square One TV.*